D1531569

ASTROSTYLE

Star-studded Advice
for Love, Life, and Looking Good

Tali and Ophira Edut

A FIRESIDE BOOK
Published by Simon & Schuster
New York London Toronto Sydney Singapore

FIRESIDE
Rockefeller Center
1230 Avenue of the Americas
New York, NY 10020

For information regarding special discounts for bulk purchases,
please contact Simon & Schuster Special Sales at
1-800-456-6798 or business@simonandschuster.com

Designed by Jaime Putorti

Manufactured in the United States of America

10   9   8   7   6   5   4   3   2   1

Library of Congress Cataloging-in-Publication Data
Edut, Tali.
    Astrostyle : star-studded advice for love, life, and looking good / Tali and
Ophira Edut.
      p.   cm.
    "A Fireside book."
    Includes bibliographical references (p.).
    1. Astrology. 2. Teenagers—Miscellanea. I. Edut, Ophira. II. Title.
    BF1729.T44E38   2003
    133.5—dc21   2003050384

ISBN 0-7432-4985-2

A SPECIAL MESSAGE
FROM TALI AND OPHIRA

Because we are identical twins, birthdays are a topic we always seem to be discussing. Once people realize that we look almost exactly alike, they start asking questions like "What day were you born?" (December 2) or "How many minutes apart are you two?" (Four—Tali's the older one) We know the drill and we never get sick of it. Our birthday is our bond, even if we *have* fought over some two-for-the-price-of-one presents before.

Our interest in birthdays soon led us to astrology. We grew fascinated by the endless ways we fit the profile of our sign, Sagittarius. For example, the stars say we Sagittarians are into publishing. The two of us have worked on everything from books to websites to magazines like *Teen People* where we write our astrology column. Our sign is also known for giving advice—and sometimes going a little overboard with the, ahem, honesty and winding up with our foot in our mouths. Oops! We admit, this has happened before. Sorry, world! We're blaming it on the stars.

We've also noticed cosmic patterns among the people in our lives. For example, the Cancers we know can always be counted on to offer a shoulder to cry on. The Aquarians are guaranteed to add a wacky and hilarious spin to any situation. The Geminis are always up for an adventure—the more hardcore, the better. Learning about astrology helps us understand people and become better friends. We know which buttons to push (or not) in order to bring out the best in the ones we love.

While there's no doubt that people are people, we believe that each sign has a unique way of approaching and experiencing life, which we share with you in this book. We hope you can use this star-studded guide to navigate through the challenges that come up for you as an individual and in your interactions with friends, family, love interests, and the people you simply have to deal with whether you like it or not. Bon voyage!

Tali & Ophira

CONTENTS

ASTROSTYLE

ASTROLOGY 101

SIGN LANGUAGE: ALL ABOUT THE SIGNS

THE TWELVE ZODIAC SIGNS

SIGN	DATES	RULING PLANET/ COSMIC RULER
Aries	March 21–April 19	Mars
Taurus	April 20–May 20	Venus
Gemini	May 21–June 20	Mercury
Cancer	June 21–July 22	Moon
Leo	July 23–August 22	Sun
Virgo	August 23–September 22	Mercury
Libra	September 23–October 22	Venus
Scorpio	October 23–November 21	Pluto (with minor rule by Mars)
Sagittarius	November 22–December 21	Jupiter
Capricorn	December 22–January 19	Saturn
Aquarius	January 20–February 18	Uranus
Pisces	February 19–March 20	Neptune (with minor rule by Jupiter)

WHAT'S MY SIGN?

Your "sign" is also your sun sign. It is actually the part of the zodiac that the Earth was traveling through at the exact time you were born. The Earth travels through a different part of the zodiac every thirty days or so. If it was traveling through the Gemini part when you were born, for example, you're a Gemini. While your sun sign tells the essentials of who you are, there are nine other planets that make up your personal horoscope, and they can be in many different signs. So the next time someone asks, "Hey, baby, what's your sign?" remember that they're really asking what your sun sign is.

WHAT DOES IT MEAN TO BE "BORN ON A CUSP"?

If you were born on or around the day the Earth moved from one sign to another, astrologers call this being born on a cusp—or a borderline between signs. The Earth moves from one sign into the next around the third week of every month—but the exact time and date vary slightly from year to year. Since most astrology books don't have enough pages to include this information, they just list approximate dates. Naturally, this has caused some confusion. For example, a person born on August 23 may wonder, "Am I a Leo or a Virgo?" since she has probably seen herself listed as both. Some astrologers believe that cuspers are a blend of both signs. Others insist you're either one or the other.

Fortunately, the matter can be settled if you know your birth time. You can find out which sign you "officially" are by checking an *ephemeris*—which is an almanac charting the exact time that the sun (and all other planets) changed signs in your birth year. You can also visit websites, such as Astrology.com (www.astrology.com), and create a free computerized chart.

WHAT'S A CHART?

Your chart is a map of the universe at your birth—and a guide to your personality, challenges, and strengths. At the exact moment you were born, every planet was revolving around the sun at its own pace—and was thus traveling through a different part of the zodiac. If you took a snapshot of our solar system at this precise moment, you would have your birth chart. To figure out your chart, you'll need the exact time (hours and minutes), date, and place that you were born. This will be listed on your birth certificate. If you don't know your birth time, use an approximate time—or just use 12:00 noon. This could give you an inaccurate moon or rising sign, but the rest of your chart should be on point. From there, you can hire a professional astrologer to calculate your chart. Or, you can create a free sample chart for yourself online at Astrolabe (www.alabe.com) or Astrology.com.

THE ELEMENTS: FIRE, EARTH, AIR, AND WATER

The twelve zodiac signs are grouped into four "elements"—fire, earth, air, and water. Each of these elementary groups has distinct traits. Together, they form the natural world, so each is in some way dependent on the other.

FIRE SIGNS: Aries, Leo, Sagittarius
EARTH SIGNS: Taurus, Virgo, Capricorn
AIR SIGNS: Gemini, Libra, Aquarius
WATER SIGNS: Cancer, Scorpio, Pisces

FIRE

Fire signs tend to be passionate, dynamic, and temperamental. Fire can keep you warm, or it can do great destruction. While fire burns out quickly without fuel to keep it going, it can also regenerate its power from the ashes. A single spark can set off a forest fire. As a result, fire signs need to be nurtured and managed carefully.

EARTH

Earth signs keep it real. They are the "grounded" people on the planet, the ones who bring us down to earth and remind us to start with a solid foundation. Slow and steady, these "builders" are loyal and stable, and stick by their people through hard times. On good days, they're practical; at worst, they can be materialistic or too focused on the surface of things to dig into the depths.

AIR

Air signs are all about action, ideas, and motion—they are the "winds of change." When a strong gust hits you, you can't help but move. While some within their ranks may be true-life "airheads," others are as powerful as a gravity-defying G-force. Air signs bring everyone a breath of fresh air when things start to get stale. Like the breeze, they can't quite be caught, and you never know where they'll drop you once they sweep you up. The encounter will almost always be an adventure, though.

WATER

Intuitive, emotional, and ultrasensitive, water signs can be as mysterious as the ocean itself. Like water, they can be refreshing, or they can drown you in their depths. These signs often have intense dreams and borderline psychic intuition. Security is important to them—after all, water needs a container, or it dries up and disappears.

YIN AND YANG: IS YOUR SIGN POSITIVE OR NEGATIVE?

Like the ancient symbol for yin and yang, the zodiac is also divided in half between yin (negative) and yang (positive) signs, which form a universal balance. The terms *positive* and *negative* shouldn't be taken literally—they don't imply that you've got a good or bad attitude. They refer to your energy style. Positive signs, like the positive part of a magnet, are more active and charged. Negative signs, like the negative part of a magnet, are more receptive, and may need an outside force to pull them into action. Some astrology guides also label positive signs as "masculine" and negative signs as "feminine," but since we think that's kinda sexist—and inaccurate—we didn't.

THE POSITIVE (YANG) ELEMENTS: FIRE AND AIR

Aries, Gemini, Leo, Libra, Sagittarius, Aquarius
Positive signs like action. They are the "doers" of the zodiac, and move at a quick pace. They tend to be extroverted, dynamic, and aggressive. Positive signs are independent and feel driven by achievement and competition. They also tend to be self-starters.

THE NEGATIVE (YIN) ELEMENTS: EARTH AND WATER

Taurus, Cancer, Virgo, Scorpio, Capricorn, Pisces
Negative signs are the "feelers" of the zodiac. They can be traditional and conservative, and are driven by their emotions. They may be introverted and prefer stable, nurturing relationships. Negative signs like to build security and will move at a slow, steady pace to achieve it. Change freaks them out unless there's a good reason for it.

As a rule, fire and air are compatible because they're the positive signs, and earth and water click because they're negative signs. Every element also fits naturally with more of the same—fire likes fire, water likes water, and so on. However, every combo has its pros and cons. It's a matter of balancing the ingredients.

YOUR SIGN'S QUALITY: WHAT ROLE DO YOU PLAY ON A TEAM?

Are you a starter, a doer, or a finisher? The signs are categorized into *qualities* that can determine this. Each quality plays an important role in the world, and it's good to have a balance of each on every team. If you were putting together a record deal, for example, it would work like this: *Cardinal signs* would be the stars, the promoters, or the trendsetters who create the act. *Fixed signs* would be the studio technicians who produce the album. *Mutable signs* would be the editors who take the near-finished product and do the final mastering and remixing. Which one are you?

CARDINAL SIGNS

Aries, Cancer, Libra, Capricorn

These signs start every season—Aries kicks off spring; Cancer starts summer; Libra begins fall, and Capricorn is the first winter sign. Thus, they are the leaders and "idea people" of the zodiac. These signs prize originality and like to be first in everything they do. They're the trendsetters and trend-spotters, the ones who get the party started and the crowd hyped. Count on them to initiate a winning idea or plan.

FIXED SIGNS

Taurus, Leo, Scorpio, Aquarius

These signs fall in the middle of every season. They're the stabilizers—the ones who set up a solid goal or foundation, then start building. Fixed signs can take the enthusiastic ideas that cardinal signs spark, and craft them into something real. They pick up the ball when the cardinal sign passes it, and run the distance to the goal. Fixed signs are the trustworthy types who like to-do lists and fancy titles. If a cardinal signs says, "Let's go on vacation!" the fixed sign will call the travel agency, book the tickets and hotel, and send everyone a list of what to pack.

MUTABLE SIGNS

Gemini, Virgo, Sagittarius, Pisces

These signs end every season—and have learned the hard lessons taught by spring, summer, fall, and winter. They know that all good things come to an end, and their role is to prepare everyone for the changing of seasons. Mutable signs are the adapters of the zodiac, a little bit older and wiser. More flexible and comfortable with change than other signs, they can "chameleon" themselves to fit into a variety of situations. Mutables are also the editors of the zodiac—the ones who complete the package with a winning touch. A plan can be sparked by a cardinal sign, built by a fixed sign, then perfected with the critical eye of a mutable sign.

THE PLANETS

HOW DO THE PLANETS AFFECT ME?

Every planet orbits the sun at a different speed, the revolution being slower the farther away a planet is. Each planet, as well as the sun and moon (which aren't technically planets but are sometimes referred to as such), is said to affect a different part of your personality.

PLANET/ CELESTIAL BODY	DETERMINES . . .	MOVES INTO A NEW SIGN APPROXIMATELY . . .
Sun	your basic personality	every month
Moon	moods and emotions	every two to three days
Mercury	mind and communication	every two to four weeks
Venus	love and attraction	every four to six weeks
Mars	drive and energy	every two months (with exceptions)
Jupiter	luck, growth, and wisdom	every year
Saturn	discipline, fears, and challenges	every three years
Uranus	change and originality	every seven years
Neptune	dreams and healing	every ten years
Pluto	power and transformation	every twelve years

The sun, moon, and the "inner planets"—Mercury, Mars and Venus—move quickly through the zodiac. As a result, they affect your day-to-day life, moods, and habits. The "outer planets"—Jupiter, Saturn, Neptune, Uranus, and Pluto—move slowly, changing signs every one to twelve years. For this reason, they shape the bigger trends in your life. In fact, Neptune, Uranus, and Pluto orbit the sun so slowly that they're said to mold entire generations. Each planet is associated with a zodiac sign, and members of that sign will exhibit traits of the planet. For example, turbo-charged Aries is ruled by energy planet Mars. Cheerful Sagittarius is ruled by optimistic Jupiter.

YOUR MOON AND RISING SIGNS

Along with your sun sign, these two star players can tell a lot about your personality. Your *moon sign* (where the moon was when you were born) shapes your emotions and your soul. It colors all the subconscious stuff going on below the surface—your deepest needs and what helps you feel emotionally secure. Your moon sign can also influence how strongly your sun sign is expressed. For example, if you're a fiery Aries with a mellow Taurus moon, your aggressive nature may be toned down by the steady Taurus influence. Or, if you're a watery Scorpio with a watery Pisces moon, you could be extra emotional and intuitive, since these are the traits of water signs. Want to find your true soul mate? Check out your moon sign and his. Chances are, your moons are in compatible signs, or your sun and moon are in similar signs.

Your *rising sign*, also called your *ascendant*, is the sign that was rising over the eastern horizon when you were born. It can affect your appearance, your attitude, and the way you come across to others. For example, a conservative Capricorn with a Leo rising can appear to have some Leo-like features—she may have wild hair, an outgoing personality, and a more expressive style than the average Capricorn. If people always peg you for a sign other than your own, don't be surprised to discover that it's actually your rising sign.

How do you calculate your moon and rising signs? The moon moves into a different sign every two to three days, and the rising sign changes every two hours. You'll need to check an ephemeris that lists moon and rising signs to determine which signs are yours.

section 2
LIFE

ASTROLOGY PROFILES
FOR EVERY SIGN

ARIES
(March 21–April 19)

SYMBOL: The Ram

COSMIC RULER: Mars—the planet of war and ambition

BODY PART: The head, face, and brain

ELEMENT: Fire

POLARITY: Yang (extrovert, doing)

QUALITY: Cardinal

GOOD DAYS: Energetic, encouraging, unstoppable, bold, devoted, heroic, caring

BAD DAYS: Proud, self-centered, impulsive, bossy, stubborn, reckless, jealous

FAVORITE THINGS: Video games, new clothes, road trips (in fast red cars), mind-challenging activities, expressing themselves through conversation

WHAT THEY HATE: Sharing their toys, being ignored, cramped spaces, losing, the word *no*

SECRET WISH: To be number one

HOW TO SPOT THEM: High foreheads, distinctive hair, focused or manic energy, aggressive stance

WHERE YOU'LL FIND THEM: Earning a fifth-degree black belt, writing and producing a solo album, working on Wall Street, trying out for *American Idol*

ASTROTURF—HOW THEY HANG OUT

When They're On

Superstar Aries like lots of attention, so when they're on, they prefer smaller gatherings where they can make a big impact. Even in a crowded room, they'll make sure you notice them—even if that means being quiet and mysterious while everyone else is yapping away. Not ones to shy away from a competition, Aries are always ready to get in the game, especially if there's a chance that they might win!

When They're Off

When it comes to personal space, Aries need their own solar system. As much as they love themselves, Aries are also their own worst critics. They not only need an escape from the world, but from their own over-active brains! During their downtime, distractions are essential—video and strategy games, puzzles, or novels if they're feeling low-key; a vigorous workout (with the headphones pumping) if they're hyped up.

FRIENDS

Aries as Friend

Aries were born expecting the best, and they take that attitude into the realm of friendships. Even if they only have a few friends, these will be high-quality connections that will stand the test of time. In public, Aries put on the good face—these private types don't like airing their dirty laundry to the world. They need plenty of one-on-one time with their friends so that they can talk through their issues without people listening in and judging them. Aries are hard enough on themselves as it is—any extra criticism can push them over the edge. When things don't go their way, they've been known to throw a temper tantrum or ice out an offender with an endless silent treatment.

While they require a little extra understanding, Aries are ready, willing, and able to offer friendship in return. They will listen with surprising patience and help friends find wise and sensible solutions. This kind of advice doesn't come around every day, since most people are too wrapped up in their own lives to really put themselves into another's world. A little dose of Aries wisdom is an inspiring gift, which makes friendships with these sometimes-difficult people worth all the trouble.

Friends of Aries

"Only the strong shall survive" could be the motto of Aries' friendships. To form an alliance, one must pass a strict application process. Do you respect them? Can you be trusted? Will you try to outshine them? Achieving the top spot is important to Aries, and they aren't looking for friends who are going to compete with them or stand in their way to success. They prefer cooperative types who are willing to go along with their exciting plans and who also bring something valuable to the mix.

Praising Aries will keep them coming back for more, since these natural-born stars love to be adored. It's gotta be sincere, though—these guys are no suckers for flattery, or anything else. That said, pushovers need not apply. Once Aries discover they can run all over someone, they're bored and on to the next challenge. Friends of Aries must give them tough love, setting limits in a firm but gentle way. By keeping things managed before they get out of control, friendships with Aries can be intense and rewarding experiences.

Got an Issue?

Paranoia

Being the first sign of the zodiac, Aries are all about number one. Trusting people, particularly groups, does not come easily. What Aries understand is independence and self-sufficiency, not following the leader or relying on others. When they see crews forming, they get uncomfortable—the group mentality is too unfamiliar to them. (Unless, of course, these crews are their own fan clubs!) Their sign believes in conspiracy theories, and it will do little good to try to convince them otherwise. Before they'll join in the reindeer games, they have to make sure their need for individuality will be respected. Often, they take this to extremes, questioning people's motives and wondering if others are plotting against them. Coworkers, classmates, family members—no one is above suspicion. As a result of this paranoia, they may push away people who are simply trying to be their allies. Or, they may decide to "play it safe" and keep to themselves, thereby missing out on key friendships and essential team activities. Aries should push themselves to sit through the early discomfort of group situations. What's on the other side is surprisingly powerful. With a little patience, there's a high probability that they will actually become the leaders of the pack!

Paranoid Aries: After the release of J. Lo and Ja Rule's "I'm Real," which allegedly used the same sample and style as a song Aries Mariah Carey was due to release, she accused forces within the music industry of trying to ruin her career.

ⓢ Destiny's Child: Career Paths for Aries

comedic actor

entrepreneur

defense attorney

holistic healer

professor

motivational speaker

military officer

stuntperson

hairdresser

salesperson

negotiator

magazine editor

political leader

⌾ Gifts That Keep On Giving

✳ Action-oriented things such as sports equipment, gym memberships, or a series of yoga classes
✳ Video-game console and/or video games (preferably fighting games, since Aries is the sign of war)
✳ Mental-strategy games such as chess or crossword puzzles
✳ A gift certificate to a bookstore (Aries love to make their own selections.)
✳ Fire toys like candles and candlestick holders or a George Foreman Grill

* Jewelry that accents the face (Aries rules the head) such as earrings and hair accessories
* A trip to the salon for a facial or haircut
* Red accessories such as a wallet, purse, baseball cap, backpack, datebook, or cell-phone cover

ARIES STARMATES

GUYS: Method Man, Heath Ledger, Haley Joel Osment, Biz Markie, Hayden Christensen, Q-Tip, Ewan McGregor, Mark Consuelos, MC Hammer, Eddie Murphy, Martin Lawrence, Redman, Steven Tyler, the Undertaker, Babyface, Eric McCormack, Jack Black, Chester Bennington, Jackie Chan, Steven Seagal, Al Gore, Adrien Brody, Deryck Whibley, Jason Kidd

GIRLS: Reese Witherspoon, Mariah Carey, Mandy Moore, Kate Hudson, Da Brat, Keri Russell, Claire Danes, Julia Stiles, Ashley Judd, Jennifer Garner, Shannen Doherty, Jennifer Capriati, Lara Flynn Boyle, Diana Ross, Chaka Khan, Victoria "Posh Spice" Beckham, Kidada Jones, Jill Scott, Alyson Hannigan, Sarah Jessica Parker, Sarah Michelle Gellar, Talisa Soto, Celine Dion, Norah Jones, Amanda Bynes

TAURUS
(April 20–May 20)

SYMBOL: The Bull

COSMIC RULER: Venus—planet of love and beauty

BODY PART: Neck, shoulders, throat

ELEMENT: Earth

POLARITY: Yin (introvert, feeling)

QUALITY: Fixed

GOOD DAYS: Patient, organized, supportive, romantic, careful, dedicated

BAD DAYS: Overindulgent, stubborn, lazy, vain, cheap, too cautious

FAVORITE THINGS: Photography, the mountains, really good music, really good food, satin sheets

WHAT THEY HATE: Being rushed, wasting money, dirty things, sleeping away from home, mornings

SECRET WISH: To own the best of everything

HOW TO SPOT THEM: Deep, soulful eyes; long, elegant necks, delicate jawlines

WHERE YOU'LL FIND THEM: Comparing prices on a luxury purchase, singing in the school choir, working three jobs, displaying paintings at an art gallery

ASTROTURF—HOW THEY HANG OUT

When They're On

Like raging bulls, hyped-up Tauruses literally percolate with nervous energy. It's not enough for them to dream about something; they have to make it happen. This sign loves to coordinate events like throwing a massive party. Bonus if they get to prepare the food and pick out the decorations—they are all about the details! Tauruses love music, so any type of concert will get their blood pumping. Don't be surprised if they lose their composure and jump in the mosh pit!

When They're Off

Home-loving Tauruses can lounge like nobody's business. This sign knows how to relax; in fact, they've turned sleeping into an art form! Listening to music is a spiritual thing for Tauruses, and they're quite happy to lie in bed all day with the stereo cranking. As an earth sign, they get a buzz from the great outdoors. Taking in natural beauty can help recharge their senses, and they're likely to enhance the experience by bringing along a camera and a picnic basket full of gourmet goods.

FRIENDS

Taurus as Friend

Hardworking Tauruses approach their friendships in much the same way that they approach everything else in life—as serious tasks that must be attended to. They are basically down to earth, and, thus, like to find out who people *really* are and what they believe in. Feeling needed gives them a sense of importance, and they'll talk about your problems until the cows come home. If you think you're better off alone, forget-about-it! Tauruses will charge forward, until your walls have been broken down.

Loving as Tauruses may be, sometimes their "helpful advice" can border on harsh or judgmental. Little things mean a lot to them, and, as a result, they don't easily forget or forgive an oversight. They also have a tendency to turn a minor issue into a major ordeal—at the first sign of trouble, they may press the panic button, blowing things out of proportion and driving people away. Perspective is an important thing for Tauruses to gain. Learning to stop and breathe before charging at a so-called red cape can help them enjoy a peaceful coexistence with others in the ring.

 Friends of Taurus

While Tauruses are generally willing to help those in need, if you want to make it past "charity case" status, you're going to have to present yourself as responsible, reliable, and straight-up. Their sign is represented by the bull, so it should come as little surprise that they can recognize bullcrap from a mile away. Word is bond, so say what you mean and mean what you say. Have a job—or get one quick. Material comfort is a must for Tauruses. While they're willing to share at first, user-friendly connections will ultimately cost you their respect.

Essentially, Tauruses are looking for friends who bring some peace, love, and harmony to their lives. The Beautiful People will dazzle them, too, but their best friends are often low-key types who have plenty going on below the surface. The expression "still waters run deep" is one that Tauruses know well. While aggressive types will send Tauruses scurrying for shelter, they can be swept away by a quiet storm. A little mystique goes a long way—at first. Ultimately, they will want to get to know you. People who know the art of keeping it real are the ones with whom Tauruses will form genuine and lasting connections.

❷ Got an Issue?

Stubbornness

Like heavy, plodding bulls, Tauruses are hard to move once they've chosen a position. Once they've made up their minds, that's it—and you're going to have to wave a serious red flag if you want them to give way. While this trait may serve Tauruses well when it comes to pursuing their dreams, it can cause major issues in their personal relationships. Without compromise, someone's getting bulldozed. Nine times out of ten, it's not going to be Taurus. While they may end up the "winners," their refusal to budge also leaves them standing alone—a hollow victory if one ever existed. At the heart of their stubbornness is a desire to do the right thing and to show people how things "should" be done. Unfortunately, the message often gets lost. By refusing to compromise, Tauruses often make people feel wrong, punished, or rejected. Even those who bend to Tauruses' will may later scurry away with their tail between their legs. To get a handle on this, Tauruses should let go of the idea of "right vs. wrong" and push themselves to listen to the other person's side *before* making a final decision.

Stubborn Taurus: Donatella Versace stubbornly carries on her signature look of bleached-blond hair and vampy makeup no matter how many trends come and go.

 ## Destiny's Child: Career Paths for Taurus

salon owner

makeup artist

engineer

film director

banker

art dealer

singer

department manager

interior designer

 ## Gifts That Keep On Giving

* Music, music, music—anything from a CD to concert tickets
* Stereo equipment, a keyboard, or a karaoke machine (They love to sing!)
* Good-smellin' things such as colognes, perfumes, and bath sets
* A basket full of comfort foods such as chocolate-chip cookies and gourmet teas
* Simple jewelry such as tiny gold earrings or a basic choker
* Black clothes and accessories made of leather or velvet
* Plush pillows or high–thread count sheets for sleeping the day away
* A long massage (They rule the neck and shoulders.)

TAURUS STARMATES

GUYS: Tony Hawk, Enrique Iglesias, Busta Rhymes, the Rock, Jason Biggs, Darius Rucker, Craig David, Mike Bibby, Lance Bass, Al Pacino, David Beckham, Trent Reznor, Jason Lee, Barry Watson, Tim McGraw, Jacob Underwood, Krist Novoselic, Bono, John Corbett, Pierce Brosnan, Andrew W.K., Derek Luke

GIRLS: Kirsten Dunst, Renée Zellweger, Jamie Lynn Sigler, Janet Jackson, Jessica Alba, James King, Penelope Cruz, Kelly Clarkson, Jordana Brewster, Donatella Versace, Cher, T-Boz, Enya, Rosario Dawson, Cate Blanchett, Carnie Wilson, Madeline Albright, Eva "Evita" Peron, Kim Gordan, Michelle Pfeiffer, Josie Maran, Emily VanCamp, Sarah Hughes

GEMINI
(May 21–June 20)

SYMBOL: The Twins

COSMIC RULER: Mercury—planet of communication

BODY PART: Shoulders, arms, hands

ELEMENT: Air

POLARITY: Yang (extrovert, doing)

QUALITY: Mutable

GOOD DAYS: Fascinating, original, resourceful, charming, wise, adventurous

BAD DAYS: Restless, distracted, two-faced, judgmental, depressed, overwhelmed

FAVORITE THINGS: Cell phones and two-way pagers, fast cars, trendy clothes, obscure music, gadgets

WHAT THEY HATE: Small-minded people, dress codes, authority figures, silence, routines

SECRET WISH: To have all the answers

HOW TO SPOT THEM: Mischievous twinkle in their eyes, talking with their hands

WHERE YOU'LL FIND THEM: Behind the camera, in the deejay booth, in a chat room, arguing both sides on the debate team

ASTROTURF—HOW THEY HANG OUT

☻ When They're On

Active Geminis have gotta be free. Their sign rules short trips, so anything from wandering around the mall to racing across town on a motorcycle will keep them happily occupied. Since they have the energy of two people in one, they require stimulation for all five senses. Variety shows, festivals, and theatrical productions—any event or activity that combines sights, sounds, tastes, and smells will bring them the rush they're looking for.

☻ When They're Off

Communicative Geminis may shut down, but they never really shut off. Their minds are always cranking away, dreaming up a new invention or trying to figure out the who-what-where-why-and-how of it all. Should they decide to skip a party, they'll find their way into a chat room. The concept of doing nothing is unfamiliar to them. If they're actually at home, it's a good bet that there's either a phone glued to their ear or a stack of reading materials close at hand.

FRIENDS

☻ Gemini as Friend

There's never a dull moment when Geminis roll into town. They have the ability to see life from many different perspectives and, as a result, get along with people from all walks of life. Lively and energetic, they love to talk—especially about the latest and greatest ideas going through their head. Sometimes, they get so carried away that they wind up talking *at* people instead of actually talking *to* them. Fortunately, they're usually gushing about an interesting topic. Who needs the Discovery Channel when Geminis are so full of facts?

Their enthusiasm is contagious, and they have little trouble gathering a crew to follow them on their adventures. What these "followers" often fail to understand is that Geminis inevitably get bored with most everything that they become obsessed with—and that may even include friends! One minute, they're totally in love with something; the next minute, they're sooo over it. This could be one of the reasons why their sign has earned a rep for being two-faced! Of course, this is not to say that Geminis can't be trusted. The fact is they are looking for soul twins—people whom they can connect with on a deep and spiritual level. Those who pass the test will be rewarded with Gemini's loyalty and a lot of bizarre and interesting experiences to boot!

Friends of Gemini

It's easy for friends to get jealous of Geminis. There are so many things to compete with—their hobbies, their work, their devoted worshipers. Scheduling time with them is like trying to get tickets to a playoff game. You're going to have to think on your toes and pin them down way in advance if you want to be there for the main event. Geminis are not the types to stop for anyone. If you can't beat 'em join 'em. Often, the best way to be in their world is to simply jump in on their many projects and adventures.

This does not mean that friends should consider becoming Geminis' personal assistants. They are the sign of the twins, after all, and they are looking for competent equals. Balance is essential to their peace of mind, and they are more than happy to pair up with people who have a skill that they are lacking. Ultimately, friends who can pick up where Geminis leave off are the ones they'll keep around forever.

Got an Issue?

Indecision

Represented by the symbol of the twins, Geminis have a tendency to talk out of both sides of their mouths. Making up their minds is a difficult thing, since they can always see the positive and the negative in every situation. As a result, they may drive friends crazy obsessing over the details. "Should I, or shouldn't I?" These conversations can go on forever. Opportunities pass them by, and they're still sitting there wondering. They may find themselves making promises they have no intention of keeping and even stringing people along while they take their time deciding. Seeing the big picture is not their strong suit, so they tend to think of every situation as the final frontier. To help alleviate this, Geminis should always have a Plan B and Plan C. That way they can learn the art of choosing without the fear of losing.

Indecisive Gemini: As a judge on American Idol, *Paula Abdul was encouraging and nurturing to all the contestants even though she was also eliminating them from their shot at a dream.*

💰 Destiny's Child: Career Paths for Gemini

editor

researcher or inventor

PR agent

stand-up comedian

interpreter

political commentator

psychiatrist

detective

brain surgeon

financial analyst

🔑 Gifts That Keep On Giving

✳ Funky gadgets such as a wireless Internet device or an electronic dictionary that translates words into five different languages

✳ DJ equipment and a crate full of old vinyl

✳ Tickets to a comedy club

✳ Well-designed computer equipment such as an iMac or flat-screen monitor

✳ Costume or vintage jewelry

✳ Trendy clothes or clothes that are "two-in-one," such as a reversible sweater or jacket with zip-on sleeves

✳ Short, adventurous trips to places such as an amusement park, or venues that offer rock-climbing or skydiving

✳ The latest best-selling book or anything else that captures their curious minds

GEMINI STARMATES

GUYS: Shane West, Lenny Kravitz, Dave Navarro, Mike Myers, Uncle Kracker, Brian McKnight, Allen Iverson, Noel Gallagher, B-Real, Billy Gilman, Johnny Depp, Andre 3000, Jesse Bradford, Ice Cube, Jamie Kennedy, Joshua Jackson, Tupac Shakur, the Notorious B.I.G., Colin Farrell, Prince, Fabrizio Moretti, Maxwell

GIRLS: Natalie Portman, the Olsen Twins, Angelina Jolie, Courtney Cox, Alanis Morissette, Jewel, Elizabeth Hurley, Faith Evans, Anna Kournikova,

Kylie Minogue, Heidi Klum, Zoë Saldana, Paula Abdul, Nicole Kidman, Melissa Etheridge, Tara Lipinski

CANCER
(June 21–July 22)

SYMBOL: The Crab

COSMIC RULER: Moon—celestial body of moods and emotions

BODY PART: Heart, chest, stomach

ELEMENT: Water

POLARITY: Yin (introvert, feeling)

QUALITY: Cardinal

GOOD DAYS: Helpful, patient, compassionate, nurturing, romantic, creative

BAD DAYS: Gossipy, cliquey, isolated, uncommunicative, hypersensitive, overly competitive

FAVORITE THINGS: Gourmet meals, intramural sports, hosting parties, working with kids, museums and art galleries

WHAT THEY HATE: Tacky clothes, frozen dinners, public speaking, being rushed, paying full price

SECRET WISH: To take care of friends and family

HOW TO SPOT THEM: Walking with their chests puffed out; round, "moonlike" facial features

WHERE YOU'LL FIND THEM: Shopping for antiques and rare finds, creating a masterpiece with a guitar or art supplies, listening to live bands, in the kitchen

ASTROTURF—HOW THEY HANG OUT

 When They're On

Social Cancers like to be surrounded by a group of close friends. Conversation is their favorite way to bond, and they prefer loungey environments where they don't have to shout to share the latest gossip. Going out to dinner with a crew is a favorite pastime for this food-loving

sign—the more exotic the restaurant, the better. Music and art charge them up, so listening to live bands, attending a poetry reading, or getting lost at an art gallery will bring them the creative buzz they live for.

When They're Off

Cancers like to retreat to a private space when they're in the mood to veg. As one of the zodiac's home-loving signs, they're happy to lock themselves in their room and dream the day away. Creative pursuits help them relax their minds. Whether they're knitting a scarf or tinkering around with a guitar, they like to occupy themselves with a project. This sign loves to eat, and they also love to cook. A day at home inevitably involves a trip (or three!) to the kitchen to prepare a rich and tasty little somethin'-somethin'.

FRIENDS

Cancer as Friend

On a good day, friendships with Cancers can feel like chicken soup for the soul—warm, healing, and comforting. Sensitive to moods and feelings, Cancers naturally tune in to people's emotions. They like to nurture their loved ones and feel guilty turning their back on people in pain. In spite of their giving nature, they are quite private when it comes to themselves. In the beginning, Cancers will know their friends better than their friends know them. However, this sign is not looking for superficial relationships. They want real friends whom they can connect with on a deep level. Once they've opened up, Cancers will gather their closest friends into cozy little families.

Don't judge a book by its cover, though. No matter what Cancers show on the surface, there's a lot going on behind the scenes. Ruled by the ever-changing moon, they can be quite moody. Crabbiness will come up and can confuse friends. Usually, these downswings are a result of Cancers holding too many feelings inside. By learning how to be more open and self-accepting, Cancers can create a consistent vibe within their friendships.

Friends of Cancer

Say cheese! Sentimental Cancers like to surround themselves with photos of loved ones. If you make it to their inner circle, there will be a flashbulb popping in your eyes. It's getting into the picture that's the hard part. Self-protective Cancers do not let people in very easily—and they don't let go easily, either. Their "getting to know you" ritual may feel like a gang initiation, so you'd better be tough enough.

Ultimately, Cancers are looking for a safe haven where they can open up. If you truly want to befriend them, you must be willing to reveal your "weaknesses" first. Cancers will rush in for the save, telling you about their own experiences and how they can relate. Once this occurs, it becomes easier to start asking Cancers some more personal questions. And keep asking, even if they attempt to keep you at arm's length with small talk. A word to the wise, however: Be prepared to deal with the true emotions that you are tapping into, or you may unleash a violent fury from the Cancer you scorn.

Got an Issue?

Possessiveness

Although they are social creatures, Cancers only truly reveal themselves to a select few. Like the crab that represents their sign, coming out of their shell makes them feel vulnerable. At the first sign of danger, they will retreat and even use their claws as defense. Cancers are born under a sentimental sign that is deeply attached to family and old friends. They can become quite possessive of loved ones, using these people to form a protective shell around themselves in social situations. If they feel these people moving away from them, they will cling and hold on for dear life. Unfortunately, this pinch can injure their loved ones, and may even cause them to retreat. Cancers should challenge themselves to become more independent. Experiencing things on their own can help them learn to trust their own strength, which ultimately, makes them less clingy and more desirable.

Possessive Cancer: "Stand by your man" Pamela Anderson is seldom seen or photographed without possessively clutching the arm of her significant other.

Destiny's Child: Career Paths for Cancer

writer/editor

clothing designer

child-care worker

marine biologist

music critic

financial manager

restaurant owner

history professor

real-estate agent

nurse

Gifts That Keep On Giving

✳ Handmade items such as a knit sweater or scarf

✳ Picture frames, vintage photo albums, or a tiny locket with a picture of the two of you inside

✳ Tickets to a live music performance, preferably by an underground band

✳ Expensive dinners at hip restaurants (Just make sure it's quiet enough to talk!)

✳ One-of-a-kind clothes from a secondhand store or tiny boutique

✳ Books about art or Do-It-Yourself manuals with lots of bright pictures

✳ Musical equipment such as a home stereo, amplifier, or guitar

✳ Home-decor items, especially anything for the kitchen

CANCER STARMATES

GUYS: Tom Cruise, Josh Hartnett, Carson Daly, Vin Diesel, Tobey Maguire, Prince William, Mike Tyson, Jason Schwartzman, Derek Jeter, Scott Foley, Billy Crudup, Carlos Santana, David Spade, Eddie Griffin, Simon Rex, Beck, Harrison Ford, Michael Weatherly, John Cusack, John Leguizamo, Tom Hanks, Sylvester Stallone, Evan Marriott a.k.a. Joe Millionaire, George W. Bush, Milo Ventimiglia

GIRLS: Michelle Branch, Liv Tyler, Lil' Kim, Selma Blair, Pamela Anderson, Edie Falco, Gisele Bundchen, Juliette Lewis, Ashley Scott, Jessica Simpson, Michelle Rodriguez, Missy Elliot, Selma Blair, Courtney Love, Tia and Tamera Mowry, Princess Diana, Lisa Rinna, Busy Phillips, Solange Knowles, Michelle Kwan

LEO
(July 23–August 22)

SYMBOL: The Lion

COSMIC RULER: The Sun—center of our universe

BODY PART: Heart, upper back

ELEMENT: Fire

POLARITY: Yang (extrovert, doing)

QUALITY: Fixed

GOOD DAYS: Courageous, kind, generous, loyal, protective, nakedly honest, entertaining

BAD DAYS: Arrogant, greedy, sloppy, coldhearted, jealous, aggressive, vain

FAVORITE THINGS: Theaters, cameras, DVDs, rich desserts, red roses, exchanging gifts

WHAT THEY HATE: Being ignored, silver medals (instead of gold), bland food, being alone, good-byes

SECRET WISH: To rule the world

HOW TO SPOT THEM: Distinctive mane of hair, regal posture, catlike noses

WHERE YOU'LL FIND THEM: Producing, directing, and starring in their own independent films, swept away in a romantic escapade, building their own megaenterprises, running for president

ASTROTURF—HOW THEY HANG OUT

 ## When They're On

Active Leos like to keep busy, and have a habit of turning hobbies into major-league productions. It's not enough for them to join an activity. These natural-born leaders want to run the show! They come to life when the cameras start rolling—whether they're in the starring roles or filming the world around them. Romantic and playful, they enjoy physical adventures such as dancing the night away in the arms of a beautiful stranger.

When They're Off

Adventurous Leos seldom make time for a break. When they do decide to settle back on their throne, they'll take themselves on an exploration in their minds. Reading is big with them, and they like to study up on politics, culture, and spiritual concepts. They're sure to tell you about these new ideas later—Leos love to show off what they know! If they're not actually on stage, they like to watch a good play or movie. They're likely taking notes, thinking of ways to improve their own performances. Don't forget the popcorn—or the dessert! Little indulgences are the treats Leos require to keep life sweet.

FRIENDS

 ## Leo as Friend

Overachieving Leos have as many friends as they do projects. In fact, many of their friends *are* their projects! Noble Leos like to help people—it makes them feel like the important and powerful royalty that they are. Doing favors is a big part of their friendships. These are the friends whose couches you can crash on night after night. They won't mind a bit—but they won't forget, either. Leos expect favors to be repaid. Should they need something in return, the answer had better be yes—or else! If they don't roar at you, Leos will sulk, and their guilt trips can be just as hard-core as their meltdowns.

Should the scorecard remain even, Leos make dynamic companions. They love to play around and are always up for an adventure. They'll stay up all night living life to the fullest. Friends seldom have to worry about coming up with ideas—Leos always have a plan or two lined up. Their sign is ruled by the sun, so they sometimes forget that the world doesn't revolve around them. Learning to step out of the take-charge role and go along with other people's plans can help Leos relax and discover new ways of having fun.

Friends of Leo

Loving Leos are looking for give-and-take relationships. They'll dole out support, but they also need plenty of it in return. Since they tend to take on more than the average mortal, they also get overwhelmed on a regular basis. While their expressions may be saying, *I've got it all together,* often what they are thinking is, *What did I get myself into?* Friends must learn to form a cheerleading squad, pumping up their Leos' self-confidence.

Being the royalty that they are, lavish Leos like to spend money. No matter how much they're making, they never quite seem to have enough cash. Friends should help them put the brakes on their spending—and say no when Leo asks for a loaner! Bonus points go to those who give Leos gifts and compliments. Leos are suckers for flattery and are easily won over by random acts of kindness.

❷ Got an Issue?

Ego-tripping

Dramatic Leos like to make an impact on other people. Some are obvious about it, wanting to be adored as the kings and queens of the jungle. Others are more subtle, trying to be everyone's best friend or the teacher's pet. The point is they want to be noticed and they want to be praised. Ignoring them will basically drive them crazy. Criticizing them will send them off the deep end. Even modest Leos might overexaggerate their sense of importance, taking blame for things that are beyond their control. Or, they may fish for compliments, putting themselves down so that others will object and tell them how worthy they are. After a while, these dramatic plays for attention can make people feel duped, unsure who these Leos really are and if their situations are *really* as wonderful or as horrible as they've been made out to be. Loved ones may also feel drained by the highs and lows of their Leos' mood swings. One too many of these ego trips can send even the most patient person packing! If Leos are to truly win people to their side, keeping it real is essential. Instead of simply trying to impress, they must also learn how to make other people feel important. Getting off stage and into the audience will help develop true and lasting bonds with the people in their lives.

Ego-tripping Leo: Jennifer Lopez sings a song called "Jenny from the Block" about how she's just a regular old girl from the Bronx, then shoots a video for it flaunting her wealth and celebrity mate Ben Affleck

Destiny's Child: Career Paths for Leo

playwright
children's book author
movie star
world leader

bodyguard

language specialist

coach or trainer

lead singer

education director

department manager

filmmaker

 ## Gifts That Keep On Giving

✳ Expensive and eye-catching jewelry with plenty of bling-bling! (Like J-Lo's pink-diamond engagement ring)

✳ Accessories for their "lion's mane" such as hair products or hats, or a haircut from a posh salon

✳ Tickets to a Broadway play or a movie premiere

✳ A DVD player or home-theater system . . . or just a brand-new DVD

✳ Cameras (preferably video) and camera equipment

✳ Classically romantic gifts such as a dozen red roses and a box of chocolates

✳ A rare treasure from another part of the globe—Leos are worldly signs

✳ Clothes or accessories engraved or embroidered with Leo's initials

LEO STARMATES

GUYS: Ben Affleck, Matt LeBlanc, Daniel Radcliffe, Matthew Perry, Fred Durst, JC Chasez, Tom Green, Scott Stapp, Ed Norton, Robert De Niro, Kevin Spacey, the Edge, Ashley Parker Angel, Billy Bob Thornton, Kevin Smith, Antonio Banderas, Wesley Snipes, Pete Sampras, Sir Mix-A-Lot, Omar Epps, Bill Clinton, Chuck D, Fat Joe, Lil' Romeo

GIRLS: J. Lo, Madonna, Halle Berry, Kate Beckinsale, Charlize Theron, Debra Messing, Vivica Fox, Emily Erwin, Hilary Swank, Hallie Kate Eisenberg, Lisa Kudrow, Mila Kunis, Angela Bassett, Carrie-Anne Moss, Soleil Moon Frye, Tori Amos, Sandra Bullock, Anna Paquin, Vanessa Carlton, Monica Lewinsky, Whitney Houston, Kim Cattrall, Tamyra Gray

VIRGO
(August 23–September 22)

SYMBOL: The Virgin

COSMIC RULER: Mercury—the planet of communication

BODY PART: Stomach

ELEMENT: Earth

POLARITY: Yin (introvert, feeling)

QUALITY: Mutable

GOOD DAYS: Dedicated, resourceful, helpful, hardworking, witty, practical

BAD DAYS: Preachy, self-destructive, overwhelmed, self-pitying, uptight, critical

FAVORITE THINGS: Laptops, magazines, long showers with aromatherapy soaps, outdoor concerts, childhood friends, Trivial Pursuit

WHAT THEY HATE: Lazy or vulgar people, dive bars, spicy food, leaving home, toothpaste squeezed from the top of the tube

SECRET WISH: To be a hero

HOW TO SPOT THEM: Baby faces, roving eyes that are sizing up or analyzing a situation

WHERE YOU'LL FIND THEM: Baby-sitting for the neighbor's kids, running errands on their endlessly long to-do lists, building something with their own two hands, anywhere help is needed

ASTROTURF—HOW THEY HANG OUT

 ## When They're On

Generous Virgos give the world service with a smile. They are the worker bees of the zodiac, so the concept of "just hanging out" is a little unfamiliar to them. Even when they're at a party, they like to pitch in and lend a helping hand. They'd rather be the host than one of the guests. While they enjoy experiencing new things, they like to plan and research in advance, gathering data rather than rushing ahead blindly.

When They're Off

Detail-oriented Virgos need outlets to help slow down their racing minds. Getting organized is essential to their success, and jotting down notes or making lists will help them relax and see what's ahead. Information gatherers that they are, Virgos also love to read. Self-improvement or spiritual books are favorites with this sign, since they are always striving toward perfection. Virgos also like to work with their hands, so crafty projects such as knitting or tinkering around with a car or computer will provide a happy distraction.

FRIENDS

Virgo as Friend

Generous Virgos make helpful and supportive friends. They like order, and they'll happily come in and organize other people's lives. In their own world, however, they prefer to be in total control. They don't believe in asking for help in return; in fact, they get nervous when other people move things around in their living space or schedule. A handmade or sentimental gift is a better way to show appreciation to a supportive Virgo.

Nothing turns Virgos on quite like a deep conversation. They love to analyze every little detail, and will stay up half the night gossiping or helping friends iron out their issues. They expect results, however, and can be quite critical of people who don't live up to their standards. This sign has sent enough people on guilt trips to open a travel agency! The truth is, Virgos tend to give too much and as a result wind up resentful when people don't immediately return the favor. Learning to speak up for their own needs can help Virgos relax and get the support they need to make friendships work.

Friends of Virgo

Virgos are worriers, and friends who can calm them down will be highly valued. Soothing words won't do the trick. Virgos need facts, and those facts had better be backed up by statistics. If you're not the type who likes to read, you won't get far with this sign. Knowledge ranks high on their list of respectable qualities. If you can't hold your own in a conversation, your chances are slim to none.

While Virgos are willing to make sacrifices for the ones they love, friends should be sensitive enough not to take advantage of their kindness. One too many favors asked can provoke a tirade from tapped-out Virgos. Relaxing is not something this sign knows how to do naturally, and friends who are able to put their minds at ease will enjoy the fun-loving and hilarious personalities hidden inside every Virgo.

Got an Issue?

Perfectionism

Being the virgins of the zodiac, it follows that Virgos want everything simple, fresh, and clean. They can't help but notice that speck of lint dirtying up the surface of your crisp white shirt. After a few minutes, its mere presence will begin to offend them until they have to get up and brush it off you. Virgos are critical thinkers who see nothing wrong with pointing out the flaws in a situation. In their mind, they are only trying to help. They would want to know if they made a mistake so that next time they can do a better job. They expect perfection from themselves, and therefore expect it from the people in their lives. Their high standards can border on unforgiving. Ultimately, people will let them down, or they will let themselves down. That's when the overanalyzing begins. Virgos will turn a situation over endlessly, trying to figure out where things went wrong and why. They will ask the people in their lives for their opinions on the situation, inadvertently spreading gossip or even coming across as petty. At the heart of the problem is their belief in the idea of perfection; the idea that there is one right way of doing things. Learning to accept humanness and see the beauty in the flaws can help Virgos find inner peace and be more loving to the people they care about.

Perfectionist Virgo: Throughout his long and prolific career, Michael Jackson has been a study in evolution with his never-ending plastic surgeries. The "perfection" he hopes to achieve began to backfire long ago, but he seems unable to realize it.

Destiny's Child: Career Paths for Virgo

therapist or counselor

nutritionist

religious leader

accountant

critic

office manager

journalist

doctor

architect

🔑 Gifts That Keep On Giving

* Organizers such as photo albums, datebooks, and storage boxes (Virgos are pack rats!)
* Small tools and gadgets such as an electric shaver or power drill, since Virgos like to work with their hands—or even a trip to the salon for a manicure
* An elegant desk lamp or bedside reading lamp
* Leather-bound journal for jotting down their observations about life
* Clothes and accessories in earthy fibers or clean and simple white
* Membership to a health club or a series of Pilates classes
* Party-hosting items like a set of funky glasses or Moroccan pillows for floor seating
* A laptop computer for working whenever, wherever

VIRGO STARMATES

GUYS: Ryan Phillipe, Keanu Reeves, Luke Wilson, Ludacris, Kobe Bryant, Marc Anthony, Michael Jackson, Macaulay Culkin, Jimmy Fallon, Adam Sandler, Chris Tucker, Julian Casablancas, Xzibit, Paul Walker, Mario, Wes Bentley, Wade Robson, Nas, Liam Gallagher, David Arquette, Jonathan Taylor Thomas, Rich Cronin, Prince Harry, Mystikal, Tony Kanal, Guy Ritchie, Sean Connery, Craig Nicholls, Yao Ming, Hugh Grant

GIRLS: Pink, Beyoncé Knowles, Cameron Diaz, Alexis Bledel, Foxy Brown, Molly Shannon, Stella McCartney, Sanaa Latham, Jada Pinkett, Fiona Apple, Shannon Elizabeth, LeAnn Rimes, Lisa Ling, Alexa Vega, Asia Argento, Faith Hill, Rose McGowan, Macy Gray, Angie Everhart, Sophie Dahl, Salma Hayek

LIBRA
(September 23–October 22)

SYMBOL: The Scales

COSMIC RULER: Venus—planet of love and beauty

BODY PART: Lower back, booty

ELEMENT: Air

POLARITY: Yang (extrovert, doing)

QUALITY: Cardinal

GOOD DAYS: Charming, lovable, fair, sincere, sharing, hopelessly romantic

BAD DAYS: Vain, indecisive, melodramatic, manipulative, spoiled, delusional

FAVORITE THINGS: Concerts at large venues, poetry, expensive jewelry, designer clothes, rich food

WHAT THEY HATE: Dull or practical people, bullies, being pressured to decide, saying good night, hearing the word *maybe*

SECRET WISH: To love and be loved in return

HOW TO SPOT THEM: Small symmetrical features, dimples, gentle eyes

WHERE YOU'LL FIND THEM: Dancing the night away at a warehouse party, philosophizing about life at a coffeeshop, tucked away at home writing a novel, shopping at a designer outlet

ASTROTURF—HOW THEY HANG OUT

 ## When They're On

Being the sign of relationships, Libras like to be around people, even if they are just people-watching. They like to observe, and anything from a sports event to a concert will captivate them. They'll have plenty of opinions to share afterward, so make sure there's time left over for talking—and eating! This sign can chow down like no other. Dinners at expensive restaurants are a favorite pastime, but a diner or coffeeshop will do if Chez Pierre is closed.

🪬 When They're Off

Libras have a tendency to get thrown off balance by all the thoughts swimming around in their heads. Writing long letters or poems and jotting down their many opinions help them sort things out. Conflicts truly do upset this harmonious sign, so books by relationship experts can help them put their overactive minds at ease. They love luxury. Scented bubble baths or indulgent massages do wonders to help them relax.

FRIENDS

 ### Libra as Friend

Loving Libras make gentle, patient, and sweet friends. Being the sign that rules relationships, they are genuinely interested in knowing people. They don't mind getting involved in friends' dramas. In fact, they will stand by their friends' side from beginning to end, helping them work through the issue one step at a time. Because of their abilities to look below the surface, many Libras develop deep connections with people from different backgrounds—in fact, many of them even get "adopted" into another culture.

As much as they can dish it out, however, Libras seem to have trouble taking their own advice. In the name of keeping things harmonious, they often put other people's needs in front of their own. When it comes to making decisions about their own lives, they can get stuck endlessly weighing the pros and cons. If they don't learn how to let go and take a chance on themselves, Libras may become bitter and jealous, turning away from people and choosing the loner route. Learning to find the balance between giving to themselves and giving to others can help Libras enjoy the satisfying friendships they crave.

👥 Friends of Libra

Family and old friends are important fixtures in the lives of sentimental Libras. Simply put, Libras crave unconditional love. They are hard on themselves, so they need people they can talk to; people who will listen patiently as they figure out how they *really* feel about a situation. Closed-up or cold people will only send Libras into a downward spiral, making them wonder, "Am I overreacting?"

At the end of the day, Libras just want a partner-in-crime or two to accompany them on their various explorations. While they crave adventure, they often hesitate before taking a chance. Friends of Libras must be inspiring, even daring. Whether that means holding their hand or just stepping out first and taking a risk, helping Libras face the fear factor is one of the most valuable gifts a friend can give them.

❷ Got an Issue?

Rebellion

Represented by scales, Libras seek balance in all that they do. Too often, however, they swing to extremes, seeing themselves as the forces that must fill in the blanks where other people leave off. If their families are conservative, then they're giving 'em a punk-rock shake-up. If everyone else is on an express train to Loserville, Libras will hop off and prove to the world that they can make it despite the odds. Little do they realize, this rebellion can actually be a trap. Instead of charting out their own destinies, Libras often get stuck reacting to what everyone else is doing. They waste years being angry at so-called authority figures, when all they really need to do is stop giving those people so much power. It's as simple as turning off a light switch. With a flick, Libras can turn their enemies into allies. The key for Libras is to let go of the idea that *different* always means "better." Learning to be comfortable in their own skin—whether they blend in or not—can help them tap into the natural harmony of the universe.

Rebellious Libra: Eminem has gone where few would dare, verbally bashing his mother, his baby's mother, and even himself. Ironically, while he writes fiery rhymes about "white America," his fan base includes people of all races, including his own.

💰 Destiny's Child: Career Paths for Libra

judge
party promoter
diplomat
food critic
fashion designer
art dealer
massage therapist
novelist
interior designer

Gifts That Keep On Giving

* Expensive dinners at large, airy restaurants
* Framed artwork or oversize mirrors
* A manicure or spa treatment
* Box set of CDs or a mix-tape made specially by you
* Gift certificate to Sephora or a cosmetics counter; scented lotions or colognes
* Payment of a month's worth of bills (Libras often overspend on luxury items and forget the necessities)
* Book of poetry or fiction or a biography about a famous hero
* Sweaters in classic black, brown, or gray
* Tickets to a stadium-size concert, exclusive party, or sports event

LIBRA STARMATES

GUYS: Matt Damon, Will Smith, Eminem, Russell Simmons, Simon Cowell, Ginuwine, John Lennon, Seann William Scott, John Mayer, Erik-Michael Estrada, Usher, Bam Margera, Snoop Dogg, Evander Holyfield, Shaggy, Jermaine Dupri, Sting, Kieran Culkin, Eric Benet, Ralph Lauren, Flea, Kevin Richardson, Nick Cannon, Viggo Mortensen

GIRLS: India Arie, Gwyneth Paltrow, Ashanti, Avril Lavigne, Alicia Silverstone, Sharon Osbourne, Bridgette Wilson, Mira Sorvino, Neve Campbell, Jenna Elfman, Serena Williams, Kelly Preston, Mya, Naomi Watts, Catherine Zeta-Jones, Ani DiFranco, PJ Harvey, Kelly Ripa, Rachel Leigh Cook, Hilary Duff, Donna Karan

SCORPIO
(October 23–November 21)

SYMBOL: The Scorpion

COSMIC RULER: Pluto—planet of transformation; Mars—planet of war and ambition

BODY PART: Reproductive organs

ELEMENT: Water

POLARITY: Yin (introvert, feeling)

QUALITY: Fixed

GOOD DAYS: Magnetic, passionate, loyal, protective, trendsetting, brave

BAD DAYS: Obsessive, possessive, jealous, secretive, vengeful, manipulative

FAVORITE THINGS: Underground music, spicy food, an air of danger, one-of-a-kind objects, wireless devices, vinyl

WHAT THEY HATE: Simplistic people, flattery, personal questions, living at someone else's house, feeling vulnerable

SECRET WISH: To have complete and total control

HOW TO SPOT THEM: Intense eyes, a hawklike gaze, smooth movements

WHERE YOU'LL FIND THEM: In the studio producing a platinum album, sitting at the corner table of an underground bar, taking things apart and figuring how to put them back together again

ASTROTURF—HOW THEY HANG OUT

 ## When They're On

Spicy Scorpios crave intense situations. They like hanging in small groups where they can ask probing questions and get into people's heads. If they're not in the mood to talk, they'll rock out to live bands in dark, underground clubs. Or, they'll take over the VIP section, letting the world see that they've got the power. They don't mind creating a little envy—or mystery. As long as they leave an impression, their mission is accomplished.

 ## When They're Off

When it feels as though things are slipping out of their grasps, it's time for Scorpios to take a break. Getting a hobby is a good idea, since making something with their own two hands can help them regain a sense of control. They need plenty of privacy and like to escape into a quiet space where they can lock the door and be alone. Water rejuvenates them, so a walk around a lake, or a hot bath, will soothe their souls.

FRIENDS

Scorpio as Friend

Secretive Scorpios take a long time to open up. The idea of sharing their vulnerabilities frightens them, since one of their deepest fears is that people will use this personal information against them. They prefer to feel people out first by listening and asking lots of questions. To shift the spotlight off themselves, they give people plenty of focused attention. This trait is incredibly charming—after all, most people love to talk about themselves!

As friendships develop, Scorpios can go to extremes. If they do decide to share themselves, it can be an intense and overwhelming experience. At best, they are loyal friends who will go to the ends of the earth to protect their loved ones. At worst, they can be possessive and jealous, scaring people off with their suffocating hold. Learning to be less "all or nothing" in their approach can help Scorpios relax and enjoy friendships that are about fun instead of control.

Friends of Scorpio

Trust doesn't come easy to Scorpios, so friends may have to go through a fraternity-style hazing in order to prove their loyalty. Those who make the cut will be treated like family—in a Sopranos sort of way. Scorpios are looking to build a tight inner circle. Respecting their privacy and sharing their little secrets will be the glue that bonds you together.

Scorpios are drawn to mystery, but only if the surprises are small and the risks are calculated. Too much wondering makes them suspicious; not enough bores them. They need smart and competent friends who can help them stay grounded when they start obsessing about all the behind-the-scenes details. Power turns them on and they like to surround themselves with VIPs who not only make them look good but can also help them make their own success story come true.

Got an Issue?

Destructiveness

Scorpios are ruled by Pluto, the planet of transformation. Change both scares and fascinates this sign, and often they'll stir up trouble just to see what happens. They understand that sometimes things have to be broken down in order to be built back up. Their goal is ultimately to do good, as Scorpios are highly generous to the ones they love. But before someone gets close to them, they must first pass the test. Scorpios will push potential allies away or injure them with their notorious sting. They want to see what happens after someone breaks: Who are they *really* when their defenses are down? While Scorpios themselves may feel a sense of control from this, it can be quite destructive to the people in their lives. There's a thin line between love and hate for this sign. Often the ones they love the most are the ones they treat the worst. Learning to give people the benefit of the doubt is a valuable lesson for them. Along with imagining the worst-case scenario, Scorpios should also push themselves to visualize the best-possible outcome. Doing this will help them to drop their defensive attitude that pushes away the powerful alliances they crave.

Destructive Scorpio: While putting together a rap group on MTV's Making the Band, *Scorpio Sean "P. Diddy" Combs tried to break the contestants down by putting them through a rigorous process, including boot camp!*

Destiny's Child: Career Paths for Scorpio

dramatic actor

critic

nightclub owner

real-estate broker

record-label producer

research scientist

computer programmer

talent scout

psychiatrist

tax attorney

surgeon

detective or spy

Gifts That Keep On Giving

* Spy equipment, a tiny camera or a voice recorder
* Digital goods such as laptops, studio equipment, or their own network servers (Scorpios are highly technical)
* Diary or journal—with a lock!
* Black leather clothes cut for a sexy rock star

- ✳ Tickets to hear a live band perform or passes to an exclusive underground club
- ✳ Sexy lingerie or silk boxers
- ✳ How-to and self-improvement books (Scorpios like to know how things work)
- ✳ Bedroom accessories such as down comforters, vintage lamps, or curvy mirrors

SCORPIO STARMATES

GUYS: Nelly, Sisqo, Anthony Kiedis, Gavin Rossdale, Leonardo DiCaprio, Scott Weiland, Owen Wilson, Trevor Penick, RuPaul, Old Dirty Bastard, P. Diddy, Sammy Sosa, David Schwimmer, Nick Lachey, Vanilla Ice, Matthew McConaughey, Joaquin Phoenix, Ben Foster, Rev Run, Jack Osbourne, Isaac Hanson, Phife Dawg, Ethan Hawke, Patrick Fugit, Ryan Adams, Justin Guarini, Calvin Klein

GIRLS: Kelly Osbourne, Julia Roberts, Tara Reid, Brittany Murphy, Eve, Thandie Newton, Winona Ryder, Calista Flockhart, Monica, Piper Perabo, Rebecca Romijn-Stamos, Mayte Garcia-Nelson, Chloe Sevigny, Taryn Manning, Pepa, Björk, Jane Pratt, Demi Moore, Anne Hathaway, Jodie Foster, Famke Janssen, Maggie Gyllenhaal, Trista Rehn ("The Bachelorette")

SAGITTARIUS
(November 22–December 21)

SYMBOL: The Archer

COSMIC RULER: Jupiter—the planet of luck and expansion

BODY PART: Hips, thighs

ELEMENT: Fire

POLARITY: Yang (extrovert, doing)

QUALITY: Mutable

GOOD DAYS: Honest, fair-minded, inspiring, optimistic, enthusiastic, encouraging, dedicated

BAD DAYS: Argumentative, reckless, flaky, preachy, tactless

FAVORITE THINGS: Dares, flirting, pets, pop music, international travel, laughter

WHAT THEY HATE: Prejudice, routines, being bored, taking things too seriously, the words *you can't*

SECRET WISH: To make the rules

HOW TO SPOT THEM: Strong legs, laughing eyes, comedic facial expressions

WHERE YOU'LL FIND THEM: Organizing a school talent show, publishing a tell-all 'zine, cracking inappropriate jokes in the middle of math class, selling ice to Eskimos

ASTROTURF—HOW THEY HANG OUT

 When They're On

Adventurous Sagittarians crave constant stimulation and like to be in environments where they can chat up new people. As the zodiac's class clowns, they have a blast doing campy things such as bowling or karaoke—nothing keeps them going like an appreciative audience to laugh at their jokes. Energizers that they are, they need lots of physical activity. Outdoor sports such as hiking and biking can rev them up. At night, they'll hit the dance floor and stay on it till the sun comes up.

 When They're Off

This is not a sign that knows how to relax. Even in their spare time, Sagittarians are probably building a website, planning a new business venture, or wandering the earth in search of answers and inspiration. When they're lounging, you can bet that there's reading material or a communication device nearby—like a cell phone, TV, book, or Internet-wired computer. Staying connected to the latest and greatest ideas is important to Sagittarians, so they like to read—especially magazines, since they are impatient and tend to have shorter attention spans than other signs.

FRIENDS

 Sagittarius as Friend

Sagittarians are the truth seekers of the zodiac. No information is too gruesome, too horrifying for them, as long as it is spoken from the heart. Opening up to them is surprisingly easy, since they are less judgmental than most. They will, however, spew out advice and may wear friends' patience thin with their preaching. Although they are loyal, they often lack tact. At times, they can get carried away with the, ahem, "honesty," and may offend people with their blunt observations. Learning to think before they speak is a key lesson for this sign.

Getting close to a Sagittarius is a challenge in itself. They don't have much patience for b.s. and are quick to cut people off at the first sign of drama. Talking about your problems is one thing, but they'd rather not be weighed down by them. If things get too heavy, they may disappear without a trace. Oddly enough, should a real crisis occur, they will reappear out of nowhere, ready to lend support regardless of how many years have gone by since you last spoke.

😊😊 Friends of Sagittarius

If Sagittarius threw a party, the guests would look nothing like a police lineup. In fact, you'd wonder how these people wound up in the same room together in the first place. Sagittarians are the zodiac's travelers, and they like to have friends from all walks of life. Traditional or stuffy types won't even register on the Sagittarius radar. People who have a sense of humor and an open mind will meet the general requirements. Exploring ideas is a big part of Sagittarians' friendships, and they are drawn to dreamers and revolutionaries above all others. "Power to the people" could be the Sag motto.

Getting Sagittarians' full attention can be an exercise in futility, since this sign is all about more, more, more. You're going to have to stand out in the crowd if you want them to notice you. While they crave genuine friendships, they don't like the idea of anyone depending too heavily on them—it just cramps their style. Jealous or clingy types may get Sag sympathy for a while, but it won't last long. Independent people who can travel as freely as Sagittarians are the ones who will be invited back round after round.

❓ Got an Issue?

Doing things the hard way

When it comes to advice, Sagittarians can dish it out. Taking it, however, is another story altogether. They prefer to do things their way—even if that means doing it the hard way. Impatient and restless, they tend to jump into situations headfirst when the impulse hits them. As the zodiac's gamblers, they believe that every risk could also bring a big payoff. They've already pawned off their family heirlooms before they realize that—*Hello! Maybe I just got myself in too deep!* Challenges don't deter them; they only fuel their fire. Sagittarians may actually choose complex and frustrating situations by falling for the illusion that they will be bored by anything that's too easily won. What could be an exercise in teamwork often turns into a complicated Sagittarius solo mission. Once the thrill of the victory wears off, Sagittarians pay the price in the battle scars they suffer. By this time, they may have already lost the support of friends who tried in vain to help but eventually couldn't bear to watch Sag struggle. Dropping the know-it-all routine and getting the facts straight is essential to Sagittarians' success. Sure, they may miss out on a few opportunities, but they will also save themselves a lot of disappointments. Ultimately, this wiser approach will increase their odds of truly hitting the jackpot.

Sagittarius on the hard road: While her superstar voice could catapult her to the heights of fame, Christina Aguilera insists on dressing like a trashy pop star, costing herself respect and causing people to question her judgment skills.

Destiny's Child: Career Paths for Sagittarius

magazine publisher

pop star

animal trainer

salesperson

sportscaster

game-show host

comedian

international newscaster

motivational speaker/coach

Gifts That Keep On Giving

* On-the-go technology such as a laptop, digital camera, or portable DVD player (Sagittarians love long road trips!)
* Fitness equipment, a gym membership, or a series of kickboxing classes
* Self-help books
* Colorful, eye-catching boots or sneakers
* Outdoor equipment such as a surfboard or two-person tent
* Karaoke machine for clowning around and showing off

* Oversize backpacks for all their books and projects
* A trip to Vegas to satisfy their gambling urges

SAGITTARIUS STARMATES

GUYS: Brad Pitt, Ozzy Osbourne, Jay-Z, Samuel L. Jackson, Tom DeLonge, Tyson Beckford, Colin Hanks, Jake Gyllenhaal, Aaron Carter, Jakob Dylan, Brendan Fraser, Johnny Rzeznik, Benjamin Bratt, Jimi Hendrix, Mos Def, DMX, Montell Jordan, Andy Dick, Jamie Foxx, Mekhi Phifer, Sean Patrick Thomas, Chris Robinson, Jim Morrison, Jon Stewart, Ben Stiller, Frankie Muniz

GIRLS: Britney Spears, Katie Holmes, Lucy Liu, Alyssa Milano, Tyra Banks, Anna Nicole Smith, Trina, Anna Faris, Shiri Appleby, Christina Aguilera, Robin Givens, Nelly Furtado, Christina Applegate, Tina Turner, Bette Midler, Monica Seles, Milla Jovovich, Julianne Moore, Jennifer Connelly, Kim Basinger

CAPRICORN
(December 22–January 19)

SYMBOL: The Goat

COSMIC RULER: Saturn—the planet of discipline

BODY PART: Knees, skin, bones, teeth

ELEMENT: Earth

POLARITY: Yin (introvert, feeling)

QUALITY: Cardinal

GOOD DAYS: Loyal, family-minded, hardworking, devoted, honest, fearless

BAD DAYS: Pessimistic, unforgiving, cold, materialistic, snobbish, has feelings of hopelessness

FAVORITE THINGS: Business cards, official titles, being in charge, exclusive clubs, "leg sports" such as soccer or track

WHAT THEY HATE: Quitting, shouting in public, careless mistakes, traveling without an itinerary, doing things "just for the heck of it"

SECRET WISH: To have every need taken care of

HOW TO SPOT THEM: Distinctive jaw, strong teeth, wise look in the eyes

WHERE YOU'LL FIND THEM: Enjoying quality time with the family, working obsessively on a large-scale project, running for team captain or student-council president

ASTROTURF—HOW THEY HANG OUT

When They're On

Endurance-oriented Capricorns love to take on a challenge. As the sign of the mountain goat, they get a rush from outdoor sports such as rock-climbing or soccer. Success and status turn them on, and they love the honor of hanging out at exclusive, members-only clubs. It's all about being seen in public and looking their best. A black-tie party, formal awards ceremony, or networking event will put these born achievers in an upbeat mood.

When They're Off

"Work hard, sleep hard" could be the Capricorn motto, so don't bother trying to wake them up on those days off. Family time is important to this sign, and they'd prefer to just hang out at home playing cards, renting videos, and scarfing down hot meals. It's all about refueling their tank. As an earth sign, nature holds a special appeal for them. A drive through the country will relax their minds. The farther, the better, since Capricorns prefer to take the long and winding road.

FRIENDS

Capricorn as Friend

Time is of the essence in Capricorn friendships. These are not "here today, gone tomorrow" people. This devoted sign prefers to take things one step at a time, creating a strong foundation and building up from there. Rather than outgrow people, Capricorns are more likely to hold on past the expiration date, dredging up old memories that others have long since forgotten.

Capricorn is the "father sign" of the zodiac, and those it rules like to be seen as teachers or authority figures to their friends. They don't mind stepping back and hooking up their friends with behind-the-scenes help. As useful as they like to be to their buds, they get a little uncomfortable when others try to return the favor. At times they may actually push away support. As a result, they are often misjudged as distant or cold. Learning to receive as well as give can help Capricorns create a more even flow in their friendships.

☺☺ Friends of Capricorn

Hardworking Capricorns like to mix business with pleasure. They often develop tight bonds with people they meet on the job or through a team project. They are the "popular people" of the zodiac, so friends who can help them increase their status are valuable assets. Make Capricorns look good, and they'll stay by your side for eternity. Not that they won't hang out with the rebels and slackers. People who allow Capricorns to mentor them will also provide this sign with a much-needed power surge.

Family comes before everyone, though. Second on the list are the people who knew them back in the day. (These people are like family to Capricorns.) Capricorns are looking for friends who will stand the test of time. Chasing after people doesn't interest them. When all is said and done, they are too practical to waste their time like that. A consistent effort will win Capricorn's trust and will win you a friend for life.

❓ Got an Issue?

One-track mindedness

Capricorns were born with their eyes on the prize. Once they've set their sights on something, they begin to climb slowly and steadily toward that goal. Often they become so focused on reaching the finish line that they fail to pay attention to the journey, looking neither to the right nor the left. Changes occur in the atmosphere around them, and Capricorns ignore these factors, as if giving them attention might cause them to lose motivation. They believe that if they just keep pushing ahead, eventually they'll get what they want. In truth, Capricorns' persistence does often lead them to their destination. By the time they get there, however, they may discover that this thing they worked so hard to achieve doesn't bring the feeling of complete satisfaction that they believed with all their hearts it would. Sadly, this refusal to explore their options brings Capricorns as much pain as it does reward. In their uphill climbs, they often wear themselves down to the point of burnout and destruction. Learning to create smaller steps within their master plans can help Capricorns let go and enjoy the beauty that change can bring.

Capricorn with a one-track mind: Capricorn Kid Rock has been producing genre-fusing funk-metal-rock-rap albums since the early 1990s, when the

sound was considered ahead of its time. Refusing to compromise his style, he continued making music until the world eventually caught up and he became a commercial success.

Destiny's Child: Career Paths for Capricorn

film producer

manager

politician

police officer

stockbroker

doctor

president

school principal

business owner/CEO

⚷ Gifts That Keep On Giving

✳ Handcrafted leather clothes and accessories such as jackets, wallets, and watchbands

✳ Palm pilot or datebook for scheduling all their social and work engagements

✳ Hiking or rock-climbing equipment (Capricorn is the sign of the mountain goat)

✳ Membership to an exclusive club

✳ Tickets to the World Cup, the Grammys, or the Olympics

✳ A home-cooked candlelight dinner (best done as a surprise)

✳ Thick, hand-knit sweater or cashmere cardigan in a neutral or conservative color

✳ One-day rental of a luxury vehicle or sports car

CAPRICORN STARMATES

GUYS: Jude Law, Ricky Martin, Verne Troyer, Kid Rock, Tiger Woods, Jim Carrey, Nicholas Cage, Elvis Presley, Taye Diggs, Wesley Snipes, Martin Luther King Jr., Ray J, Mel Gibson, Kevin Costner, Muhammed Ali, David Bowie, Tyrese, Christian Burns, Orlando Bloom, Joey McIntyre, Shabba

Ranks, Morris Chestnut, Dave Matthews, Rob Zombie, Raekwon, Michael Stipe, Jonathan Davis, Tom Dumont, Eddie Veder, Zack de la Rocha, A. J. McLean, Jared Leto, Michael Imperioli, Ryan Seacrest

GIRLS: Estella Warren, Mary J. Blige, Kate Moss, Dido, Amanda Peete, Dolly Parton, Angie Martinez, Aaliyah, Joey Lauren Adams, Mia Tyler, Kate Bosworth, Sade, Christy Turlington, Donna Summer, Annie Lennox, Gaby Hoffmann, Julia Louis-Dreyfuss, Tia Carrere, Eliza Dushku

AQUARIUS
(January 20–February 18)

SYMBOL: The Water Bearer

COSMIC RULER: Uranus—planet of originality

BODY PART: Ankles

ELEMENT: Air

POLARITY: Yang (extrovert, doing)

QUALITY: Fixed

GOOD DAYS: Communicative, original, open-minded, fair, logical, inviting

BAD DAYS: Guarded, detached, destructive, out-of-touch, irrational, desperate

FAVORITE THINGS: Computer programming, teaching, team sports, anything with a cause or mission, independent films

WHAT THEY HATE: Injustice, drama queens, feeling isolated, owing money or favors, having to choose just one thing

SECRET WISH: To experience total freedom

HOW TO SPOT THEM: Cute smile, quirky movements, darting eyes

WHERE YOU'LL FIND THEM: Backpacking through the Swiss Alps, picketing a company with unfair hiring practices, coaching a Little League team

ASTROTURF—HOW THEY HANG OUT

 ## When They're On

Aquarians love to hang with a crew, and "the more, the merrier" could be their motto. They're always down for a party, especially if it offers a chance to meet new people. Discovering things gives them a thrill, and they'll happily wander the earth in pursuit of an unusual thrill. They love the great outdoors, particularly the mountains, so anything from snowboarding to hiking will charge them up and give them a chance to flex their powerful leg muscles.

 ## When They're Off

Active and alert Aquarians aren't good at doing nothing. On a day off, they'll surf the web or head to the bookstore in search of the meaning of life. Taking in new information recharges them, and they get a rush from independent films and gallery exhibits. At times, they can get panicky about the future and should resist the urge to dial a psychic hotline. They're better off channeling this energy into some volunteer work, which can help these team players feel positive about the world again.

FRIENDS

Aquarius as Friend

Aquarius is the sign of friendship and teamwork, and Aquarians tend to be more focused on the group than the individual and often have trouble letting themselves get *really* close to people. Aquarians dream of making the world a better place and may actually be more generous with the general public than they are with their own friends and family. Running off and joining the Peace Corps they can handle. Should a friend show up bawling on their doorstep, however, they may be overwhelmed by the intensity of it all. Their hearts are big, and they will try to help. But they'll feel a little bit trapped by the situation, too.

Freedom is important to Aquarians, which is why they like to keep things light. That way, they won't feel bad about running off to the opposite corner of the world at a moment's notice. At times, this strategy backfires, leaving them feeling lonely and disconnected. Or they may pick one—and only one—person to open up to and get attached to the point of near obsession. Like the rest of us, they need people. It is only their fear of being needed in return that keeps them from expressing this. Learning to relax and form deeper bonds is a powerful lesson for this sign. If they open up—even just a little—they will be surprised to find how many people are waiting to support them in whatever their freedom-loving hearts desire.

Friends of Aquarius

Thinking Aquarians don't like dummies or bores. They're just too quick for that. You've gotta stimulate their minds or make them laugh if you want to get in the door. They appreciate a little quirky or eccentric twist and have some real weirdos for friends. Not dangerous weirdos, mind you. Just unique people who love freedom as much as they do. Aquarians love to talk and analyze, particularly about philosophical ideas, bizarre mysteries, and strategies for making their world more exciting. If they sense that you're capable of stimulating conversation, expect to be meeting them at a coffeeshop on a regular basis.

Emotions, on the other hand, are not Aquarians' favorite thing to deal with—unless they are being analyzed in a logical way. (They'd rather hear you start a sentence with "I think" than "I feel.") Weeping drama queens and self-destructive types need not apply. These people will send shivers down Aquarians' cool and logical spines. Calm and patient (and private!) people who do not push Aquarians to open up before they're ready are the ones with whom Aquarians will ultimately share their deepest secrets.

❷ Got an Issue?

Hiding behind other people

Ruled by unpredictable Uranus, Aquarians are famous for making sudden changes—and they need to feel free to switch it up at any point. While they do crave fame, they also shy away from solo careers. The thought of going it alone makes them squirm, since that level of responsibility may also prevent them from shifting gears suddenly. The fact that Aquarius also happens to be the sign of teamwork doesn't make things any easier. In many cases Aquarians will stay in groups that they've long since outgrown, attempting to hide behind other people. This is no easy task, since quirky Aquarians always stand out in the crowd with their original style or eccentric viewpoints. Rather than take a chance on their own abilities, they let others latch on and benefit from their talent. Problems arise when another person gains fame from Aquarians' hard work and original ideas. Anger can bubble up out of nowhere—and hell hath no fury like an Aquarius scorned! Learning to step out and accept their own star power can help Aquarians enjoy the glory their free-thinking nature has earned them.

Aquarius in hiding: Although he has experienced his own success as a rapper, Aquarius Dr. Dre prefers working behind the scenes, producing hits for other artists like Eminem and Snoop Dogg.

Destiny's Child: Career Paths for Aquarius

inventor

futurist

nonprofit worker

computer programmer or technician

teacher or coach

astronomer

psychic healer

scientist

talk-show host

author

researcher

Gifts That Keep On Giving

* Electrical equipment such as computers, stereos, amplifiers, or any plug-in household gadgets
* Classic clothes with a cutting-edge twist that gives them a one-of-a-kind feel
* Dinner at a hip and trendy restaurant, preferably with outdoor seating
* Software to help them keep track of their finances
* Adventure-sport equipment such as mountain bikes and snowboards
* Books about astrology or any New Age or spiritual subject
* Silver costume jewelry
* Club or concert passes for Aquarius and ten of her closest friends (Aquarians love to roll in a group.)

AQUARIUS STARMATES

GUYS: Justin Timberlake, Elijah Wood, Michael Jordan, Dr. Dre, D'Angelo, Vince Carter, Nick Carter, Ice T, Chris Rock, Bobby Brown, Rob Thomas,

Seth Green, Joey Fatone, Oscar De La Hoya, Jerry O'Connell, Jam Master Jay, Cam'Ron, Danny Moder, Rakim, Ross Powers, Mike Shinoda, Billie Joe Armstrong, David Gallagher, Big Boi, Robbie Williams, Axl Rose, Wes Borland, John Travolta, Jerry Springer

GIRLS: Jennifer Aniston, Brandy, Shakira, Alicia Keys, Minnie Driver, Kelly Rowland, Denise Richards, Sheryl Crow, Christina Ricci, Mena Suvari, Natalie Imbruglia, Alice Walker, Beverly Mitchell, Paris Hilton, Heather Graham, Mia Kirshner, Willa Ford, Yoko Ono, Oprah Winfrey, Lisa Marie Presley

PISCES
(February 19–March 20)

SYMBOL: The Fish

RULING PLANET: Neptune—planet of dreams and imagination

BODY PART: Feet

ELEMENT: Water

POLARITY: Yin (introvert, feeling)

QUALITY: Mutable

GOOD DAYS: Romantic, helpful, wise, comforting, imaginative

BAD DAYS: Gullible, self-pitying, out of touch with reality, self-destructive, clingy, masochistic

FAVORITE THINGS: Dancing, romantic encounters, laughing and crying, walks on the beach, creative pursuits, candles and incense

WHAT THEY HATE: Reality, throwing away the Christmas tree, drill sergeants, daylight, bad design, noisy music

SECRET WISH: To find unconditional love

HOW TO SPOT THEM: Large, dreamy eyes; soothing voice; glamorous "old photo" look

WHERE YOU'LL FIND THEM: Printing photos in the darkroom, people-watching in the shadows of an underground club, holding hands under the table at a romantic restaurant with a sunset view

ASTROTURF—HOW THEY HANG OUT

 ## When They're On

Sensory overload! Pisces need plenty of visual aids and sound effects to turn them on. Watching a performance is a favorite pastime—be it an underground band or just a group of interesting people mixing it up. As long as there's music pumping, Pisces will escape into the happy dream-world that gives them a mind-body-soul kind of rush. Their sign rules the feet, so dancing or jogging on the beach will help them clear their heads.

 ## When They're Off

Sensitive, intuitive Pisces can easily become overwhelmed by the sights and sounds they take in. Finding the words to express these feelings is tough, so they require creative outlets to help them vent. A set of oil paints, audio and video recording equipment, a notebook for jotting down poems—these tools not only help Pisces free their minds but turn their struggles into masterpieces.

FRIENDS

 ## Pisces as Friend

Beauty-loving Pisces are charming and magical friends. Compassionate to no end, they love to help out in times of crisis. Feeling needed gives them a rush, and they don't mind if the people in their lives depend on them—at first. But, inevitably, the tide turns, and these fish get swept off into another dreamworld. This schizo behavior can both baffle and wound loved ones. One minute, Pisces are so attentive; the next minute, they disappear without a trace.

Underneath it all is the fact that Pisces simply hate to disappoint people. But, like the best of us, they also need time to take care of them-selves—and they actually feel guilty about this! So guilty, in fact, that it takes them forever to call and apologize for this "flakiness." To avoid these conflicts, Pisces must make peace with the fact that they have needs. Yes, they are human! It's okay to cancel plans or to say no. Instead of letting their guilt get the best of them, Pisces need to remember that people won't be crushed if they can't make it for the big party. But friends will be pissed off if their Pisces don't give them a courtesy call.

Staying in touch—with themselves and their loved ones—can make their friendships flow smoothly.

😊😊 Friends of Pisces

"Keep your friends close, keep your enemies closer"—this could be the Pisces mantra. Looking at the groups of people they surround themselves with, one may wonder how exactly Pisces call these people friends. Troubled types attract the naturally compassionate fish, but can also suck them down. A careful screening process is necessary before Pisces get too heavily involved, or they may find themselves caught in destructive or user-friendly relationships.

The best friends for Pisces are stable types who don't actually *need* anything from Pisces, but can appreciate the imagination and romance that Pisces bring into their world. Although, initially, Pisces may judge these types as dull, in the end these people are the very rocks that the fish will thank their lucky stars to have in their lives.

❷ Got an Issue?

Escaping reality

Ruled by watery Neptune, Pisces see the world through a hazy veil, much like a photographer who covers his lens with a piece of gauze. Through this filter, everything has a dreamy quality, which is just how the zodiac's fish like it. When it comes to sweeping things under the rug, Pisces have been known to ignore the dirt until it piles up into a mountain. Then, they're trapped by it. The bill collectors start calling. Term papers are due in four hours, and they haven't even begun the research. Their perfect loves turn out to be scandalous two-timers. Instead of dealing, they may go into denial, believing that if they wish hard enough, everything will become magically delicious again. Sadly, it never quite works out that way. And the cleanup is a mother.

On the flip side, many Pisces have learned to see the "beauty in ugliness." These types run the risk of getting dragged so deep into the underground that they become trapped below the surface. All the drama can be avoided, if Pisces simply wait until they see the picture clearly before diving in. Reality checks are essential to their success—even if that means relying on friends to keep them grounded.

Reality-escaping Pisces: A hopeless romantic, Drew Barrymore is known for saying "I do" first and asking questions later. Her two marriages both lasted less than a year.

Destiny's Child: Career Paths for Pisces

therapist

nurse

marine biologist

massage therapist

musician or music critic

graphic designer

photographer or filmmaker

actor

nutritionist

Gifts That Keep On Giving

* Photography and video equipment
* Portable CD or MP3 player for listening to music on the go
* Passes to a water park or scuba-diving lessons
* Canvas, easel, and paints for their creative jones
* Romantic surprises such as a picnic for two, overlooking a beautiful setting
* Tiny calculator for figuring out how much money they *really* have—or don't have
* Dance classes for two, such as salsa or swing dancing (Pisces rule the feet)
* Relaxing bedroom accessories such as scented candle sets, silver picture frames, plush pillows, and dream diaries

GUYS: Jon Bon Jovi, Bow Wow, Mark McGrath, Shaquille O'Neal, Freddie Prinze Jr., Bruce Willis, D. L. Hughley, Quincy Jones, Mark Hoppus, Billy Corgan, Taylor Hanson, Brian Littrell, Ja Rule, Johnny Knoxville, Benicio del Toro, Chris Martin, Chris Klein, Sean Astin, Joe Hahn, Kurt Cobain, Jay Hernandez, Billy Zane, Tone Loc, Seal, Timbaland, Rob Lowe, Joel and Benji Madden, Kerr Smith, Danny Masterson

GIRLS: Drew Barrymore, Jennifer Love Hewitt, Queen Latifah, Cindy Crawford, Chelsea Clinton, Juliette Binoche, Kristin Davis, Chilli, Mia Hamm, Thora Birch, Lauren Ambrose, Lisa Loeb, Lea Salonga, Veronica Webb, Camryn Manheim, Chynna Phillips, Melissa Auf der Maur, Jackie Joyner-Kersee, Sharon Stone, Ali Larter, Laura Prepon

section 3
LOVE

Who do you love? Spin the cosmic wheel of fortune and see. While there are certain astro-factors that may help compatibility, we believe that any two signs can make a relationship work. The trick is to know which obstacles could lie ahead. After all, every relationship has its challenges. This section breaks down some general rules of attraction, which are based on the distance between signs. We've outlined the good, the bad, and the ugly that can happen between every possible astrological combo. Use this advice to max out your enjoyment of *any* relationship you choose.

YOUR MATCHING ELEMENT

Your sign's element (fire, earth, air, or water) can give clues to compatibility. In general, the positive signs (fire and air) get along with one another, and the negative signs (earth and water) vibe best.

YOUR ELEMENT	SMOOTHEST ATTRACTION	A LITTLE MORE WORK
Fire (Aries, Leo, Sagittarius)	Air (Gemini, Libra, Aquarius)	Earth (Taurus, Virgo, Capricorn)
	Fire (Aries, Leo, Sagittarius)	Water (Cancer, Scorpio, Pisces)

Continued

YOUR ELEMENT	SMOOTHEST ATTRACTION	A LITTLE MORE WORK
Earth (Taurus, Virgo, Capricorn)	Water (Cancer, Scorpio, Pisces)	Air (Gemini, Libra, Aquarius)
	Earth (Taurus, Virgo, Capricorn)	Fire (Aries, Leo, Sagittarius)
Water (Cancer, Scorpio, Pisces)	Earth (Taurus, Virgo, Capricorn)	Air (Gemini, Libra, Aquarius)
	Water (Cancer, Scorpio, Pisces)	Fire (Aries, Leo, Sagittarius)
Air (Gemini, Libra, Aquarius)	Fire (Aries, Leo, Sagittarius)	Earth (Taurus, Virgo, Capricorn)
	Air (Gemini, Libra, Aquarius)	Water (Cancer, Scorpio, Pisces)

THE SECRET OF DISTANCE

Astrology is all about geometry, and the distance between your sign and another has everything to do with how you get along. This relationship can either cause friction or rub you the right way. So before you add someone to your romantic-buddy list, here's a quick roadmap to scope out what's in store.

SAME SIGN—ATTACK OF THE CLONES

Dating someone of the same sign can either create sibling rivalry or a beautiful reflection. On the upside, a person who's so much like you could have a lot of natural tolerance for your strange habits, since he probably shares them. You often want the same things from life, and could flourish with each other's support. At other times, you may be too similar to offer valuable perspective or balance out each other's neuroses. If you're both moody Cancers, who's gonna bring the sunshine? If you're both ambitious Capricorns, who's gonna keep the home fires burning? You could end up feeling more of a brother-sister vibe than a romantic one. Ultimately, you've gotta come home to yourself anyway, so why not enjoy a second helping? Play it right, and you can share more seasons than the cast of *Friends*.

SMOOTH SAILING: Jennifer Lopez and Ben Affleck (Leos), Catherine Zeta-Jones and Michael Douglas (Libras), Redman and Method Man (Aries)

CHOPPY WATERS: Tupac Shakur and Notorious B.I.G. (Geminis), Christina Aguilera and Britney Spears (Sagittarians), Bill Clinton and Monica Lewinsky (Leos)

ONE SIGN APART—NOSY NEIGHBORS

Aries: Pisces, Taurus	Taurus: Aries, Gemini	Gemini: Taurus, Cancer
Cancer: Gemini, Leo	Leo: Cancer, Virgo	Virgo: Leo, Libra
Libra: Virgo, Scorpio	Scorpio: Libra, Sagittarius	Sagittarius: Scorpio, Capricorn
Aquarius: Capricorn, Pisces	Capricorn: Sagittarius, Aquarius	Pisces: Aquarius, Aries

Curiosity is the magnet that draws these two extremely different signs together. Because of their closeness on the zodiac, they feel a karmic connection, and each has something to learn from the other. However, they have no *elements* or *qualities* in common. You are likely to approach life, love, and relationships from very different places. The sign after yours is said to be an "evolved" form of you, with that sign's personality traits formed in reaction to the hardships you suffer. Like next-door neighbors, you'll always be curious about each other. (Once you glimpse into somebody's living-room window, don't you want to know more?) However, there's a reason most neighbors keep a fence up to separate their personal property. Johnny-Next-Door's house may be fun to visit, but do you want his tacky lawn furniture and weed collection unleashed on your well-manicured English garden? A one-sign-apart romance is a gamble similar to that in the TV show *Trading Spaces,* where next-door-neighbor couples redecorate a room in each other's home. The results will either devastate or amaze you.

SMOOTH SAILING: Freddie Prinze Jr. (Pisces) and Sarah Michelle Gellar (Aries), Madonna (Leo) and Guy Ritchie (Virgo), Gwen Stefani (Libra) and Gavin Rossdale (Scorpio), Jada Pinkett (Virgo) and Will Smith (Libra)

CHOPPY WATERS: Ike Turner (Scorpio) and Tina Turner (Sagittarius), Nicolas Cage (Capricorn) and Lisa Marie Presley (Aquarius), Nicole Kidman (Gemini) and Tom Cruise (Cancer), Moby (Virgo) and Eminem (Libra)

TWO SIGNS APART—BEST FRIENDS WITH BENEFITS

Aries: Sagittarius, Aquarius	Taurus: Pisces, Cancer	Gemini: Aries, Leo
Cancer: Taurus, Virgo	Leo: Gemini, Libra	Virgo: Cancer, Scorpio
Libra: Leo, Sagittarius	Scorpio: Virgo, Capricorn	Sagittarius: Libra, Aquarius
Capricorn: Scorpio, Pisces	Aquarius: Sagittarius, Aries	Pisces: Capricorn, Taurus

These natural-born chillers just "get" each other, and can enjoy never-ending hangouts and conversation. That's because they're made up of compatible *elements*. They'll either be a combo of negative signs (earth and water), or positive signs (fire and air). According to astrology, earth and water signs tend to be gentle and conservative, while fire and air signs tend to be more dynamic and expressive. Although romance isn't a guarantee, communication will flow, and you won't have to constantly explain yourself to this person. Often, this relationship will form after years of platonic friendship. One day, this person magically changes from buddylicious to bootylicious.

SMOOTH SAILING: Penelope Cruz (Taurus) and Tom Cruise (Cancer), Brad Pitt (Sagittarius) and Jennifer Aniston (Aquarius), Halle Berry (Leo) and Eric Benet (Libra)

CHOPPY WATERS: Britney Spears (Sagittarius) and Justin Timberlake (Aquarius), Angelina Jolie (Gemini) and Billy Bob Thornton (Leo), Kirsten Dunst (Taurus) and Tobey MacGuire (Cancer)

THREE SIGNS APART— BATTLE OF THE BANDS

Aries: Cancer, Capricorn	Taurus: Aquarius, Leo	Gemini: Pisces, Virgo
Cancer: Aries, Libra	Leo: Taurus, Scorpio	Virgo: Gemini, Sagittarius
Libra: Cancer, Capricorn	Scorpio: Leo, Aquarius	Sagittarius: Virgo, Pisces
Capricorn: Aries, Libra	Aquarius: Scorpio, Taurus	Pisces: Gemini, Sagittarius

A sign that's three away from yours shares the same *quality* (cardinal, fixed, or mutable), so your goals may be similar. However, this person's sign is in an incompatible *element* (fire, water, air, or earth), and that can stir up tension. For example, Aries is a fire sign, which usually gets along with air signs or other fire signs. The key to an Aries relationship with an earth or water sign is balancing the ingredients. Throw too much water or dirt on a fire, and the flame goes out. At the same time, a fire must be built on the earth, and a little water can help manage a fire that's burning too fast. These two will have to constantly compromise to keep from dominating or draining each other. They'll have to switch between nurturing each other and helping each other get established. Expect your inner children to raid the playground on a regular basis. If you take the challenge, you'll have to stay on your toes—the work could be as rigorous (and potentially rewarding) as *Making the Band*. Jump in *only* if you're up for the challenge.

SMOOTH SAILING: Courtney Cox (Gemini) and David Arquette (Virgo), Richie Sambora (Cancer) and Heather Locklear (Libra), Julia Roberts (Scorpio) and Danny Moder (Aquarius)

CHOPPY WATERS: Nas (Virgo) and Jay-Z (Sagittarius), Pink (Virgo) and Britney Spears (Sagittarius), Mike Tyson (Cancer) and Evander Holyfield (Libra), Mariah Carey (Aries) and Derek Jeter (Cancer)

FOUR SIGNS APART— SWEET HOME ALABAMA

Fire: Aries-Leo-Sagittarius
Air: Gemini-Libra-Aquarius

Earth: Taurus-Virgo-Capricorn
Water: Cancer-Scorpio-Pisces

It's so nice to come home to somebody who understands you. Somebody who wants the same things from life, who accepts you for who you are, who doesn't make you work overtime for love. It's so . . . zzzzzzz . . . Wait, did we just fall asleep? These are some of the easiest relationships, since you're never "out of your element." Fire is most comfortable with fire, earth likes earth, and so on. The only potential hazard is that things are *so* comfortable, it's easy to get lazy. Keep the passion alive. Don't cut off the rest of the world, even if you've built a paradise for two. Just because your relationship is as smooth as butter doesn't mean it can't become a country crock if you take each other for granted. Change out of the sweatpants and comb your hair. Hang out with other friends to keep the energy flowing.

SMOOTH SAILING: Talisa Soto (Aries) and Benjamin Bratt (Sagittarius), Venus Williams (Gemini) and Serena Williams (Libra), Jessica Simpson (Cancer) and Nick Lachey (Scorpio), Missy Elliott (Cancer) and Timbaland (Pisces)

CHOPPY WATERS: Lauryn Hill (Gemini) and Wyclef Jean (Libra), Carson Daly (Cancer) and Tara Reid (Scorpio), Shannen Doherty (Aries) and Alyssa Milano (Sagittarius), Gisele Bundchen (Cancer) and Leonardo DiCaprio (Scorpio)

FIVE SIGNS APART—
ALL-STAR CHALLENGE

Aries: Virgo, Scorpio	Taurus: Libra, Sagittarius	Gemini: Scorpio, Capricorn
Cancer: Sagittarius, Aquarius	Leo: Capricorn, Pisces	Virgo: Aquarius, Aries
Libra: Pisces, Taurus	Scorpio: Aries, Gemini	Sagittarius: Taurus, Cancer

Fasten your seat belt, because you're going on an emotional roller-coaster ride. The highs and lows, the devastating drops and terrifying climbs . . . this relationship has 'em all. Even after you puke your guts out, you'll want to ride this twisted beast again and again. But your hopes of conquering your fears may be in vain. These relationships can be the most passionate—and the most painful—in the zodiac. Expect to wave at least six flags when declaring one of your many truces. You should also plan to work hard . . . just to get the relationship hardly working. Your two signs have no compatible qualities or elements, so you're as different as night and day. There's always something about the other person that remains an unsolved mystery. As a result, attraction and frustration will burn bright. Every day will somehow feel like a first date, and the butterflies will remain in your stomach no matter how many years you stay together. Breakups could haunt you for the rest of your lives. This temptation island may leave no survivors—or it could send you on a lifelong adventure finding clues for a buried treasure.

SMOOTH SAILING: Reese Witherspoon (Aries) and Ryan Phillipe (Virgo), Hillary Swank (Leo) and Chad Lowe (Capricorn), Usher (Libra) and Chilli (Pisces), Ashanti (Libra) and Ja Rule (Pisces)

CHOPPY WATERS: Tom Green (Leo) and Drew Barrymore (Pisces), David Blaine (Aries) and Fiona Apple (Virgo), Lenny Kravitz (Gemini) and Lisa Bonet (Scorpio), Johnny Depp (Gemini) and Kate Moss (Capricorn)

SIX SIGNS APART—BALANCING ACT

Aries-Libra
Cancer-Capricorn

Taurus-Scorpio
Leo-Aquarius

Gemini-Sagittarius
Virgo-Pisces

Your opposite sign is your "other half"—like the Dr. Evil to your Austin Powers. Falling in love with this beautiful stranger can feel a little trippy at times. The relationship will either be rocked by major sibling rivalry, or you'll balance each other out beautifully. From the great distance across the zodiac, you can see each other in full, shagadelic color. As a result, you can offer amazing perspective—as long as you're willing to hear the hardcore truth about yourself in return. If you're not ready for that jelly, save your mojo for somebody else. But if you're up for some major growing pains in the name of love, this one will be simply groovy, baby.

SMOOTH SAILING: Pamela Anderson (Cancer) and Kid Rock (Capricorn), Uma Thurman (Taurus) and Ethan Hawke (Scorpio), Mark Consuelos (Aries) and Kelly Ripa (Libra), JC Chasez (Leo) and Justin Timberlake (Aquarius)

CHOPPY WATERS: Limp Bizkit's Fred Durst (Leo) and Wes Borland (Aquarius), Whitney Houston (Leo) and Bobby Brown (Aquarius)

WHO DO YOU LOVE?
A SIGN-BY-SIGN GUIDE
TO YOUR RELATIONSHIPS

How do you groove with each sign of the zodiac? We've synced up every star-studded combo here, and tossed in advice on how the toughest astro-matches can run smoothly. Save your relationships from drama with a few cosmic shortcuts. Use this as a guide for friends and family, too.

FIND YOUR MATCH!

ARIES IN LOVE

ARIES: (March 21–April 19)

★ What They Need in a Mate

* Attention—to be spoiled and babied
* Freedom—a confident, non-clingy partner who won't cramp their style
* A good listener—they always have something to say
* To feel like number one—Aries love to win!
* To have it their way, right away
* Control—a chance to be the boss
* A mate with a sense of humor, adventure, and perspective
* Directness and honesty—anyone *too* easy to push around bores them

☆ What They Offer a Mate

* Passionate intensity—both in love and war
* Adventure—you'll never be bored!
* A chance to get in touch with your spontaneous side
* A seat on their pedestal—either temporary or permanent
* Inspiration with an occasional headache—don't bother trying to win an argument here
* Creative conversation—Aries have plenty of ideas and adventures to talk about

ARIES
(March 21–April 19)

+

ARIES
(March 21–April 19)

STAR COMBO: actors Sarah Jessica Parker and Matthew Broderick, married

THE BREAKDOWN

Energetic Aries like to be first in everything, and the competition could get fierce between these two. As the zodiac's first sign, Aries are childlike by nature and may act like screaming infants if their basic needs aren't met. Both Aries will need plenty of attention *and* freedom, and they'll understand this duality in each other. As long as they're able to work out an even give-and-take system, this can be a relationship of passion coupled with a fiercely loyal friendship.

COMMON GROUND

Aries are aggressive, dynamic, and competitive. These are macho men and liberated women—even the ones who play innocent have a fierce streak in them. Attention is an issue—they want to be taken care of, and may go for a mate who is willing to spoil them. Aries rules the nervous system, and they can drive people crazy with their issues such as "germophobia" or bizarrely specific food preferences.

VIVE LA DIFFÉRENCE

Are they a ram or a lamb? The ram Aries are fiery, quick to anger, and impulsive, filling a room with their supercharged energy. Impulsive and direct, they know what they want, and go for it. The lamb Aries are generally those who weren't properly attended to as kids, or whose free spirits were somehow crushed. They hide their true, fiery natures behind a timid, "sheepish" front. The lambs are best off shearing most of this wool, since they can't pull it over people's eyes anyway.

HOW TO MAKE IT LAST

Keep the fires hot, but don't burn each other out. Have your own individual lives, but don't forget to support each other—this is a team effort, after all. Take turns being in charge and play "follow the leader"—make your Aries feel like a confident star. Give plenty of praise and admiration. Stay active—Aries have lots of energy to work off. Watch the egos and tempers, which can rage out of control.

HOW TO END IT FAST

With your fierce independence, your lives may not intersect enough to hold this together. If the relationship looks like an endless episode of *Who's the Boss?*, somebody may get fired. The diva-style blowups and angry righteousness could cause a communication collision, with nobody willing to back down and "lose" the match. If you insist on having it "your way, right away," the list of demands could be returned unfulfilled. Grow up, or find somebody who enjoys taking orders.

ARIES
(March 21–April 19)

✚

TAURUS
(April 20–May 20)

STAR COMBO: singer Victoria "Posh Spice" Beckham (Aries) and soccer player David Beckham (Taurus), married

THE BREAKDOWN

Although the combo of next-door-neighbor signs can be tricky, this one seems to work—at least for a while. Straight out the gate, it's all romance and compliments and TLC, which both signs love. Then . . . the big difference shows up. Taurus wants to settle down. Aries wants to run around. Aries doesn't necessarily want to run around on Tauruses in a cheating kind of way. They just need to get out of the house and star in a magical personal drama—and they can't help it if life has cast them to play the lead. Tauruses love a good show, but they'd rather catch it on DVD and watch from the couch, where they can fall asleep promptly at the closing credits, curled up in fleece pants and popcorn crumbs.

COMMON GROUND

Although Aries are more energetic than Tauruses, many Aries have a homebody side, too—and nobody can bring it out like a Taurus. Aries are not always as wild as their reputation suggests, and they'll happily snuggle in front of the TV. Both signs can be stubborn, and both like to be babied. If their emotional bottle-feeding and diaper changes happen on different schedules, then everyone gets to go home happily burped in a fresh pair of Pull-Ups. If not, you've got a couple of screaming infants with no Similac in sight.

VIVE LA DIFFÉRENCE

Taurus is a patient earth sign. Aries is an *imp*atient fire sign. Aries need to feel like they're divas on a faraway adventure, even when they're chilling at home. Tauruses need to feel like they're wearing silk pajamas and munching fresh-baked cookies, even when they're out at a club. Aries needs to release energy through high-intensity physical action, and Taurus is always frantically saving it up by living in a deep-lounge state. They could make great poster children for the "before" (Aries) and "after" (Taurus) of an energy-conservation campaign.

HOW TO MAKE IT LAST

Taurus will have to avoid being a stick-in-the-mud, and Aries will need to burn on a lower flame. In a balanced combo, Taurus will slow down

Aries' tracks just enough to mix in a few smooth, stabilizing beats. Aries will warm up the frozen earth of a Taurus ice queen or king, bringing out the passion. Taurus will be the *rock*—lending Aries a stable foundation to shoot flames from. Aries will be the *roll*—leading Taurus toward an exciting future, and keeping the two of them in motion.

HOW TO END IT FAST

If Aries embarrasses Taurus in public with a tacky remark, mismatched outfit, or temper tantrum, the bull will plod off elsewhere. Likewise, Aries will hang out at home only if Taurus doesn't order the ram around or suggest that Aries spend a "romantic" evening rolling up loose change. They'll both need to find lots of outside sources of attention, or else they could grow restless and frustrated. If Taurus tries to saddle Aries with too many responsibilities, the ram will roam toward more adventurous pastures. Stubbornness could turn this peaceful pasture into a battlefield, and a charging ram and bull can do plenty of damage when they lock horns.

ARIES
(March 21–April 19)

GEMINI
(May 21–June 20)

STAR COMBO: actors Matthew Broderick (Aries) and Helen Hunt (Gemini), exes

THE BREAKDOWN

Aries rules the head, and Gemini rules the intellect—what a meeting of the minds. As two of the best verbal communicators in the zodiac, they usually find an instant understanding. In most cases, they won't suffocate each other, since they both love freedom. However, attention-hungry Aries may be unsure they'll get the babying they need; long-winded Geminis may bore impatient Aries if they take too long to get to the point.

COMMON GROUND

These adventurers like to "think different," and love anything that challenges their minds. Debating is their forte, and they can twist words like a pair of pretzel vendors. Both signs are often articulate speakers, writers, and thinkers who love to talk for hours. They won't be told what to believe or who to become, so don't step to them with unsolicited advice unless you want to be told where to put it. Neither sign is a master of tact, and they prefer brutal honesty to pretty lies. When they want something, get out of the way unless you want to be bulldozed. In relationships, they're easily bored, always ready to run off to the next adventure.

VIVE LA DIFFÉRENCE

Fire-sign Aries need passion and emotional intensity, while air-sign Gemini prefers a cool, logical approach. Aries is the sign of the self and needs a lot of focused attention from partners. Gemini is the sign of the twins—with a built in "imaginary friend," they're far less needy. Although both signs are impulsive when it comes to new relationships, Aries usually gets more attached and involved, while Gemini holds back a bit. Aries is ruled by Mars, planet of passion and energy, and is often very physically expressive. Gemini is ruled by cool, analytical Mercury, and is reserved and unaffectionate by comparison.

HOW TO MAKE IT LAST

Sit still and stop those wandering minds. Drop your "I don't care" act and admit that you like each other, even if you met because neither one of you wanted to be tied down. Show some vulnerability, unless you want this to dissolve into a battle of wills. Build a strong friendship, then stop pretending that you're "just friends." Gemini, keep a few of those blunt opinions to yourself, especially if they wound Aries personally—the Aries ego is easily challenged. Aries, give up your need to be babied—Geminis don't do "adult diapers." They'll give you plenty of other things, so learn to be satisfied with what you get.

HOW TO END IT FAST

Too much independence could stall this at the gate—who's gonna keep the home fires burning? Aries need a place to unwind at home, and Geminis may be too busy on their own adventures to build the nest. Jealousy can flare, since both signs like to flirt yet can't stand their mate looking at anyone else. If these independent rebels don't recognize that being together is a choice—and an adventure—they may never get to the full-on commitment, even if it's obvious that they belong together.

ARIES
(March 21–April 19)

✦

CANCER
(June 21–July 22)

STAR COMBO: singer Mariah Carey (Aries) and athlete Derek Jeter (Cancer), exes

THE BREAKDOWN

Aggressive, radical Aries and sensitive, conservative Cancer will have to adjust to each other's style if they hope to ease their natural tension. Cancer is the mother of the zodiac, and Aries is the baby—this can be a relationship with a lot of nurturing *and* a lot of demands. Both of their inner children need emotional security, and finding it here will be an on-again, off-again thing. However, they can grow a lot from compromise, and their bond may remain even after they've learned their lessons and moved on.

COMMON GROUND

These two natural leaders love the taste of victory and hate to show their weaknesses. Both may come off as aloof or grumpy at times, giving people the false impression that they're unfriendly. With their strong verbal abilities, they can be gifted speakers and writers. Both signs have bouts of irrational jealousy—they may push down feelings, then release them in emotional outbursts. Neither sign trusts easily, and may bring out each other's paranoia.

VIVE LA DIFFÉRENCE

Aries is direct and outgoing, while Cancer is secretive and reserved. If there's a problem, Aries wants to talk it out, while Cancer withdraws into a moody silence. Aries's energy is raw and primal, while Cancers are more concerned with being cool. Independent Aries like to roam free with no demands or limitations—they'll travel the world solo and make friends along the way. Cancers stick to a comfortable crew of close friends, taking a homelike feeling with them even when they leave the nest.

HOW TO MAKE IT LAST

Take care of each other, offering lots of emotional security in the style your partner needs. Aries, give Cancers space and soothing when their insecure moods flare. Don't take things personally if one of you needs space. Cancers, pay attention to Aries—they hate to be ignored, so if you're slipping into a mood, reassure them first. Say "I love you" even when you feel like saying "go away." Mix adventure and comfort so that Cancer always feels the safety of home while Aries gets the thrill of conquering new terrain. Communicate openly and directly, keeping no secrets and checking your shared tendency to pout.

HOW TO END IT FAST

If Cancers' mothering turns into smothering, Aries will find somebody else to tuck them in at night. Nurturing is all good, but nagging is out—after all, Aries need to be the boss! If Aries acts flamboyant and tacky around Cancer's friends, the crab may disapprove sternly, leaving Aries feeling humiliated and angry. Watery Cancer's moodiness and pessimism will cool fiery Aries' temperature. Aries' hot temper and demands for immediate attention will drive Cancer deeper into sullen, silent spells—or provoke Cancer's own fearsome anger. A pissed-off crab will deliver a stunning pinch before withdrawing, sending the outraged ram smashing its horns against the Cancer's resistant shell. When the ram is ready to charge, Cancer will scurry away to safety.

ARIES
(March 21–April 19)
+
LEO
(July 23–August 22)

STAR COMBO: athlete Jason Sehorn (Aries) and actor Angie Harmon (Leo), married

THE BREAKDOWN

Lights, camera, action! The drama starts the second these two prima donnas meet, and it never stops. Aries rules the self and Leo rules the ego. They're both self-centered, bossy, and demanding . . . *and* generous, passionate, and independent. Whew! Sharing the stage will be hard unless they have very different starring roles, with zero competition for airtime and attention.

COMMON GROUND

As stunningly selfish as they can be, these signs can also be amazingly generous. It all depends on their mood. Both can be great listeners and nonstop talkers—with their endless energy, they're like walking power plants. They have natural star quality, and like to be praised—even worshiped—for what they do. (Early in her career, Leo Madonna told Dick Clark that her ultimate goal was "to rule the world.") These glamorous divas and regal dons hate to lose, and can have world-class temper tantrums—such as those of Aries Shannen Doherty and Steven Seagal, or Leos Whitney Houston and Fred Durst.

VIVE LA DIFFÉRENCE

Sun-ruled Leos are the kings/queens of the universe, and conduct themselves in an appropriately regal style—roaring only when their rulership is questioned. Aries is ruled by war-god Mars, and often has a more raw and aggressive style. Leos are often polite and smiling, and are more cooperative in a team situation. Aries often wear a mask of anger, and prefer to run the show, no questions asked. When their egos are challenged, which happens easily, these two signs respond with different tactics. Leos fear invisibility, while Aries fear criticism. When Leos want praise, they put on a show or play humble. In desperate hours, they may even confess to a weakness (they're faking it) or put themselves down so that you'll reassure them. Aries would never lower themselves that way. At the slightest scent of criticism, they talk themselves up and inflate their accomplishments to distract you from seeing their mistakes.

HOW TO MAKE IT LAST

Build a stadium-size stage—or better yet, perform in different megadomes. Be equals in your power. Leos, nurture Aries, but don't try to "parent" or boss them around unless you want a showdown. Aries, try a little tact around sensitive Leos, and never push them around. You're dealing with royalty, so grow up and show some respect. Be generous, passionate, and gush endlessly about your mutual admiration—never let up on the support. You'll both be busy, so make sure you have plenty of other sources of attention and reassurance.

HOW TO END IT FAST

Battle for the throne. Demand more attention than you're willing to give. Order each other around and put on haughty airs—the clash of these titans always ends in mortal combat. Act like spoiled babies and refuse to share your toys or compromise in any way. Let anger and aggression boil over and cloud your good judgment. Burn out trying to please each other, control each other, or prove each other wrong. Too much drama could stop the show, and too many ego trips will ruin the perfect vacation.

ARIES
(March 21–April 19)

+

VIRGO
(August 23–September 22)

STAR COMBO: actors Reese Witherspoon (Aries) and Ryan Phillipe (Virgo), married

THE BREAKDOWN

Finally—somebody who works as hard for Virgo as Virgo does for everybody else. Virgos bring out spoiled-brat Aries' "responsible" side. Aries awaken uptight Virgos' passion, and draw out their secrets. Here, Aries is the worker, and Virgo is the diva—a strange role reversal that could keep them locked together simply because they can't figure out how it happened.

COMMON GROUND

Neither sign likes to show their vulnerability up front. They respect privacy and may hold back on the self-expression until they've surveyed a whole situation, or allowed other people to show their hands first. With their 007 style, they would make great spies. These are "thinking" signs with neurotic tendencies—Aries rules the brain, and Virgo is powered by Mercury, planet of the mind. Both signs also share a certain innocence. Aries is the "infant" first sign of the zodiac, and may look at the world with a childlike wonder. Virgo is the sign of the virgin, and likes everything pure and untainted. Neither sign tolerates criticism well, especially not from each other. When they feel wronged or accused in any way, both react with dramatic displays of self-righteousness, either freezing the other out or going off on a blaming, exaggerated tirade.

VIVE LA DIFFÉRENCE

Virgos are simple, practical, and responsible, willing to put aside their desires and handle uneventful tasks that others consider a drag. Aries are complex, impulsive, and often irresponsible, following their whims all over the map, with zero patience for anything that isn't going to pay off. Aries' energy is intense and physical, while Virgo's is mellow and mental—although both can be quite athletic. Aries are more ambitious and demanding, while Virgos usually take what they get without complaining, and feel uncomfortable asking for anything.

HOW TO MAKE IT LAST

Aries need a mommy/daddy type to spoil them, and Virgos like to take care of everyone. This can work, as long as the roles get switched up now and again. Virgo, pamper Aries, show some passion, and keep the criticism constructive. Aries, don't get too high-maintenance or babyish—show Virgos that you have some sense in that active brain of yours if you want to keep their respect. Aries Reese Witherspoon and Virgo Ryan Phillipe admit to seeing a marriage counselor—a good idea, since this relationship requires constant adjustments and compromise to keep it on track.

HOW TO END IT FAST

Tyrannical Aries may foolishly assume that Virgos enjoy waiting on them like butlers, and could pile on the demands. Virgos may give service with a smile, but if the load gets too heavy, they start building up a storehouse of resentment. Rather than expressing this directly, Virgos may launch cruel, subtle attacks on Aries' ego with snide little criticisms. Or, Virgos could become suddenly cold, leaving Aries feeling like abandoned infants, desperate to win back love and attention. Oh, the cruelty! Virgo's rigid routines may clash with passionate Aries' need for impulsive adventures. If they criticize each other's intelligence or try to change each other's vastly different nature, there could be nothing but trouble in paradise.

ARIES
(March 21–April 19)

LIBRA
(September 23–October 22)

STAR COMBO: actors Heath Ledger (Aries) and Naomi Watts (Libra), flames

THE BREAKDOWN

Aries loves a battle, and Libra loves peace, but these opposite signs can balance each other out. Fierce Aries can help gentle Libras put some fire into their step. Smooth-flowing Libras can teach the Aries warriors how to refine their raw aggression and use their anger constructively. As the zodiac's first sign, Aries rules the self, and prizes individuality. Libra is the sign of partnership and cherishes relationships.

COMMON GROUND

Libra is symbolized by the scales of justice; Aries is ruled by war-god Mars—both fight unfairness and like to debate. They can deliberate on a topic for hours, and love a lengthy, lively conversation. Opinionated and liberated, the women of both signs have plenty of spice to go along with their sugar, and the men are competitive leaders. Both signs can be very social and charming people, with more than a touch of the spoiled prima donna in them. They speak candidly and like to drive home their points in a way that makes people laugh *and* think.

VIVE LA DIFFÉRENCE

Aries are ruled by Mars, the red-hot planet of passion and energy. Libras are ruled by Venus, the planet of beauty and love. As a result, Aries are rough around the edges, sporty, and tough—they may look intimidating even though they're big babies on the inside. Libras are more refined—their features are delicate and dimpled, even if there's a bold spirit beneath. Most Aries have an innate aggressive quality, while most Libras are more laid-back. Libras are sweet-talking diplomats, while Aries are known for their trademark rude comments. Although they're both competitive, Aries want to win and Libras want everyone to be happy.

HOW TO MAKE IT LAST

Aries, polish up the crude performance and show some class if you want to be seen on refined Libra's arm. Libra, loosen up and get your hands dirty—you may enjoy a roll in the mud with Aries more than you realize. Both signs can be self-absorbed and need lots of attention, so make sure this is a true give-and-take. Aries, listen to Libra's sound judgment and look before you leap. Libra, get a clue from Aries and make a bold move, instead of wasting years making up your mind.

HOW TO END IT FAST

Too much fiery Aries energy could tip Libra's scales way out of balance. Libras like to take it slow and will resist being trampled in an Aries stampede. Aries impulsiveness could send Libra searching for a more stable partner. Libra's constant analyzing and "wimpiness" could find Aries playing with a new action figure. This affair will burn out if you exhaust each other with demands for attention, or try to have it all on your terms. You'll need to have separate hobbies, friends, and lives. Both signs rebel against anyone who tries to boss them around or tells them how to live. Resist the urge to do that to each other.

ARIES
(March 21–April 19)

+

SCORPIO
(October 23–November 21)

STAR COMBO: actors Dennis Quaid (Aries) and Meg Ryan (Scorpio), divorced

THE BREAKDOWN

They're competitive, controlling, and slow to trust—so who's gonna open up first? The heat is intense, and the passion is in overdrive, and all is well if they're equally committed. Compromises will have to be made between Scorpio's insatiable need for security, and Aries' unquenchable thirst for freedom. Scorpio possessiveness could ignite the quick Aries temper. Aries' roving eye and flirtatious style could work Scorpio jealousy into a frenzy. Nobody wants to be around either of these signs when they're upset.

COMMON GROUND

These signs are passionate and powerful—they don't feel anything halfway, and may carry many scars. Aries is ruled by aggressive Mars, and Scorpio is coruled by Mars and power-planet Pluto. Both signs are ambitious and driven—when they want something, they'll stop at nothing to get it. Once they are mad, they're often blinded by rage, and can be deeply unforgiving. Both signs are control freaks with fragile egos, ruthless determination, and a desire to be untouchable in their game.

VIVE LA DIFFÉRENCE

Aries are a freedom-loving fire sign, and they're not quick to be tied down in a commitment. Scorpios are a security-seeking water sign—once they bond, they don't want to break it off. Although both signs anger easily, Aries gets mad, and Scorpio gets even. The rams charge enemies with a brutal head-butt, although rarely is the wound fatal. Scorpios' vengeful strike is pure poison. Their seduction tactics are different, too—Aries is direct, and Scorpio is sneaky. Scorpio studies its prey like a hawk, patient and plotting, always fearing the pain of rejection. Aries goes in for the kill, and moves on quickly if things don't work out.

HOW TO MAKE IT LAST

Find lots of energy outlets. Aries' should be physical and mental, and Scorpio's should be mental and spiritual. Don't compete. Give each other lots of attention, and focus on an outside project together—blend your amazing brain power. Aries, don't trample delicate Scorpio, because your insensitivity will get you stung. Scorpio, watch those cutting remarks—Aries doesn't like criticism. Aries, if you can't commit, don't play with this one—Scorpio demands blood loyalty.

HOW TO END IT FAST

Control and pride battles will be this relationship's downfall, with these signs' shared capacity to be envious and demanding. Wanna cause destruction? Hold on to anger or let rage distort your vision. Use your strong seductive powers to make each other jealous. Try to control each other. Compete ruthlessly and crush each other in pursuit of your own agendas. Scorpio can be secretive when Aries wants to talk, or may get stuck on a single topic when Aries wants to move on. Aries can exhaust and enrage Scorpio with wild energy bursts and unfaithfulness.

ARIES
(March 21–April 19)

✳

SAGITTARIUS
(November 22–December 21)

STAR COMBO: actress Kate Hudson (Aries) and Black Crowes' vocalist Chris Robinson (Sagittarius), married

THE BREAKDOWN

Finally—these two fearless fire-sign adventurers have found a kindred spirit. Few people love freedom and honesty as much as these two— and they can take it in large doses. Sagittarians help Aries see the big picture and channel their drive into supersize ventures worthy of

Aries' boundless energy. Aries bring out Sags' creativity and romantic expression. Because both signs are impulsive spenders, they may need to lock some of their cash away—in a place where the other can't find it.

COMMON GROUND

As fire signs, they're driven, passionate, and expressive. They were born to be pop superstars, like Sags Christina Aguilera and Britney Spears, or Aries Mariah Carey and Celine Dion. They're temperamental and impulsive, but thoughtful and thirsty for knowledge and new frontiers. Both signs have attention-deficit disorder—Aries can't *get* enough attention, and Sag can't *pay* enough of it. Crashing, burning, and blazing up again may be the story of their lives.

VIVE LA DIFFÉRENCE

Impulsive Aries is the "infant" of the zodiac, symbolized by a charging, headstrong ram. Sag is a philosopher, a half-human, half-horse centaur who aims arrows of truth at a target—this sign's intentions may be a little more directed. Aries can be a polished glamour-diva who needs lots of attention, while Sag is more of a down-to-earth "dirty hippie" who craves wide-open space. Ruled by aggressive Mars, Aries is a natural competitor who likes to win. Sag loves a challenge, too, but cares more about making everyone happy than about winning—the archer's abundant ruler Jupiter has enough goodies for everyone.

HOW TO MAKE IT LAST

Play follow the leader—and make it a treasure hunt. Aries, chill on the jealous routine and double standards. You don't want anyone telling you where to go and whom to talk to, and Sagittarius is exactly the same. Sag, sit still and give the focused attention that Aries needs. Travel together—literally or figuratively. Expand your minds and horizons; send your restless spirits on an international quest for inner peace. Watch your notorious tempers and brutal honesty—you're both as sensitive as you are tactless.

HOW TO END IT FAST

Aries' demands can drain Sagittarius, especially if the entrepreneurial archer is busy envisioning a huge new project. Sag's scattered focus and hundreds of unfinished projects could make Aries feel sidelined, and the ram needs to be numero uno. Sags' habit of remaining friends with all their exes could challenge Aries' ego again. The macho, bossy Aries routine will cease to amuse when Sag gets treated like the "little lady" or "man-slave." Not here, baby. Sag's ruthless honesty will no longer tickle Aries when the comment cuts the ram down in any way. Prepare for attack! If you battle for independence or sample a side dish, you could find yourselves as single as a slice of cheese.

ARIES
(March 21–April 19)

➕

CAPRICORN
(December 22–January 19)

STAR COMBO: singer Celine Dion (Aries) and manager René Angelil (Capricorn), married

THE BREAKDOWN

Aries is the "baby" of the zodiac who wants to be spoiled, and Capricorn is the "daddy," looking to take care of somebody special. It can be a family affair as long as they're both comfortable in these roles. Energetic Aries can lighten Capricorn's heavy spirits, while disciplined Cap can direct Aries' impulsive energy into a solid structure. As with Aries Celine Dion and her Capricorn manager-husband, René Angelil, this combo works best when Aries is the star and Capricorn is the quiet background producer—and they rise to the heights of status and fame together.

COMMON GROUND

Both signs are self-centered and ambitious—they want to be at the top, pampered, and livin' it up. They can be stubborn and pushy, refusing to compromise when they want something. Without a solid goal, these high achievers may get lost in unhappiness and frustration. They both like to win, and need to feel admired and respected in their game. An MVP award would be the ultimate achievement.

VIVE LA DIFFÉRENCE

Aries is the ram, charging headfirst into everything and rarely stopping to think first. Capricorn is the mountain goat, climbing cautiously up a rocky trail toward its goal, trying not to lose its footing. Capricorn is a down-to-earth realist; Aries is the impulsive idealist. They may not see eye to eye. Capricorns like money, rules, and traditions—they have a settled, elder-adult energy. Aries are like hyperactive, rebellious kids who want it all and then some. In relationships, Aries heat up fast, and may charge off to the next best thing before the first even takes off. Capricorns are loyal and steady—if they finally commit, they're in it for the long haul.

HOW TO MAKE IT LAST

If they have common goals, Aries will intrigue and amuse Caps with their childlike energy. If not, Aries will become a frustrating burden, demanding attention while goal-focused Cap is trying to get some work done. Aries will have to show Caps that they are loyal and trustworthy. Capricorn will need to loosen up and take some risks—don't be stern or uptight when Aries wants to play. Snap out of those depressive Cap moods when Aries gets the party started.

HOW TO END IT FAST

Workaholic Cap ignores emotional needs in order to get the job done. The Aries baby can't wait for the bottle. If Capricorn neglects Aries, or Aries doesn't find other sources of attention, the babe may seek a new crib. People-pleasing Capricorns may drain themselves by trying to keep up with Aries' whims. These signs will have to follow their own energy patterns, instead of trying to imitate each other's foreign nature. Aries, when Capricorns gets depressed, be supportive and don't push and demand that they talk to you—unless you're prepared to hear "good-bye."

ARIES
(March 21–April 19)

+

AQUARIUS
(January 20–February 18)

STAR COMBO: singers Jill Scott (Aries) and D'Angelo (Aquarius), exes and parents

THE BREAKDOWN

This lively relationship is full of friendly competition and energy. These quick-thinking, innovative signs love to delve into out-there topics and toss around exciting ideas. Conversation could run nonstop, and their social calendar could be packed. Passion could be a stumbling block, however, at least in the beginning. At times, Aries may wish cool Aquarius would warm up, and Aquarius may pray that hotheaded Aries would just chill out. They'll both have to check their temperatures if they want to keep the fever burning.

COMMON GROUND

Both signs are competitive, ambitious, and love to win. They react impulsively and decisively to most things; ideas are their fuel. They have strong wills and highly defined personalities—they prize their individuality and are usually born with a star quality. Both signs can be generous friends and true revolutionaries with the power to reform society. Like

Aries Gloria Steinem and Aquarius Oprah Winfrey, these signs rebel against unfair rules—neither will be restricted by gender, race, or any label placed on them. Anything new and never tried before excites them.

VIVE LA DIFFÉRENCE

Though both can be dramatic onstage, off-camera Aries is a passionate energy burst, while Aquarius is usually detached and chill. Aries needs attention; Aquarius needs space. In love, Aries can be demanding and high-maintenance when compared to self-sufficient Aquarius. Although the sound and the fury of both signs' anger can be unrivaled, Aries' tempers flare on the regular, while Aquarians stuff down anger until they snap, seemingly out of nowhere. As the first sign of the zodiac, Aries rule the self, and they may gratify themselves before getting around to other people. Aquarius is the sign of groups and friends—Aquarians will give friends everything and leave nothing for themselves, which is why they eventually burst with resentment.

HOW TO MAKE IT LAST

You're both impulsive, so build a strong friendship before diving into something more intense. Aries, curb the jealousy and constant demand to be babied when Aquarius floats around like a social butterfly. Aquarius, warm up and show some passion and connection—Aries needs to feel reassured that the bond is tight, and will need lots of nurturing as proof. This may feel uncomfortable and confining to Aquarius, but it's better than being trampled in a neglected ram's stampede. Don't tarnish your beautiful minds with too many private or suspicious thoughts. If Aries gets neurotic, or Aquarius gets psychotic, you'd better start talking to each other—fast.

HOW TO END IT FAST

Constantly catering to Aries' mood swings or babyish demands for attention will turn Aquarius into a storehouse of resentment. Aquarius will eventually lash out, leaving Aries stunned, then infuriated—and things can only get ugly from there. Aquarius's emotional distance can provoke Aries' abandonment issues, and nothing's sadder than a needy, neglected ram. When it's time to build a solid foundation, Aries immaturity and Aquarius restlessness can leave these two stuck on the ground floor.

ARIES
(March 21–April 19)

✛

PISCES
(February 19–March 20)

STAR COMBO: actors Sarah Michelle Gellar (Aries) and Freddie Prinze Jr. (Pisces), married

THE BREAKDOWN

Aries is the first sign of the zodiac, and Pisces is the last. Their relationship completes a strange karmic circle. Aries rules birth and self-awareness—clear-cut individuality and a "me first" attitude are classic traits. Pisces rules endings and selflessness—the boundaries between these people and others are blurred, and their lives may be filled with great sacrifices. The world can look like an enchanted wonderland to both, seen through Aries' innocent eyes, or Pisces' dreamy, mystical ones. As a couple, Pisces can teach Aries how to give, and Aries can teach Pisces how to receive—an important lesson for both.

COMMON GROUND

Rose-colored glasses are always perched on these signs' noses, since neither one is a big fan of harsh reality. Although they're both capable of putting on a tough act, as Pisces Queen Latifah or Aries Julia Stiles has shown, they also resonate with a certain vulnerability. Both signs are suspicious of "the man," and neither one likes being told what to do. Aries rules the head and Pisces rules the imagination, and both are highly receptive to messages and energy in their environments. They must manage their thoughts and feelings carefully, or negativity and stress can literally make them sick.

VIVE LA DIFFÉRENCE

This is the match of the champion and the underdog. Aries can be a bragging bully who feels entitled to the best and hates to suffer. Pisces relate personally to the poor and suffering. Energetic Aries is direct and aggressive with an open, talkative style. Slow-moving Pisces is indirect and passive, a keeper of secrets. Aries love attention and tend to attract it easily. Pisces like solitude, and feel guilty wanting anything for themselves. If Aries want something, they demand it. Pisces circle around, using tragic tales and cryptic hints until people feel sorry enough to give them whatever they want.

HOW TO MAKE IT LAST

Build a romantic fantasyland—then step out to live your separate lives. Aries needs room for ambitions and adventure; Pisces needs space for dreams and privacy. Pour all your intense feelings onto each other, but don't drown. Champion a cause together, with fiery Aries as the spokesperson and Pisces as the devoted foot soldier who volunteers healing energy. Aries can teach Pisces how to stand up for themselves (Note to the fish: don't try your new skills on the ram). Aries, let Pisces' soothing energy relax your busy brain. Pisces, don't be so agreeable that you let Aries bulldoze you.

HOW TO END IT FAST

Suffering Pisces can bring out the bully in Aries, who have little patience for other people's emotional "weakness." Pisces may express anger indirectly, escaping Aries' domination by cheating, manipulating, or staging a guilt-riddled drama. Try to deceive an Aries and they'll charge at you headfirst. Aries can shatter Pisces' dreamy state with pushy demands and hotheaded outbursts. Pisces can push back in their own way, sucking Aries down in an emotional undertow and putting out their fire in the process.

TAURUS IN LOVE

TAURUS: April 20–May 20

What They Need in a Mate

* Sense and sensibility—practical Taurus is ruled by the five senses
* Loyalty, ambition, and good character
* Beauty and attention to your appearance
* Affection and pampering (even if they don't admit it)
* Classiness, manners, and good taste
* Sentimental gestures—don't forget anniversaries, birthdays, or other special occasions

☆ What They Offer a Mate

* Steadiness, dedication, and persistence
* Traditional romance with all the trimmings
* A solid foundation—you can always lean on them
* Loyalty with a touch of possessiveness
* Someone to sleep, eat, dance, cuddle, and indulge with
* Strong values and solid opinions—changeable types need not apply

Taurus-Aries: *See Aries-Taurus.*

TAURUS
(April 20–May 20)

✛

TAURUS
(April 20–May 20)

STAR COMBO: actors George Clooney (Taurus) and Renée Zellweger (Taurus), exes

THE BREAKDOWN

This combo can either look like two contented cows or too much bull to handle. On good days, they'll offer each other amazing amounts of patience and consideration. They'll stuff their faces with their favorite foods, give each other massages, and cuddle to their favorite CD. These stubborn types hate to back down from an opinion, so disagreements can last as long as the good times.

COMMON GROUND

Thrifty as they are, bulls occasionally like to charge—and these two can whip out the credit cards when the occasion calls for it. As long as it makes them look and feel good, it's worth it. Tauruses believe they can buy anything—love, reputation, even friends. Whatever they can't buy with money, they'll pay for with their time—clocking long, hard hours to prove their dedication. Once they get the gig, they may occasionally fall asleep on the job, but only if they feel 100 percent secure.

VIVE LA DIFFÉRENCE

There are sitting bulls . . . and there are charging bulls. The sitting bulls are peaceful grazers who mind their own business. They may look tough, but as long as nobody bothers them or stops them from eating, they're all love inside. (Think of Tauruses Janet Jackson and Jason Biggs.) The charging bulls are the ones to watch. You can spot them by the steam coming out of their nostrils, or their refusal to sway from an opinion. Like an angry toro in a bullfight, these charging Taureans refuse to see anything but their target. Many intense political figures have been charging-bull Tauruses, such as Malcolm X, Eva Peron, Golda Meir, and Saddam Hussein.

HOW TO MAKE IT LAST

If two Tauruses want to make it last, they should buy a clock radio. First, it will wake them up from the long naps they like taking. Second, it will wake them up with music, which they both love. And lastly, it will remind them to set a time when they'll clock out of their jobs and get home to each other already—affection is their magic pill that can melt their stubbornness. When they get stuck in a rut, they can set the alarm to buzzer mode. It will shock them out of bullheadedness and into reality—not the reality that they *think* they know, but an even better one. After all, Taurus always wants the best.

HOW TO END IT FAST

The only other danger is that their relationship could turn into a snoozefest. Too much of the same-old same-old doesn't exactly help when it's time to make a major life change and nobody wants to take action. Two Tauruses might stay together only because they don't want to change. They're comfortable simply knowing each other's favorite foods, special massage spots, and worst habits. The more predictable, the better. From that same fear of rocking the boat, they could turn a blind eye to major relationship problems, and could avoid taking responsibility for their actions. These two will be the last in line for couples counseling.

TAURUS
(April 20–May 20)

+

GEMINI
(May 21–June 20)

STAR COMBO: singer Enrique Iglesias (Taurus) and tennis star Anna Kournikova (Gemini), flames

THE BREAKDOWN

Have you ever stepped off a carnival Tilt-a-Whirl, and continued to feel like the world was slanted and your body was still spinning? That's the sensation Gemini can leave Taurus feeling: dizzy and taken for a ride. No matter how honest Geminis may be, Tauruses will never fully trust them. Honesty, in a Taurus's eyes, doesn't change. It's the truth, like the law—it is what it is, and that's final. To Gemini, the truth means expressing what you see and feel in any given moment, even if it's completely different from what you were feeling half an hour ago. Taurus is already out the door.

COMMON GROUND

Both signs are ambitious and can win any debate—Geminis, through mental dexterity, and Taurus, through sheer determination. They're creative and hardworking, but stubbornness can thwart their goals. Taurus may refuse to change, and Gemini may refuse to settle into one track—in the end, it can leave them both frustrated and unfulfilled. As a result, both signs can be their own worst enemies.

VIVE LA DIFFÉRENCE

Tauruses need affection like a DJ needs a record collection, and Geminis may often forget to spin the more touchy-feely tracks. Geminis approach everything with the logical vibe of a math whiz doing an algebra equation, forgetting to show their deeper feelings. Taurus wants guarantees, answers, and the right to remain silent. Gemini wants freedom, constant chitchat, and the right to ask questions. Taurus wants to impress people by being moral, modest, and mainstream. Gemini loves to shock people by breaking every rule and getting away with it.

HOW TO MAKE IT LAST

To make this combo work, Gemini will have to (gulp) get emotional sometimes—and show it. A little bit of kissing and sweet-talk goes a long way with Taurus. Taurus will have to break a few traditions and open his mind—go ahead and give your Gemini girlfriend a skateboard instead of perfume, for example. In many cases, they're better off having a wild fling where the only "conversation" is the sound of spit-swapping. They should just let their imaginations go crazy, and never, ever rush to say the "C word" (*commitment*)—at least not seriously.

HOW TO END IT FAST

Serious Taurus can feel like a tether on Gemini's leg, a romantic parole officer who restricts Gemini's freedom. And Geminis, who think they're above the law anyway, will always be tempted to violate parole. Tauruses, who respect the law as though they wrote it themselves, will keep bringing down harsher sentences, until there's either a jailbreak, or two extremely frustrated people who turn themselves in to the authorities. Conversation will probably be another source of frustration. Geminis are like windup toys on long-life batteries. They jump from one topic to the next, and twist people's minds into intricate knots that only they can untie. Tauruses tend to get stuck on a single topic and stampede it to death like a raging bull. Refuse to compromise, and it's over.

TAURUS
(April 20–May 20)

+

CANCER
(June 21–July 22)

STAR COMBO: actors Penelope Cruz (Taurus) and Tom Cruise (Cancer), flames

THE BREAKDOWN

You know those stories about high-school sweethearts who've been happily married for sixty years? That's what a Taurus-Cancer love combo can look like. Both signs share a quest for security—emotional and financial—and balance each other out nicely. They love kitties, puppies, and little babies. The sweetness could send their friends into sugar shock. Since both signs are attached to their families, this could quickly turn into a successful "meet the parents" scenario.

COMMON GROUND

Both Cancer and Taurus are thrifty and feel better when they've got coins in their piggy banks. The idea of being caught without a safety net gives them both the willies. Both signs can pout with the best of them, and it's tough to break the spell once Taurus falls into a stubborn silence, or Cancer into an emotional storm. The magic touch for both is lots of gentle, soothing affection and understanding. A cookie or present also works, since these signs love to eat well and be pampered.

VIVE LA DIFFÉRENCE

Although both are thrifty, they may have different approaches to spending. Taurus saves up for something top-of-the-line, while Cancers are just as happy to Dumpster-dive, or buy a bunch of cheap stuff that eventually falls apart. Taurus may shop wholesale, but they'll rarely go secondhand—unless it's a vintage designer piece. Arguments can be tricky, too. With Cancers, a fight's not over until they're sure you've *felt* what they're feeling. For Tauruses, it's over once you've heard their opinion a couple hundred times—and, hopefully, agreed with it.

HOW TO MAKE IT LAST

Ultimately, home is where the heart will beat for these two nest-building types. Cancer, who rules the heart, may occasionally frustrate Taurus by trying to save the world and forgetting who's waiting patiently at home. Tauruses must learn to soothe moody Cancers with sympathy, not coolheaded logic. The bulls may have to lay the compassion on a little thicker than they think the situation merits. Cancers tend to be secretive and indirect about their feelings, so most breakdowns can send the Taurus Eagle Scout on a scavenger hunt without a flashlight. Tauruses hate to back down, but that attitude won't fly here. With Cancer, it's a lot less work to kiss and make up in fifteen minutes than to let your stubbornness drag out the drama another fifteen hours.

HOW TO END IT FAST

The pristine waters can get a little turbulent when Cancer's moodiness meets Taurus's "sensible" approach to life. Tauruses may be the Eagle

Scouts of the zodiac, but they're seldom prepared for an emotional downpour, especially if Cancer hasn't warned them to pack a raincoat. Tauruses, who can be exceptional pouters, may try to comfort Cancers by saying something like "There's nothing to cry about!" or "You're being so *unrealistic*." This will only turn the Cancerian tear ducts into Niagara Falls, or send the crab scrambling deeper into its shell. Cancer will have to return the favor when the tears dry, and pour out plenty of attention on Taurus. Too much drama will send the bull searching for greener pastures.

TAURUS
(April 20–May 20)

+

LEO
(July 23–August 22)

STAR COMBO: TLC singer T-Boz (Taurus) and rapper Mack 10 (Leo), married

THE BREAKDOWN

It all starts out so nicely. Both signs like to look good in public, and that's probably where they'll meet. From across the room, they'll sense each other's strength, and they'll be pulled together like magnets. Taurus and Leo are both fixed signs, meaning they like to walk in the door, set up shop to their own standards, and start running the show. Problem is, they've both got different ideas about how that ought to be done, and each is rarely prepared to roll with the other one's style. They may not discover that until they've already signed an exclusive deal with each other.

COMMON GROUND

A lion and a bull are both powerful, intimidating animals. They're both attractive enough to dazzle each other, too. They love luxury, beauty, and romance. Leos are the touch of royal class that Tauruses know they deserve. Tauruses appear to have good breeding, and Leos are suckers for a pretty face. These signs were born to rule and should have no problem telling other people exactly what to do.

VIVE LA DIFFÉRENCE

Sun-ruled Leos like to spend, while Venus-ruled Tauruses like to save. That goes for money *and* energy. After all, the sun's not gonna burn out, and it has no problem shining strong from morning to night. Taurus, on the other hand, is drained easily. It's exhausting to be ruled by the five senses. Tauruses don't like to gush. If they like something, they'll grunt or make some other bull-like noise. Leos don't hear applause unless it's a standing ovation from a packed stadium. Both signs need to be petted and pampered, but Tauruses are like faithful golden retrievers, while Leos are big, proud cats who need to be petted in a very specific way. If you don't attend to Leos in the royal style to which they're accustomed, they've got no problem scratching your hand, even as you're serving them a bowl of Fancy Feast.

HOW TO MAKE IT LAST

To make this one work, Tauruses will have to chuck their time-tested strategy of winning through endurance, and adopt the idea of "working smarter, not harder." They should let the Leos' sun heat them up, and shine light on the fact that praise *can* be practical—not a foolish luxury. Leos, in return, should remember that even the sun must drop out of the sky—and that Venus is one of the only planets that can be seen at night without a telescope. Perhaps Tauruses shine a little brighter than Leos think.

HOW TO END IT FAST

The problem here is a lack of appreciation. Taurus quietly supports Leo, seldom asking for acknowledgment—and thus, seldom getting it. Leos bulldoze Tauruses and complain that Tauruses never thank or praise them, simply because Tauruses aren't praising them loud enough. Tauruses often go unthanked for building the megadome where Leos perform their hits. In fact, Leo may even take credit for the structure Taurus provides. If Taurus is "unable" to acknowledge Leo's greatness, then it's fair to say that Leo is unable to appreciate the Taurean gift of simplicity and stability. Since Lion Kings and Queens need to rule, Tauruses could feel bossed around by Leos; and like bulls, they'll stubbornly resist.

TAURUS
(April 20–May 20)

VIRGO
(August 23–September 22)

STAR COMBO: Tim McGraw (Taurus) and Faith Hill (Virgo), country-croonin' husband-and-wife team

THE BREAKDOWN

This is the ultimate slow jam of relationships, a quiet storm that brews slowly and steadily. Since Virgo and Taurus are both earth signs, this combo naturally takes its time to get off the ground. Once it does, they'll get down and dirty—and stay that way.

COMMON GROUND

Taurus likes beauty, and Virgo likes perfection. At school dances, they'll hang in a corner and quietly analyze everyone's outfit. These two teacher's pets will bond over their mutual distaste about the way things are done, and their agreement that they can do it better. Virgo likes to serve, and Taurus loves to be served, so everybody's happy—as long as Taurus doesn't criticize Virgo.

VIVE LA DIFFÉRENCE

Taurus is more materialistic than Virgo, who likes everything in simple, neutral colors at dollar-store prices. Taurus likes quality for a bargain but won't always appreciate when Virgo brings home fresh-picked dandelions and Hershey's kisses instead of long-stemmed roses and a box of Godiva chocolates. Tauruses, ruled by sensual Venus, also love their honeys dipped in expensive perfume or cologne. Low-maintenance Virgos are happiest smelling like the earth itself, and may prefer a dab of essential oil, which could offend the Taurus senses.

HOW TO MAKE IT LAST

This is the couple that, in forty years, could be calling each other "Mother" and "Father" instead of "honey" and "baby." Stop being so damn polite to each other, and bring it down to earth. Virgos should tap into their natural caretaking skills, and shower Tauruses with the attention they love. Traditional Tauruses will have to exercise their amazing patience when Virgo starts considering "wilder" ideas such as spending the summer in India studying Sanskrit, instead of lifeguarding at the local pool like they always do. Preachy Virgos will have to avoid all soapboxes except the kind that come gift-wrapped with a scented bar inside. Beauty-loving Taureans will have to offer some perspective when fault-finding Virgos turn their critical eyes on everything around.

HOW TO END IT FAST

Squabbles will become shakedowns if Virgo uses cool criticism when Taurus just wants a cookie and a hug. Also, Mercury-ruled Virgo's over-analyzing could annoy Taurus, whose attitude can be: "If I wanted to dig all the time, I'd study archaeology." In exchange, Virgo could find Taurus's thinking too basic. If Taurus stubbornly sticks by too many bull-headed opinions, Virgo will charge the hell out. Both signs are also hesitant to express their needs. The slow jam could get sticky if they refuse to open up, and neither one will be ready for *this* jelly.

TAURUS
(April 20–May 20)

LIBRA
(September 23–October 22)

STAR COMBO: model Kimora Lee Simmons (Taurus) and music mogul Russell Simmons (Libra), married

THE BREAKDOWN

Both signs are ruled by Venus, planet of beauty, love, and the five senses. However, Tauruses are a fixed earth sign and like things grounded and steady. Libras are a cardinal air sign, who like to float above the ground, where they can look down on all the ordinary wonders below. Tauruses won't tolerate anyone being above them for long. They're the one sign that can get naturally spoiled Libras to serve *them*. Libras are usually too attracted to Tauruses to notice how hard they're working—after all, they look so good together. Despite strong differences, their Venus corulership can smooth out the wrinkles—and they both *hate* anything of theirs to be wrinkled.

COMMON GROUND

Libra and Taurus have a love-without-limits for music, flowers, romance, and designer clothes (although thrifty Tauruses buy theirs on sale). Paparazzi bulbs will pop when this attractive twosome parlays through town. They've got so much luck in the charm department, their combined effect is magically delicious. When it comes to commitment, both move slower than rush-hour traffic on the L.A. expressway. Taurus wants to make sure flighty Libra is serious. Libra can't make any decision before weighing all the pros and cons. An outsider could sweep either one away before they get around to a full-on commitment.

VIVE LA DIFFÉRENCE

Taurus ultimately wants forever after, and Libra wants forever and a day to "think it over." Tauruses may be patient, but they'll never go to the next level if the Libra scales swing too wildly. Taurus is a happy homebody who needs eight to fourteen hours of sleep a night. Libra will be fine with eight minutes of rest if it means hanging out with favorite pals. Conversation may be tough, and both can get heated in a disagreement. Libra loves to debate and has enough "hot air" to argue any point. Taurus is all about law and order, and saving energy. Unless the subject threatens Taureans getting their next meal, paycheck, or nap, they'd rather not waste their breath.

HOW TO MAKE IT LAST

The key to survival is *balance*—the Libra buzzword. Tauruses will have to get off the couch and socialize; Libras will have to settle for a few more nights at home. Both signs need to be pampered and spoiled, so go heavy on the affection. Possessive Taurus must understand that Libra, the sign of partnerships, needs other people. If possessive Taurus lets Libra spend time with other friends, Libra will always come back with a dozen roses, a poem, and concert tickets. As two music-loving signs, their issues can be soothed by a good piece of stereo equipment.

HOW TO END IT FAST

In the end, substance triumphs over style for Taurus. Although both signs are suckers for a pretty face, airy Libra had better supply more than charm and a good time if she hopes to be taken seriously. If solid Taurus can't figure out where Libra stands on important issues, he may look for someone more wholesome and down-to-earth. In turn, Taurus's traditional values and harsh judgments could offend Libra's delicate sense of fairness. Social Libra is fine staying in for a romantic evening now and then, but if Taurus turns every night into a Blockbuster night, Libra could get bored and restless—and her scales will tip out of Taurus's favor.

TAURUS
(April 20–May 20)

SCORPIO
(October 23–November 21)

STAR COMBO: actors Uma Thurman (Taurus) and Ethan Hawke (Scorpio), married

THE BREAKDOWN

The supercharged combo of these opposite signs always creates a power surge. It can either light up Las Vegas or cause a massive blackout. On a good day, Taurus can calm Scorpio's intense emotions, and Scorpio can break through a few layers of Taurus's earthy surface to dig up buried treasure. When these two commit to each other, it's the kind of pact that makes Tony Soprano look like *The Simpsons* good neighbor Ned Flanders. Don't mess with this tag team unless you wanna sleep with the fishes. *Capiche?*

COMMON GROUND

These are both fixed signs, meaning once they're in, they're in. Neither one likes change—Tauruses, because it causes discomfort and energy loss; Scorpios, because it makes them insecure. They can turn into real homebodies once they slip into comfort mode. Private by nature, they'll limit public appearances to events that keep them on top of the charts.

VIVE LA DIFFÉRENCE

Scorpio is a mystery and Taurus is a challenge. Ruled by tiny powerhouse Pluto, Scorpio will play power games to test Taurus's commitment. Loyal and steady Tauruses consider games an insult to their integrity and a waste of their precious energy. Taurus is far more trusting than Scorpio, and hates constantly proving devotion. If Taurus refuses to budge, Scorpio will rage against the machine. Bulls are peaceful until provoked, but mess with them and the cattle field becomes a battlefield.

HOW TO MAKE IT LAST

To keep it flowing, they should remember their animal-kingdom representations. Taurus is a large, heavy bull with sharp horns. Scorpio is a delicate creature whose only defense against the rest of the food chain is its stinging tail. It's natural for a little scorpion to keep his defenses up in case the bull steps on him. Like two mobsters, they'll go far if they swear by a code of loyalty and play strictly by the rules. Scorpio will promise not to keep secrets or be vengeful. Taurus will swear to start drinking Red Bull so she can stay awake and pay attention to Scorpio.

HOW TO END IT FAST

Their initial attraction could fade if Scorpio gets too creepy or Taurus gets too sleepy. Taurus pouting and Scorpio brooding can mean turned backs, slammed doors, and silent treatments that last longer than the Cold War. Taurus's stubborn refusal to end a fight will be outmatched by Scorpio's need for revenge. Teasing will also put this relationship on ice, as neither has much of a sense of humor about themselves, and any joke at Scorpio's expense will earn Taurus a deadly sting in return.

TAURUS
(April 20–May 20)

+

SAGITTARIUS
(November 22–December 21)

STAR COMBO: actors Kirsten Dunst (Taurus) and Jake Gyllenhaal (Sagittarius), flames

THE BREAKDOWN

Rule-following Taurus's old-fashioned values may clash with rule-reforming Sag's radical style, but the bond will be intense once it forms. They may not understand each other's basic approach to life—the bull plods along so slowly, and the archer dashes around impulsively. When the graceful Taurus model meets the wacky Sag clown, it's anyone's guess whether they'll sashay down the catwalk or wobble across a tightrope.

COMMON GROUND

Both signs are pleasure seekers at heart, who love dry humor, rich foods, and analyzing situations. They're creative, ambitious overachievers who can be bulldozers when going for a goal. Both signs have a perfectionist streak—they can be self-conscious and extremely hard on themselves. Although they fancy themselves to be realists, both secretly want to see the world through rose-colored glasses, and may take things hard when the pink-'n'-pretty lenses are shattered.

VIVE LA DIFFÉRENCE

Venus-ruled Taurus is slow-moving, loyal, and concerned with material comforts. Jupiter-ruled Sag is impulsive, commitment-phobic, and concerned with personal freedom. Taurus hates change, and Sag thrives on it. Homebody Taurus is more likely to follow rules and conventions, while world-traveling Sag makes his own rules. Taurus loves to sleep all day, while Sag hates to miss a second of the action.

HOW TO MAKE IT LAST

Indulge your senses and giant appetites—eat, shop, draw, and listen to music. Go dancing—Sag rules the hips, and Tauruses are graceful music-lovers, so you'll rock any dance floor you hit together. Sag can be the showbiz guy or entrepreneur, while Taurus is the manager who takes care of the details that weigh Sag down. Mine your human potential—set a goal for a shared creative project, then divide the work according to your skills. Sag, relax that nervous energy and spend a few more lazy nights lounging on the sofa. Taurus, help calm Sag's hyperactivity with a massage. Hippie-dippy, foot-in-mouth Sag may have to take a few grooming and etiquette tips from image-conscious Taurus—the beauty-loving bulls need a mate who won't embarrass them in public.

HOW TO END IT FAST

If Taurus takes too long to make a move, or tries to force Sag to settle into a conventional relationship, Sag will pack a suitcase and take a permanent vacation. Sag's daring style could entice Taurus into a brief affair, but the bull will quickly look for something more permanent if Sag seems too wild or changeable. Independent Sag is nobody's accessory, and traditional Taurus is nobody's plaything. Both signs are highly opinionated and "bullheaded"—if their strongest beliefs clash, they'll only lock horns.

TAURUS
(April 20–May 20)
+
CAPRICORN
(December 22–January 19)

STAR COMBO: actors Renée Zellweger (Taurus) and Jim Carrey (Capricorn), costarred in *Me, Myself & Irene* and dated briefly

THE BREAKDOWN

This is an easy combo of two status-loving and traditional earth signs. Both signs love to work hard on the j-o-b, and sleep long on their days off. Practical, loyal, and family-oriented, these signs usually end up in a no-joke relationship that's built to last. You'll have to step a little harder on the gas, though—since you're both so slow to make a move, somebody else could step in before you get it together.

COMMON GROUND

Mirror, mirror on the wall . . . These image-conscious signs like to gaze at their reflections, shop, and spend hours making sure they look good in public. They may both have "classic" features, especially a finely chiseled jaw or distinctive chin. Ruthless when chasing an ambition, these signs may come across as a bit gruff or closed off. Neither of them likes change—slow and steady is how they win the race. With their great determination, they can usually be trusted to get the job done.

VIVE LA DIFFÉRENCE

Venus-ruled Taurus is more high-maintenance and indulgent, with a stronger sensuality. Saturn-ruled Capricorn is more comfortable with self-denial and can live with fewer frills. As the "father figures" of the zodiac, Capricorns like to spoil their mates, which works just fine for the Taurus princes and princesses. Tauruses usually have a softness to them (Venus is the planet of beauty), while old-soul Capricorn may have a certain ruggedness.

HOW TO MAKE IT LAST

Step out in your finest, and make each other look good—bonus points if your reputations and salaries improve. Tease each other in a friendly way, since you both share a down-to-earth humor. Team up on a business idea, but bring in an energetic third party, since you may plod along too slowly to get this off the ground. Taurus, your sensuality and caretaking can help moody Cap get out of occasional depressed ruts. Mature Cap can offer wisdom to Taurus when the bull gets too charged up with anger.

HOW TO END IT FAST

Workaholic Capricorn may never leave the job, and homebody Taurus could be left lonely and unfulfilled. Cap's rough lack of sensuality may contrast with Taurus's affectionate style. Taurus's self-indulgence could seem too immature to Capricorn, who will frown with disapproval when Taurus starts "living it up." Taurus won't appreciate being put in the time-out chair by this stern Cap "parent," who doesn't seem to know how to appreciate music, art, and true beauty the way the bull does. Their mutual stubbornness and resistance to change could also stunt their growth.

TAURUS
(April 20–May 20)

+

AQUARIUS
(January 20–February 18)

STAR COMBO: Cher (Taurus) and Sonny Bono (Aquarius), divorced

THE BREAKDOWN

Although Aquarius is usually detached and Taurus is usually ultra-committed, this relationship can flip the script. Aquarius plays nurturer to Taurus's inner child, helping the bull get established. Taurus brings out Aquarius's take-charge side, and may help freewheeling Aquarius discover how organized he really is. Both signs will be needier than usual in this occasionally tense relationship—they'll have to balance Aquarius's wacky ideas with Taurus's traditional tastes.

COMMON GROUND

Both signs are bossy and stubborn types who stick loyally by their friends. As fixed signs, they look for stability and strive to establish themselves firmly in the world. They both rebel against unfairness, though Aquarius will try to invent a whole new game, while Taurus will try to change the system from within. In an argument, both can go from chill to explosive quickly. Watch out! When either takes a strong position, they'll defend it till the end.

VIVE LA DIFFÉRENCE

Their paces couldn't be more different. Air-sign Aquarius likes action and quick change—this sign bores easily and needs to stay on the go. Change is upsetting to earthy Taurus, who's easily contented and loves to lounge around listening to music, sleeping, and eating. Tauruses prefer commitment and traditional romance—they dream of a huge wedding and forever after. Aquarius wants freedom and has an eccentric approach to love—Aquarius Christie Brinkley had her third marriage on a ski lift. Taurus is far more materialistic than Aquarius, who doesn't care to be weighed down by possessions or anything else.

HOW TO MAKE IT LAST

Bring out your patient, sensitive sides (yes, they're in there somewhere!). Taurus, don't get overly dependent on Aquarius's strength—Aquarius may seem cool and composed, but needs some nurturing, too. Aquarius, don't get codependent trying to take care of Taurus. Unless you want to bring out the bull's lazy side, resist those blinding charms. Balance Taurus's love of low-key, romantic home time with Aquarius's need to jet-set around with millions of eccentric friends. Avoid discussing politics and religion, since Taurus's conservative values will rarely vibe well with Aquarius's radical ideas.

HOW TO END IT FAST

Taurus's judgmental style, vanity, and materialism could annoy Aquarius, who prefers to focus on people's souls more than on their images. Aquarians may go overboard with this philosophy, bringing home every freak they meet, thus earning Taureans' staunch disapproval. After all, in Tauruses' world, their mate's job is to pay attention to them. From there, it's downhill: Aquarius feels controlled and suffocated by Taurus, and is offended by someone meddling in her choice of friends. Taurus feels neglected by Aquarius, and begins to wonder how he invested in someone so irresponsible. Add in Aquarius's lack of patience and Taurus's slow pace, and they may never groove to the same track.

TAURUS
(April 20–May 20)

✦

PISCES
(February 19–March 20)

STAR COMBO: punk-rock legends Sid Vicious (Taurus) and Nancy Spungen (Pisces), flames

THE BREAKDOWN

Sensual and romantic is the way for these two love seekers, whose souls are written in poetry and music. Taurus is a romantic realist, and Pisces is a romantic idealist. Reality may bite the fish here and there, but Pisces is usually so romantic that Taurus hardly minds paying all the bills. In most cases, they'll be friends and companions who can weather their differences through any emotional storm.

COMMON GROUND

Both signs love traditional romance and appreciate the arts. They're highly sensual, creative, and sensitive, with a love of the good life—their tastes can be a bit snobbish at times. They love to shop, eat, chill with DVDs, and listen to music—indulging all of their five senses together is a favorite pastime. Both signs can be hard on themselves and may be self-conscious about their looks.

VIVE LA DIFFÉRENCE

The bull is heavy and charges toward a definite target. The fish is slippery and darts among emotional dramas (many stirred by its own fins), avoiding anything that resembles reality too closely. Practical Taurus needs material comfort and security, which may seem confining for escape-artist Pisces. Tauruses respect authority (in spite of all their complaining about teachers and bosses)—they're the builders of the zodiac and understand the need to play by the rules in the name of ambition. Pisces hate authority and may have a self-destructive side. The fish seeks change while the bull avoids it.

HOW TO MAKE IT LAST

Taurus, prepare to handle much of the reality here and keep the fish grounded. Pisces, stir up some adventure in the bull when he gets stuck. Indulge in romance and get swept away. Surround yourselves with beauty and art. Inspire each other's creative expression. Taurus, loosen up and get a little more experimental and adventurous. Don't treat Pisces like your property, unless you want a strong-but-silent resistance. Pisces, give yourself a reality check—don't bring negativity into the bull's world just because you feel like being dramatic. Taurus, be a hero for Pisces; Pisces, help high-strung Taurus unwind.

HOW TO END IT FAST

Hotheaded Tauruses can be bulldozers. Pisces rarely speak up for themselves in the face of bullying. If Tauruses push Pisces into something they're not ready for, the fish will mysteriously swim away. Pisces love trouble, and if Tauruses seem too squeaky clean, Pisces will disturb the peace with someone else. (Law-abiding Tauruses will be glad to see them go.) Tauruses like to be spoiled and don't care for messes; Pisces like things complicated, and their fantasy world may be crushed by too many Taurean demands. Taurus's conventional tastes may clash with some of Pisces' more alternative ones. Too much of Taurus's routine and stubbornness will bore the fish, who long for change and motion. If the fish get too flaky, the bulls will be off seeking greener, more reliable pastures.

GEMINI IN LOVE

GEMINI: May 21–June 20

★ What They Need in a Mate

✳ Patient amusement with their multiple personalities, arguments, and indecision

✳ An adventurous spirit—you must be comfortable with change

✳ A sharp mind—no artificial intelligence allowed

✳ Supreme confidence—don't lose your cool when Gemini wants to debate or flirts with somebody else

✳ A captive audience for their many stories and trivia bits

✳ A willingness to try anything once

☆ What They Offer a Mate

✳ Imagination unlimited

✳ A true mental challenge

✳ Wild adventure and radical ideas

✳ Variety and constant surprises—who knows who they'll be today?

✳ Common sense, blunt humor, and clever opinions

✳ Eternal youth

✳ More games than an Xbox, more drama than a video store

Gemini-Aries: *See Aries-Gemini.*

Gemini-Taurus: *See Taurus-Gemini.*

GEMINI
(May 21–June 20)

✛

GEMINI
(May 21–June 20)

STAR COMBO: singer Faith Evans (Gemini) and rapper Notorious B.I.G. (Gemini), married until his death

THE BREAKDOWN

There are at least four people in this relationship—each Gemini and both of their "twin" selves. Then there are all the other hidden personalities on top of those. Depending on which ones meet on which day, they'll either get along great or clash like mad. Communication will be a focal point of this relationship, since Gemini is ruled by Mercury, the planet of words and ideas. There will probably be plenty of talk, but they'll have to make sure there's enough action to back it up.

COMMON GROUND

Both Geminis love ideas, facts, and anything communications-related. Their curious minds move at lightning speed, and their eyes have a mischievous twinkle. Geminis are inventors and adventurers who won't shy away from a debate, but may end up taking both sides. Common sense is important to them, even if they often abandon their own. Mood swings and personality shifts happen on the regular, and they need a partner who can hang with all the action. Geminis often flow with great verbal dexterity and imaginative wordplay. (Think of Geminis Alanis Morissette, Notorious B.I.G., and Tupac Shakur.)

VIVE LA DIFFÉRENCE

Some Geminis are chatterboxes, while others are the silent types who live in their thoughts and imaginations. Many Geminis are impatient in love—it's a miracle if a relationship lasts more than two months before they get restless and bolt. Besides, Geminis love to flirt, and can't stand to give that up unless the person is really worth it. Secretly, they may withhold a piece of themselves from a partner, even after years of commitment. Other Geminis commit full-on, but their indecision runs rampant everywhere else—they switch hobbies, goals, and best friends at every turn. These Geminis flirt with ideas more than with other people but can still manage to drive themselves, and everyone else, mad in the process.

HOW TO MAKE IT LAST

Make a plan and stick with it. Limit your quota on mind changes. There's always tomorrow to try those other ten ice-cream flavors, so scoop one up and enjoy it before it all melts. Quieter Gems may be awkward with affection—warm it up a few degrees. If you don't express all those vivid thoughts, how can anyone know you're interested in them? Motor-mouth Gems should watch a tendency to "talk over" each other, too. Geminis rule high-tech communications, so send each other instant messages, digital photos, two-way pages, and text messages to keep your love connection stable.

HOW TO END IT FAST

Twist each other's minds into pretzels with constant debates. Insist on winning an argument at the expense of your partner's feelings. Dig up "facts" to prove each other wrong, then throw them in each other's face. Exhaust yourselves with constant change instead of building a foundation. Get so involved in your heads that you forget to connect with each other, or express your feelings. Or, swing to the opposite extreme and change from cold to needy without any warning. Refuse to commit to each other, or fail to make your mate more important than your "inner twin."

GEMINI
(May 21–June 20)

+

CANCER
(June 21–July 22)

STAR COMBO: actors Nicole Kidman (Gemini) and Tom Cruise (Cancer), divorced

THE BREAKDOWN

Cancer is a motherly sign, and Gemini has plenty of drama for this mama. Between Gemini's personality shifts and Cancer's mood swings, there's never a dull moment. They'll have to strike a tough compromise between Cancer's desire for emotional security and Gemini's need to feel free. The mischievous gleam in Gemini's eyes already makes Cancer a bit uneasy. Gem will have to chill on the flirting, and the crab will have to loosen up that possessive death grip.

COMMON GROUND

Both signs are moody and changeable and need a lot of reassurance. Their minds are curious and analytical, and their verbal skills are strong. They hate to be wrong and may have been kicked out of class a few times for challenging the teacher. When a feeling or project catches their interest, they're both known to get completely lost in it. Both signs wear many disguises or tend to hide parts of themselves. Geminis want to be able to switch personalities without warning, and sensitive Cancers hover under a protective outer shell. Underneath it all, both signs have quite a few soft spots, even though they throw up a tough front to keep you from seeing it.

VIVE LA DIFFÉRENCE

Intellectual Gemini is a futuristic sign and loves all forms of high-tech communication—the newer, the better. Sentimental Cancer loves history, old clothes, and anything classic. Gemini is a mentally oriented air sign, while Cancer is an emotionally driven water sign. As a result, Gemini craves change and radical ideas, while conservative Cancer wants stability and security. Geminis change their minds constantly, and go through friends faster than Jennifer Lopez goes through husbands. Once Cancers finally catch something in their claws—hobbies, friends, opinions—they tend to cling fast and never let go.

HOW TO MAKE IT LAST

Team up your creative verbal skills and flow together—as did Gemini Notorious B.I.G. and Cancer Lil' Kim. Since Cancer loves the old school and Gemini loves the new, fuse your tastes together. Cancer can dig up the classics, and Gemini can invent a totally original remix. Geminis should curb the flirting and impulsiveness if they want Cancers' trust. Cancer should chill with the clinginess and pessimism, and give air-sign Gemini room to breathe. Devoted Cancers can teach Geminis the power of love. Adventurous Geminis can show Cancers how to take life, and themselves, a little less seriously.

HOW TO END IT FAST

Gemini will skip tact to tell the truth, and believes that if you find a fact, you should share it, even if it offends somebody. In the supersensitive crab's case, the truth *does* hurt, and Cancer will withdraw if Gemini delivers their data when Cancer is in a bad mood. Speaking of moods, Gemini may break for lower-maintenance ground after too much of Cancer's nagging, clinging, and pouting. Impulse-shopping Geminis had better keep some money in their own accounts to pay the bills. Rash behavior will rock thrifty Cancers' security, and Geminis can send them searching for a more sensible investment.

GEMINI
(May 21–June 20)

+

LEO
(July 23–August 22)

STAR COMBO: Angelina Jolie (Gemini) and Billy Bob Thornton (Leo), divorced

THE BREAKDOWN

Between Gemini's imagination and Leo's colorful expression, everything is exaggerated here. If the drama makes it past the first act, there will be plenty of costume changes, and a fierce competition for the leading role. With Gemini's "twin self" and Leo's ego, both signs love themselves a little more than they love each other at times. Although they feel a natural understanding between them, they'll need to keep communication open and remember to put each other first.

COMMON GROUND

Both signs are playful and love to shock people. Many have been known to get wild in the public eye, and like to be noticed for their outrageous behavior or opinions. They're the first to say "Dare!" in a game of Truth or Dare. Both signs are communication-oriented, and have many chatterboxes among their ranks. They're also independent "busy bees," happiest when surrounded by lots of projects and plans.

VIVE LA DIFFÉRENCE

Leo is ruled by the sun, which is the center of the universe. Gemini is ruled by Mercury, the planet of the mind. As a result, Leos may have a more raw and flamboyant way about them, while Geminis are analytical and reserved. Leo is a loyal and consistent friend, while shifty Gemini can switch sides anytime. Leos want to be known and worshipped;

Geminis like to travel incognito, disappearing or changing disguises whenever the whim hits.

HOW TO MAKE IT LAST

You're both impulsive in love, so build a strong friendship first. Committed Leos will have to be patient with Geminis' indecision, and not take their hesitation personally. Geminis will have to snap out of their imaginary wonderlands and pay full attention to Leos. If Leos get the royal treatment—a date with the works, where they feel like the center of attention—their neediness will subside for a while. Both should keep busy with projects, but not so busy that they become estranged from each other, which can happen in this match. Don't get so caught up in a love affair with your egos that you forget to support each other.

HOW TO END IT FAST

Your mutual ability to be stunningly self-centered could kill this one off. Gemini may forget to praise Leo, which can be the beginning of the end. There's no sadder sight than the kings and queens of the jungle undignifying themselves by begging Geminis for attention. Geminis in turn will feel smothered, and may run for freedom. If scattered Geminis show up with a sloppy or neglected appearance, vain Leos will find somebody else to display on their arm. If Leos' warmth meets a Gemini cold front, the sun gods and goddesses may respond with some of their own fire and ice, leaving Geminis frozen out of the kingdom.

GEMINI
(May 21–June 20)

+

VIRGO
(August 23–September 22)

STAR COMBO: actors Courteney Cox Arquette (Gemini) and David Arquette (Virgo), married

THE BREAKDOWN

Both signs are ruled by Mercury, planet of intellect and communication, so their mental connection will be strong. However, Virgo is a practical earth sign, while Gemini is an impulsive air sign. They'll have to constantly balance their differences, and their communicative natures will help them talk it through. If Gemini's constant hyperactivity and chatter doesn't exhaust Virgo, and Virgo's pickiness doesn't spoil Gemini's party, they can build something solid and nurturing. If Gemini dreams up the wild ideas, and Virgo makes sure the practical details are handled, they can make a solid team.

COMMON GROUND

Neither sign likes to reveal personal secrets up front. They prefer to debate, talk about ideas, and get to know a person's mind before they let you into their hearts. As mutable signs, they're both comfortable with change, and can adapt to all types of situations and personalities. They love to analyze, solve puzzles, and dig up interesting factual tidbits—they may share a love of reading, crosswords, and clever wordplay. The mechanics of anything fascinates both signs, and nothing escapes their highly observant (and often critical) eyes. If opinions were worth money, they'd both be tycoons.

VIVE LA DIFFÉRENCE

Earthy Virgo is the zodiac's most responsible sign and likes to serve or take care of everyone. Gemini would rather jump out of an airplane than be saddled with somebody else's baggage—this excitable air sign doesn't want to be slowed down. Polite Virgos are picky in their tastes, while Geminis are always eager to try a new flavor—then tell you exactly what they think about it. Ouch! Virgo likes routine, while Gemini needs lots of variety and action.

HOW TO MAKE IT LAST

Let your minds meet, then get intimate. Balance private time with your ambitions. Virgos prefer to give more than receive, but they'll have to open up and let Geminis baby-sit their inner children. Virgos can help

Geminis get established, and can teach their scattered minds how to focus—something Geminis should endure, even though it can feel like boot camp. Take a stack of books and crosswords to the beach. Or go to a favorite outdoor spot (Virgo loves nature, and Gemini needs fresh air), and talk for hours.

HOW TO END IT FAST

Virgo criticism or stuffiness could kill the buzz when Gemini wants to do something outrageous—like skydiving, or starting a business in the middle of final exams. Although Gemini is just the person who could probably make any scheme work, flaw-finding Virgo will point out exactly how it will backfire. Gemini imagination could threaten Virgos' need for practicality and order. Geminis may talk too much or think too quickly, disturbing Virgos' need for peace and quiet. Scattered Geminis that are too all over the map may lead earthy Virgos to seek more solid ground.

GEMINI
(May 21–June 20)

+

LIBRA
(September 23–October 22)

STAR COMBO: actors Shane West (Gemini) and Rachel Leigh Cook (Libra), exes

THE BREAKDOWN

Making a decision will be as easy as winning the lottery when these two wishy-washy air signs combine. But who cares, since neither of them likes to make up their mind, anyway? For the most part, this makes for a wild adventure with occasional periods of frustration—like when one is hit by a commitment impulse and the other is still drifting in the clouds.

Although their powerful air currents can create tornadoes, they have a built-in disaster-relief mechanism, and it's often strong enough to help them weather the storms.

COMMON GROUND

As highly compatible air signs, these two are thoughtful go-getters brimming over with ideas. Both signs are outwardly focused and know how to lighten up (or leave) when things get too heavy. They love variety, and probably have lots of people and action in their lives. Communication is important to both. They're charming, flirtatious, and bold; their punch is spiked with plenty of good-humored mischief.

VIVE LA DIFFÉRENCE

Geminis are ruled by speedy Mercury, so they like quick change and can make up their minds in a snap, even if they change them later. Libras are ruled by slow-'n'-sensual Venus, and they'll take years to ponder an idea, running it through their five senses, savoring its delicious possibilities. Geminis can get worked up when angry, while Libras try to stay balanced. Gemini may seem shallow or superficial compared to Libra's stop-and-smell-the-roses approach. The truth is, these two are just different machines, so they handle data their own ways. Speedy Gemini is like a Pentium processor, while cautious Libra is more of a calculator.

HOW TO MAKE IT LAST

Patient Libras should not let Gemini moods rock their scales—they should just sit back and let Geminis amuse them with out-there ideas, most of which will never be fully activated. Radical Geminis should give Libras some (gulp) traditional romance and attention—a little appreciation goes a long way here. Gemini can get self-absorbed and detached and may feel awkward with Libra's sentimental style. Warm up and let Libra be a little sappy—remember that you can be quite the cheeseball yourself.

HOW TO END IT FAST

These two can dance around commitment forever instead of making a move and following through with it. If pushy Gemini goes into bulldozer mode, gentle Libra may rebel by taking even longer to make a decision. Gemini will lose the endurance test by rushing Libra, and Libra will be yesterday's headlines if she doesn't show a little more spine. Both signs may prefer to talk about their opinions instead of their feelings, but they'll have to go deeper into vulnerable territory when they're hurt, or the full impact may never be communicated. Without a solid force to pin them down—like a commitment or shared project—they may drift away on their own clouds, leaving them to wonder if their relationship was all an illusion.

GEMINI
(May 21–June 20)

+

SCORPIO
(October 23–November 21)

STAR COMBO: singer Lenny Kravitz (Gemini) and actress Lisa Bonet (Scorpio), exes and parents

THE BREAKDOWN

The bond can be intense when these two masterminds meet. They both want to build an empire, so why not team up? As long as they can hold back from constantly manipulating each other, they can create powerful innovations. Otherwise, it can quickly become an evil empire, with Scorpio's thirst for control and Gemini's habit of twisting people's words. Since you both hate weak-minded people, you may become exhausted, but you'll never be bored.

COMMON GROUND

Some of the biggest moguls are born under these signs, such as Gemini Donald Trump and Scorpio P. Diddy. Both signs have extremely active minds and imaginations. They can be master manipulators and are incredibly seductive. Their intuition is almost scary at times—they can pick up vibes like a satellite dish, and read people as though they were a large-print novel. Both signs have an air of mystery about them, and may wear many disguises to keep you from figuring out who they really are. They may be a little bit scared to discover that themselves. Trying to get a straight answer from either will be about as easy as finding Osama bin Laden.

VIVE LA DIFFÉRENCE

Single-minded Scorpio sets one goal and ruthlessly pursues it, working hard to establish a secure base. Multiple-personality Gemini wants to be all over the map, and can't stand to be limited to just one mission. Scorpio longs for passion, consistency, and emotional stability. Gemini wants constant change and a degree of emotional detachment.

HOW TO MAKE IT LAST

Treat life like a ten-million-piece jigsaw puzzle with a $10 million prize to the team who solves it. Yes, we said *team*—so that means don't try to outsmart each other and go it alone. Since you both have an insatiable need to know absolutely everything, team up your beautiful minds and create a masterpiece, as did P. Diddy and his Gemini soul mate Notorious B.I.G. Gemini, control your personality shifts so that Scorpio can build trust. Scorpio, release the death grip, and let Gemini be free.

HOW TO END IT FAST

Sensual Scorpio may crave more passion and devotion than distracted Gemini can offer, and Scorpio's control alarm may go crazy if Gemini acts too inconsistent. Gemini's playful words and twinkling eyes can spark Scorpio's natural suspicions. Homebody Scorpio may bore restless Gemini; Gemini's blunt chatter may anger Scorpio, should one too many tactless remarks tumble out. If revenge enters the picture, no punishment will be too cruel for either to unleash. You both like mystery, but don't be too enigmatic with each other. Open up and talk about your feelings—this relationship requires work to reach understanding.

GEMINI

(May 21–June 20)

SAGITTARIUS

(November 22–December 21)

STAR COMBO: musician Melissa Etheridge (Gemini) and actress Tammy Lynn Michaels (Sagittarius), flames

THE BREAKDOWN

If these opposite signs can focus long enough to team up, it can be a wild ride. Their lives are often too full to keep it together, but while they're in the same place, it's nothin' but a party, baby. With Sag's gambling and Gemini's crazy schemes, it will be Las Vegas wherever they go. Stakes are high, and it's anyone's guess whether this deal will pay off in the end.

COMMON GROUND

Both signs have a wild or impulsive streak. They talk big, and they can talk a lot of smack. No joke is too raunchy, no comment too blunt, no topic off limits. Both signs get fixated on an idea or opinion, and can be pushy about getting their way. New adventures get their blood pumping, but they're both just as quick to drop something as they are to start it up. With this impulsiveness, their relationships often have a revolving-door policy.

VIVE LA DIFFÉRENCE

Gemini rules everyday communications, and Sag rules the "higher" mind of philosophy. Geminis love to debate, while Sags like to ponder and discuss. As a fire sign, Sag's heat is a little more intense, while air-sign Gemini can be a chilly wind by comparison. Sag is faster to get emotionally involved, while Gemini hangs back with a detachment that the archer could never pull off. In a debate, Sag uses humor and wisdom, while Gemini argues with logic, facts, and common sense.

HOW TO MAKE IT LAST

Gemini takes a small idea and makes it a little bigger. Sag takes a big idea and spreads it through the universe. If they team up on a venture, they can go from concept to world domination. Gemini should try a little tenderness—don't shred Sag's wacky ideas with emotionless fact-finding. Remember, this is a relationship, not a debate club. Sag, don't push Gemini to open up or get affectionate—give him time to run through his personality shifts. Remain cool and unruffled through each Gemini costume change, and the twins will know that "all of them" are welcome in the archer's arms.

HOW TO END IT FAST

Impatience and impulsiveness could turn this adventure into a nightmare. Sag gets restless with Gemini's lack of passion and constant need to argue. Gemini gets sick of Sag's nosy attempts to understand all of her personalities—Gemini doesn't want to be figured out. Sag's indirect style of questioning can seem manipulative or weak to Gemini; Gemini's roughness can hurt the archer's sensitive feelings. Sags need air to keep their fires burning, but Geminis' winds may be too icy to fan the flames. Sag's heat may raise coolheaded Geminis to uncomfortable temperatures, and they may break the fever by dropping the relationship down to a more moderate climate.

GEMINI
(May 21–June 20)
+
CAPRICORN
(December 22–January 19)

STAR COMBO: actor Johnny Depp (Gemini) and model Kate Moss (Capricorn), exes

THE BREAKDOWN

Gemini's multiplayer games meet Capricorn's single-track production—they may never understand each other's flow enough to record a hit album. If life is a journey, Caps have one destination: the top. Once they reach it, they'll unpack and stay forever, chilling in executive style. Geminis usually have many destinations in mind, and plan to stay only until the next adventure sweeps them away.

COMMON GROUND

There's not a whole lot of similarities between these two, except for their shared ability to become goal-obsessed when they want something badly enough. Both signs have been known to handle people a little roughly at times and may have stepped on one or two friends in the name of ambition. Many among them may be awkward with affection and dress in a preppy style. Others swing far to the extreme, wearing outfits worthy of a fashion-police arrest—as have Caps Dolly Parton and Marilyn Manson or Gemini Helena Bonham Carter. Both signs are masters of disguise, often hiding behind blank facial expressions—or bizarre "clown suits" as have Gemini Andre 3000 of OutKast, and Capricorn Jim Carrey. No matter how serious they look or how depressed they both can get at times, *mischief* is always their middle name.

VIVE LA DIFFÉRENCE

Integrity is everything to earth-sign Capricorns, and they strive to honor their word. Gemini chatterboxes use words as toys—or as weapons to twist people's minds. Ambitious Capricorns are methodical and persistent—they'll tough out the marathon long after everyone's quit. Impulsive Geminis have no time to run a losing race. Unlike status-struck Capricorns, Geminis could care less about reputations and medals of honor. They'd rather use their mad-scientist style, while Caps prefer the old-fashioned way that's time-tested and guaranteed.

HOW TO MAKE IT LAST

Team up your different strengths. Quick-thinking Geminis can dream up the schemes, and rock-solid Caps can carry them out in a viable way. Let

Gemini be the talk, and Cap be the action that backs those words up. Lighthearted Gemini can lift old-soul Capricorn's heavy spirits. When Geminis get too scattered and lose perspective, Capricorns can reel them back to reality, where they can recover before trying again.

HOW TO END IT FAST

Capricorn's traditional values and thirty-year plans can bore Gemini to tears. Where's the adventure? the spontaneity? In turn, Gemini's impulsiveness or slick salesman routine can send Cap searching for a more stable, long-term investment. Capricorns are all about commitment when they meet the right person. Imaginative Geminis avoid lockdown, preferring to keep the relationship more like a dream than a reality. Do they really want the same thing from life? Unless they sync their mikes and do a thorough sound check, this clash of old-school classics and futuristic mixes may not make it past their first rotation.

GEMINI
(May 21–June 20)

✛

AQUARIUS
(January 20–February 18)

STAR COMBO: singers Kylie Minogue (Gemini) and INXS's Michael Hutchence (Aquarius), exes

THE BREAKDOWN

These two free-spirited air signs may both need an extra push before they'll get romantic and stop saying the other is "just a friend." If they can retire from the buddy system and move a little closer, this could be a sweet blend of two creative, quirky souls. Conversation will never bore them, and the out-there ideas will run nonstop. This tag team can move mountains when they put their minds together.

COMMON GROUND

As air signs, they both need plenty of space and freedom. They can either blow a lot of hot air or produce a forceful wind that pushes everything into motion. Both signs are often surrounded by strange friends and unusual ideas. *Adventure* and *independence* are their middle names, and they're comfortable keeping it light. Gadgets, new technology, and all things futuristic will capture their mutual interest. With their highly original ideas, they may feel misunderstood, even ostracized, by the mainstream. No surprise that Aquarius Big Boi and Gemini Andre 3000 teamed up to form a musical group called OutKast.

VIVE LA DIFFÉRENCE

Aquarians are the zodiac's humanitarians, and they're often more fascinated with people than with ideas. Gemini is the opposite. Ruled by Mercury, planet of the mind, Geminis would rather analyze facts and figures than listen to some street artist tell a sob story. Sure, Gemini might debate with the guy, if she's feeling chatty that day. But unlike Aquarius, Gemini won't invite some freak to become a best friend. Aquarius has a bleeding heart, and this sign tends to collect a crew of "strays." Impatient Gemini has no time for losers.

HOW TO MAKE IT LAST

Although Aquarians have a rebellious streak, they can also be teachers' pets—or at least, a little controlling. They should avoid getting uptight when Geminis are scattered, changeable, or indecisive. If you can't beat those tricky Geminis (and you really can't), join them. Aquarians should let Geminis inspire them to see new possibilities, and to let their own natural creativity flow. Geminis should let Aquarians rescue them when they get lost in their thoughts.

HOW TO END IT FAST

Aquarians' perfectionism and "team player" approach can annoy Geminis, who feel their individuality and freedom being stifled. Moods will have to be managed, too. Aquarians' tendency to stuff down their feelings can lead them to snap in a sudden angry outburst. Geminis will likely respond with a mind twist instead of sympathy—and the scene could become a verbal showdown. Geminis' own extreme personality changes can exhaust Aquarians, who strive to be perfect partners for their mates. Since Aquarians are already hard on themselves, they may drive themselves crazy trying to figure out what ever-changing Geminis *really want* and how to make them happy. If Gemini doesn't drop a few clues and act like a member of the team instead of a dictator, Aquarius may snap for good.

GEMINI
(May 21–June 20)

✛

PISCES
(February 19–March 20)

STAR COMBO: singer rapper Lisa "Left Eye" Lopes (Gemini) and athlete Andre Rison (Pisces), divorced

THE BREAKDOWN

Welcome to unreality. Pisces live in a world of hazy illusion; Geminis dwell in the land of make-believe. Air-sign Gemini will stir deep currents in water-sign Pisces, and they can both get sucked into the undertow. Like two surfers, they'll fight the blue crush, with Gemini trying to stay above water and breathe, and the fish trying to pull Gemini into the depths. Like the Little Mermaid and her human prince, they could be drawn together despite astounding obstacles.

COMMON GROUND

Strong imaginations drive both of these free spirits, and their minds dream up some quirky creations that are difficult to imitate. Many people born under these signs love film and video—strong visual images pique their senses. Neither sign likes to commit too quickly, and they need plenty of space for their imaginations to roam. At times, they can both be paranoid that people will take advantage of them, and may have a few conspiracy theories about "the man." Indecisiveness plagues them both—Gemini the twin is always of at least two minds, and reality-avoiding Pisces feels trapped by making firm decisions.

VIVE LA DIFFÉRENCE

Pisces is a fine artist who loves classic romance, while Gemini loves new media and flirting in a chatroom. Air-sign Gemini prefers not to get too heavy on the feelings, while watery Pisces wants to dive into the emotional depths. Their minds work differently, too. Geminis are ruled by Mercury, the planet of communications and data. They like to talk and think everything through, analyzing the facts and plotting a logical strategy. Pisces has a more subconscious process—journals, meditation, art projects, and long naps help them deal with their innermost feelings.

HOW TO MAKE IT LAST

Use your powerful imaginations to strike a creative compromise. Like that of the half-fish/half-human Little Mermaid and her prince, Pisces and Gemini's love will survive through a balance of water and air. Pisces will have to swim in somewhat shallower waters, where the air makes things choppy. When the fish start to get seasick, Gemini will have to dive a little deeper than usual. Although it's uncomfortable, focus on the payoff: The ocean is filled with enough mysteries to keep you both intrigued.

HOW TO END IT FAST

If Pisces feels like fish out of water, they may be forced to return to their natural habitat, and Geminis may not want to swim along. If intellectual Gemini can't get sensual or romantic enough, passionate Pisces could feel unsatisfied. Piscean depression and guilt trips will make Gemini run for lighter days. Gemini's constant personality changes could rock Pisces' boat too hard—the fish needs security. Their mutual fear of commitment could be an ongoing issue—deep down, each may be unsure if the other is really "the one."

CANCER IN LOVE

CANCER: June 21–July 22

★ What They Need in a Mate

* To nurture and be nurtured—Cancers are the zodiac's "mothers"
* Deep emotional security
* Comfort when they're upset—don't freak when they withdraw into their shells
* Lots of time to open up—they may be awkward or impersonal at first
* A homelike or familiar feeling at all times
* Common sense—don't threaten their security with impulsiveness

☆ What They Offer a Mate

* Lifelong friendship—Cancers respect family, history, and anyone who stays true
* Reality checks—cautious Cancers know when a scheme isn't airtight
* Financial thriftiness—the crabs like to save
* Devotion to your growth that sometimes feels like nagging
* Nurturing and a shoulder to cry on when you're upset
* Sensitivity that manifests as either compassion or moody spells

Cancer-Aries: *See Aries-Cancer.*
Cancer-Taurus: *See Taurus-Cancer.*
Cancer-Gemini: *See Gemini-Cancer.*

CANCER

(June 21–July 22)

+

CANCER

(June 21–July 22)

STAR COMBO: actors Selma Blair and Jason Schwartzman, flames

THE BREAKDOWN

Cancers are happiest in their homes, and these two sensitive, intuitive souls feel right at home with each other. Ruled by the mystical moon, they may have more psychic connections than John Edward. Security will be the focal point of this relationship, and they'll build it together with ease. Although it may be cozy, too much one-on-one time can get stifling if they don't push each other outside of their comfort zones.

COMMON GROUND

Cancers love anything that has to do with food, feelings, and history. They'll spend most of their happy time in kitchens and restaurants, creating memory books and photo albums, and digging around for old treasures. Many Cancers are also athletic, so a dash of sporty spice can heat things up for this quietly competitive twosome. They appreciate anything secure enough to stand the test of time, and love to explore old neighborhoods, read classic novels, and wear vintage clothes. They can be possessive at times, and those crab claws can pinch pennies as tightly as they hold on to the people they love.

VIVE LA DIFFÉRENCE

Cancers deal with their difficult emotions in two main ways. Some hide the true cause of their upsets and bitterly complain about everything else. Others pour out their anxiety in a tearful or raging meltdown. The complaining crabs are trying not to cry, so they'll want nothing to do with the weepier Cancers, for fear of losing their own composure. The emotionally uncorked Cancers will think their composed sign mates are cold and unsympathetic, and they'll just cry harder or steam longer until somebody finally gives them the love they need.

HOW TO MAKE IT LAST

Feed each other—constantly. Play a sport together, preferably one where you have to tackle each other (a convenient way to get past your shyness!). Pay attention to each other's deepest feelings, and show them that you take them seriously. Respect each other's moods, and always give love to the Cancer who's in a funk. Read to each other, snuggle on the couch, and hang out with each other's family. Make each other feel safe and nurtured, and you'll be inseparable.

HOW TO END IT FAST

Be so self-protective that you never let the other Cancer see who you really are. Snap your claws into cling mode when the other needs some private time. Get oversensitive and drown each other in the emotion ocean. Keep secrets from each other, then pry at the other's shell while refusing to spill your own goods. All Cancers have some kind of mommy issue. Act like Mommy when they need a partner, and they'll rebel. Forget to act like Mommy when they need to be nurtured, and they'll pout. Too many emotional roller-coaster rides could send the other Cancer searching for a new magic kingdom.

CANCER
(June 21–July 22)

+

LEO
(July 23–August 22)

STAR COMBO: actors Simon Rex (Cancer) and Jaime Pressley (Leo), flames

THE BREAKDOWN

Cancer is ruled by the moon, and Leo is ruled by the sun. They can literally be as different as night and day. Leos may outshine Cancers in the drama department, but as long as Cancers feel secure, they won't mind a bit. At their happiest, Cancer will glow softly and Leo will shine brightly. You could say that night and day are two dramatic forces competing for the same "stage"—the sky—each one having a realm of time to dominate. This sums up the eternal tension that follows Cancer and Leo, causing one to constantly surrender to the other.

COMMON GROUND

Leos and Cancers need extreme amounts of approval and attention, and lose perspective easily without a full daily dosage. Both can also be bossy—Cancer, in a "motherly" way (scolding and nagging); Leo, in an arrogant way (bulldozing and boasting). Between Cancer's mood swings and Leo's drama, the show won't stop. Leos are one-person starship enterprises—think J. Lo, Madonna, and Martha Stewart. Cancers have a few Jedi masters of their own—such as Tom Cruise, Pamela Anderson, and Mike Tyson. Both signs want to be the best (Leo publicly, Cancer secretly), and will fight for the number-one spot. In the ego department, this can be a surpising attack of the clones.

VIVE LA DIFFÉRENCE

Proud Leos let it all hang out the second you meet them, while shy Cancers tend to hold themselves back and check for safety before opening up. Leos may scare people with their roar, but inside, they're all giant kitty cats who just want to be petted and praised. Cancers, on the other hand, may *seem* all sweet and sensitive. Threaten them, however, and you'll get clipped by a crab claw (think of Cancerian boxer Mike Tyson's deadly hook). When the sun finally rests, nurturing Cancers will blanket hardworking Leos in velvety comfort. But if Leos roar too loudly or forget to return the love, Cancers will withdraw into their shells.

HOW TO MAKE IT LAST

Respect your differences and don't step on each other's turf. Just because Cancers keep the castle cozy doesn't mean Leos should treat them like royal subjects. Likewise, simply because Leos rule their domain doesn't mean Cancers have to get all insecure about it. Instead of expecting the sun to become more like the moon, or vice versa, they should celebrate their uniqueness. After all, if it wasn't for the moonlight, how would we see the other stars in Leo's universe? And if it wasn't for the sun, how would we stay warm while the moon goes through all its phases? Give each other plenty of praise, appreciation, and support if you want it to last longer than forty days and forty nights.

HOW TO END IT FAST

Pull out your best dramatic tricks in a fight and act like pouting children, each refusing to give. If Leo's fire turns from passion to arrogance, the heat will make watery Cancer steam. Cancer will strike back by dumping water on Leo's fiery dreams or by subtly causing water damage with pessimism and possessiveness. Once the sun burns out, Leo will make sure that the whole universe goes dark for Cancer. Better to let the sun keep shining, unless you want Leo to ice you out.

CANCER
(June 21–July 22)

+

VIRGO
(August 23–September 22)

STAR COMBO: musicians Courtney Love (Cancer) and Julian Casablancas (Virgo), exes

THE BREAKDOWN

This relationship will rest somewhere between the cozy and the practical, and can create deep healing as long as communication stays open. A long-term friendship could form, and years could pass before they take it to the next level. Virgo listens patiently to Cancer, who feels safer opening up than usual. Cancers drag Virgos out of their solitary confinement, and get them involved in group activities or interesting causes.

COMMON GROUND

Both signs can be reserved in public and like to kick it around the house or outdoors. They'll never embarrass each other in public, and they'll respect each other's privacy. Cancers and Virgos like to save their pennies and can bring out each other's cheap sides. Both stay true to their homies from back in the day and prefer to roll with a tight, trusted crew. Virgos are perfectionists who are ultra-picky about their partners. Cancers are slow to come out of their shells. Neither one likes to leap into relationships—they take time before they trust.

VIVE LA DIFFÉRENCE

Although their love "don't cost a thing," Virgos may take it to an extreme—these minimalists can live without a lot of the comforts that Cancer needs. Virgos can be loners and introverts, and need a lot of quiet time. If a Cancer is quiet, it's often a warning sign of a bad mood rising. Cancers like rich food and a good short story—Virgos prefer Pepto-Bismol and a computer manual or a crossword puzzle.

HOW TO MAKE IT LAST

Cancers are looking for a mommy, and Virgos want to take care of everyone. How convenient is that? Cancer should recognize that Virgo is always happy to listen, so don't be so quick to hide in that crab shell. Asking a Virgo's advice is the highest form of flattery and produces far better results than holding in your feelings until you unleash them in a tearful rage. "No More Drama" is Virgo's theme song. However, Virgos will need to relax that policy in order to give Cancers their proper sympathy. Virgo's valuable critique has its place, but trying to control Cancer's moods is like trying to stop the weather. Better to let the storm run its course.

HOW TO END IT FAST

Virgo's fault-finding eye won't be appreciated when it's turned on Cancer, who's ultra-sensitive to criticism. If Cancers unleash a few too many temper tantrums, Virgos will head back to their single life with a quickness. Virgos tend to live like nuns or monks, happy with just the bare essentials. If Virgo serves Cancer bread and water instead of milk and cookies, Cancer will run into someone else's comforting arms. Virgos can respond defensively to Cancers' mood swings by getting self-righteous, instead of keeping their amazing sense of cool. This will lead to an emotional freeze-out—they may not talk again for months.

CANCER
(June 21–July 22)

✛

LIBRA
(September 23–October 22)

STAR COMBO: Bon Jovi guitarist Richie Sambora (Cancer) and actress Heather Locklear (Libra), married

THE BREAKDOWN

Although water and air signs can be an odd mix, the planets soften the rough edges in this combo. The moon (Cancer's ruler) and Venus (Libra's ruler) are so harmonious that these two make a peaceful, loving pair. In most cases, they bring out each other's best. Libras give Cancers the security they crave; Cancers offer stable relationships that balance Libras' ups and downs.

COMMON GROUND

Both signs are highly sensitive and may try to cover it up with sarcastic jokes. While they're both the take-it-slow types, once they find each other, they may bend the rules. They are creative and verbal and share an appreciation for words that are well spoken and well written. Both can be uncomfortable with affection until they really know somebody—expect a few awkward hugs in the beginning. In the end, they both value true love, and if they find the "real thing" in each other, they'll stay together forever. They both know how to get the best for less and make an excellent shopping team. When upset, they can brood with the best of them.

VIVE LA DIFFÉRENCE

Cancer is far more intuitive and tuned into people's feelings than Libra, who takes a lighter, more intellectual approach to issues. Cancer likes to hang with a clique, and clings to a comfort zone. Libra needs to meet, greet, and mingle, and adapts to new crews with far more ease. With partners, Cancer is possessive and even clingy, while fair-minded Libra is happier to let everyone roam freely.

HOW TO MAKE IT LAST

Write each other long, meaningful letters. Pamper each other at all times and surround yourselves with beauty. Indulge in huge portions of your favorite foods—decadent meals are the way to both signs' hearts. Never, ever skip dessert. Both signs cherish true friends and family, so spend plenty of time with your closest people, preferably having a great conversation over dinner.

HOW TO END IT FAST

Turn the full-force sloppy kisses on each other in public—anything too freaky will scare the other one away. Pout for so long that you bring down the other one's mood. Neglect each other, and forget to remind the other how special he is to you. Libra will have to show more feeling when Cancer gets upset—cool logic will send her farther down the well. Cancer will have to get a grip on his moods if he notices that Libra's balance is being thrown off by too much emotion. Libra's cool exterior and indecision about commitment could cause Cancer's insecurity to rage.

CANCER
(June 21–July 22)

SCORPIO
(October 23–November 21)

STAR COMBO: pop singers Jessica Simpson (Cancer) and 98 Degrees' Nick Lachey (Scorpio), married

THE BREAKDOWN

Oh-so-satisfying on every level, these two emotional soul mates will find each other and never leave. They'll be meeting the parents by the second date and planning names for the kids by the third. They won't be able to keep their hands off each other—partly out of passion, partly because they're too scared and possessive to let go. Once again, nobody will mind. Cancer inspires controlling Scorpio to take life less seriously—making everyone in the world feel a little safer. Shy Cancers will come out of their shells with the security of Scorpios' love.

COMMON GROUND

Secrets, secrets, and more secrets—it takes a miracle for these two to trust anyone. First they'll want to see your driver's license and registration, draft a legal contract, and have a federal agent probe your personal history. Since both signs are highly intuitive, they'll sense this common distrust of all other mortals and will naturally trust each other as a result.

VIVE LA DIFFÉRENCE

Cancer has a softer side, while Scorpio has a lot more rough edges. Cancers' drive for security eases once they have a warm bed, money in the bank, and somebody to comfort them when they're upset. Scorpios drive for security *never* ends, even after they conquer the world. (Scorpio gazillionaire Bill Gates can't stop inventing new Microsoft Windows versions, even though he's far on top of the competition.) Cancer will have to understand that Scorpio's ambitions come *before* a cozy evening at home watching DVDs.

HOW TO MAKE IT LAST

There's no such thing as "too much reassurance" here. Both partners must always make the other feel secure. Since Cancers and Scorpios are both control freaks, they'll have to respect each other's boundaries as though they were the law. Scorpios like to think of themselves as hard to figure out (it's a control thing). Cancers must treat Scorpios like an unsolved mystery, even if they've already put the evidence together.

HOW TO END IT FAST

Fail to handle each other's sensitive areas with care, and you'll get a crab's pinch or a scorpion's sting. Scorpios feel comfortable only when moving at warp speed, but soft-shelled crabs will snap if Scorpio pushes them to operate at too intense of a pace. Cancer is great with the witty one-liners, but if they clown too much with Scorpio, the show will end early. Too many Scorpio power plays will upset Cancer, who prefers board games to head games. Unfounded jealousy will flare unless they check their tendency to keep secrets instead of communicating directly.

CANCER
(June 21–July 22)

✢

SAGITTARIUS
(November 22–December 21)

STAR COMBO: boxer Mike Tyson (Cancer) and actress Robin Givens (Sagittarius), divorced

THE BREAKDOWN

There's always instant chemistry here, but nine times out of ten, the chemicals end up causing an explosion if romance is added too quickly to the mixture. Problem is, these signs' chemical makeup is so different that they feel out of their element together. They make excellent friends, though, with Cancer giving supportive advice and Sag listening to Cancer's deepest secrets. Their best bet is to control their hormones and build a friendship, then slowly add other ingredients.

COMMON GROUND

Both signs love to laugh and appreciate the fundamental weirdness of life. Jokes won't stop between these two, and they may hide their insecurities behind humor. The "awkward phase" could last for months, but once they finally get to know each other, they'll bond tightly. Both signs are so sensitive that they can be *in*sensitive to others. In insecure moments, Cancers and Sags have been known to wound people's feelings with a cutting remark.

VIVE LA DIFFÉRENCE

Fire-sign Sag is the zodiac's wanderer, looking for a coadventurer to explore the world. Water-sign Cancer is a homebody, looking for somebody to help build a cozy nest. Without compromise, one of them is always gonna feel abandoned or lonely. Their common ability to hurt people's feelings stems from different places, too. Clumsy Sag hurts people's feelings with an accidentally tactless remark, then fumbles even more trying to fix it. Cancers hurt with an intentional snap of their crab claws. After the pinch, they withdraw into gloomy silence, leaving their victim wounded and alone.

HOW TO MAKE IT LAST

Take plenty of time to establish a friendship and adjust to each other's differences. Make each other laugh as much as possible. Balance time between comfortable old habits (for Cancer) and daring new adventures (for Sag). Build trust by helping and confiding in each other. Cancer needs to see that impulsive Sag will stick around for the long haul. Sag needs to see that Cancer's nurturing isn't going to suffocate her. Oddly, their best shot at romance could come if one helps the other get through a breakup or any difficult situation. They'll see each other's strengths—Cancer's care and Sag's perspective—and could fall for each other from there.

HOW TO END IT FAST

Sags may try to control or dominate Cancers, who will rebel by crawling into their shells and shutting Sags out. This will drive Sagittarians insane, and they'll strike back with brutal honesty that cuts vulnerable Cancers to the core. (Imagine the archer shooting arrows into the crab's ultra-sensitive underside.) Eventually, they'll both dissolve into tears and rage. If the watery crab clings too tightly or rains on Sag's parade, freedom-loving Sag will break away and march with another band. Too many of Sag's tactless comments and flirtatious moves could wound sensitive Cancer beyond repair.

CANCER
(June 21–July 22)
+
CAPRICORN
(December 22–January 19)

STAR COMBO: actress Pamela Anderson (Cancer) and musician Kid Rock (Capricorn), engaged

THE BREAKDOWN

These two opposite signs attract well—Cancer is the "mother" of the zodiac, and Capricorn is the "father." Cancers' sensitive touch softens Capricorns' gruffness; Capricorns' rock-steady stability gives Cancers the security they crave. Cancers love history, and Capricorns love anything that's built to last. This relationship comes with a solid insurance policy and the diesel to go the distance.

COMMON GROUND

Both signs are ambitious, crave security, and respect tradition, even if they may front like they're rebels. Underneath it all, they love children, keep friends for the long haul, and are attached to their families. They may have flings, but they're always looking for the real thing. Cancers and Capricorns are comfortable only in stable relationships that are built to last. Still, neither one is boring—they both have a few freaky little secrets tucked away.

VIVE LA DIFFÉRENCE

Cancer is more emotionally changeable than Capricorn, whose moods (both good and bad) last for long periods of time. Serious Capricorns don't like to lose their cool, and will take a lot more in stride than easily upset Cancers. Caps are an earth sign, which means they crave *material* security. Cancers are a water sign, and they crave *emotional* security. Capricorn is more likely to accept things at the face level, while intuitive Cancer always senses when something's going on below the surface.

HOW TO MAKE IT LAST

Stick by each other through thick and thin. Find every way possible to show loyalty and devotion. Love each other's family as though they were your own. Cap should take Cancer's intuitive hunches seriously (think of them as like your mother's intuition), and Cancer should listen up when Capricorn offers a reality check (think of it as a kind of fatherly support).

HOW TO END IT FAST

If Cancer acts too dependent or helpless, Capricorn will tell him to toughen up or hit the road. Capricorn can drive sentimental Cancer crazy by being too disciplined, slow-moving, or unexpressive. Capricorn can be a little selfish a times, putting her goals before everything else. If Cancer feels second best to Cap's ambitions, he'll look for a new security blanket. Capricorns are lone wolves who can go for long periods without a relationship or any of the extra comforts Cancer loves. There's no place like home for Cancer, so if Capricorn refuses to settle into the crab's cozy accomodations, Cancer may evict her and find a new shell mate.

CANCER
(June 21–July 22)

+

AQUARIUS
(January 20–February 18)

STAR COMBO: former first lady Nancy Reagan (Cancer) and former president Ronald Reagan (Aquarius), married

THE BREAKDOWN

This match may never strike hard enough to light an eternal flame. There will always be sparks, though, and they'll keep trying to blaze it up into something bigger. With their vastly different personalities, the struggle could eventually just burn them out.

COMMON GROUND

Both signs like to help people in need, and often end up in a caretaker role in relationships. They can come off as detached, although with Cancers it's all an act to cover up how sensitive they are. Both signs are part rebel, part teacher's pet. Friends are important to both Cancer and Aquarius, and they live to talk to people. They make great team captains, class presidents, and teachers. These natural-born leaders know how to bring people together and get a group excited.

VIVE LA DIFFÉRENCE

Cancers love history and are deeply attached to the past. Aquarians are inventors who focus on the future. Cancers roll with a tight-knit crew of tried-and-true homies, while Aquarians talk to strangers and will befriend just about anyone. Cancers are creatures of habit, who play it safe and have traditional tastes. Unpredictability is like oxygen to Aquarians, who have an eye for anything unusual.

HOW TO MAKE IT LAST

Pass the mic, and make sure each one gets equal time to rock it. Take turns being the MC and being the appreciative fan. Remember that go-getter Aquarians operate from logic and action, while the more passive Cancers operate from intuition and *re*action. Aquarians will have to express more than their usual dose of emotions, and should work hard to make sure Cancers feel properly nurtured. Cancers will have to think before they react around Aquarians—Aquarians, keep the emotion ocean at bay.

HOW TO END IT FAST

If Aquarius is too unpredictable, Cancer will take it as a sign of flakiness, and he'll withdraw or cling too tightly. Suffocation is not an option for air-sign Aquarius. Too much Cancer moodiness will either set off a sudden burst of Aquarian rage, or cool Aquarius's passion. Speaking of passion, Cancer is far more likely to express it, which could be another trouble spot. Aquarius likes to keep the vibe light. But if she makes it all about ideas instead of feelings, they'll never be more than just friends. Cancers need a safe environment to share their secret feelings, or they'll never open up. Aquarians could be on to the next big thing light-years before that happens.

CANCER
(June 21–July 22)

+

PISCES
(February 19–March 20)

STAR COMBO: Carson Daly (Cancer) and Jennifer Love Hewitt (Pisces), exes

THE BREAKDOWN

These two water signs can swim to the depths of passion or sink to the bottom of the sea. Their love can be titanic, as long as they don't drown in their own emotion ocean. They'll both be moody and need their private time, and at best, they'll have an understanding. But when insecurities flare on the same schedule, there may not be a dry shoulder to cry on.

COMMON GROUND

Both are emotionally driven and extremely creative. Writing, art, music, film—you name it, they've got something to say about it. They're likely to be the "artistes" themselves, and can have refined, even snobbish tastes. Both signs can have intuitive, near-psychic powers, although they may disguise it under a conservative front. Insecurity and shyness can be themes for both, though they may also cover that up with some brilliant performance art.

VIVE LA DIFFÉRENCE

Cancer likes to keep a grip on reality, while Pisces is always eager to escape it. That Cancerian crab claw can also pinch things, like pennies . . . and people who arouse Cancer's insecurities. Ouch! A wounded Pisces is more likely to sulk than strike, and he would much rather spend money than save it. Cancers are secondhand and bargain-store junkies, while Pisces can be label snobs who like the luxe life. Pisces also need to feel freedom and adventure, while Cancers need constant reassurance and stability.

HOW TO MAKE IT LAST

Let Cancer handle the money if it gets tight—or better yet, keep separate piggy banks. That way, Cancer never has to lose sleep over Pisces' wasting their hard-earned cash, and dreamy Pisces never has to be brought crashing down to earth with Cancer's talk of budgets and savings. Cancers, control the cling and give Pisces their privacy, and they'll always swim right back to your shore. Pisces, chill with the secretiveness if you don't want to arouse Cancers' suspicions—the crabs are more vulnerable than their hard shells suggest.

HOW TO END IT FAST

When your active imaginations get out of hand, suspicions can flare. If Cancer's mind starts to conjure up jealousy, Pisces will swim away at the first sign of possessiveness. Pisces' flakiness and ever-shifting opinions could also rock Cancer's boat a little too hard. When Pisces fall into a spell of self-doubt, drill-sergeant Cancers may try to force them out of it, which will drive Pisces deeper into resentment. Because they understand each other so well, they'll know exactly which buttons to push to hurt each other. Unfortunately, neither is above such underhanded tactics, since they hate to express themselves directly and they're both supersensitive. They'll have to appeal to their kinder, gentler side when soothing the other's upset feelings.

LEO IN LOVE

LEO: July 23–August 22

★ What They Need in a Mate

✳ Mutual adoration—even worship

✳ Grand gestures of devotion—Leos are in love with love

✳ Praise by the truckload

✳ Strength, courage, honor, and intelligence

✳ Gifts that show how much you truly know (and admire) them

✳ Something special or "different" about you—as long as it doesn't outshine Leo

✳ Beauty, class, romance, and luxury—the more decadent, the better

☆ What They Offer a Mate

✳ Warm, loyal love—you'll always feel safe when their sun shines on you

✳ Passion and encouragement to pursue your dreams

✳ Drama, drama, drama—you can throw out your TV and just watch them go

✳ Loyalty and devotion, as long as you offer it to them

✳ A colorful, beautiful, creative world

✳ A touch of the wild kingdom—fragile types should look elsewhere

Leo-Aries: *See Aries-Leo.*

Leo-Taurus: *See Taurus-Leo.*

Leo-Gemini: *See Gemini-Leo.*

Leo-Cancer: *See Cancer-Leo.*

LEO
(July 23–August 22)

LEO
(July 23–August 22)

STAR COMBO: actor Ben Affleck (Leo) and actress/singer Jennifer Lopez (Leo)

THE BREAKDOWN

It's a 24/7 lovefest, as long as these two royals can share the throne. Leos rule the ego—and the jungle—so their favorite word is *me*. Equal stage time is a must, and both demand as much attention as they give. As costars, they'll be each other's biggest fans, and the paparazzi won't stop snapping. There could be trouble in paradise, however, if one Leo's star rises higher or faster than the other's. The less-famous Leo won't fancy playing a supporting role, unless the favor is fully repaid.

COMMON GROUND

Leos are ruled by the sun, which is literally the center of our solar system. Is it any wonder that they expect the world to revolve around them? Both love praise and command the spotlight. They're playful, dramatic, and expressive—even the quiet Leos manage to capture attention. Leos may roar or growl, but like big cats, they purr if you pet them the right way. They're fiercely loyal and protective of their clans, and will shred their prey and competitors. A fighting spirit is also their trademark.

VIVE LA DIFFÉRENCE

Contrary to myth, not every Leo is a loudmouth show-off. Some Leos are roaring lions on the hunt, while others sit proud and silent, surveying their kingdom with a quiet confidence. The first type is playful and expressive, capable of more drama than a Broadway revue. They want all eyes on them, and they expect those eyes to shine with admiration. They can swing between arrogance and desperate attempts to get attention, as have Madonna and Limp Bizkit's Fred Durst. The quiet Leos are equally proud, but they may be reserved or haughty at times, as Martha Stewart and JC Chasez can be. A confident smirk is often the Leo's dead giveaway—think Sandra Bullock, Kevin Spacey, and Debra Messing. They may be able to laugh at themselves, but deep down they know that the world is theirs.

HOW TO MAKE IT LAST

Crown yourselves Bling and Bling, and rule the universe together in high-rolling style. Bring a touch of the jungle, and get wild. Keep the scorecard even at all costs. Shine your rays of support onto each other's dreams—it will be a dark day if one sun god/goddess burns out, so create a solar-power reserve. Plenty of honor and devotion will be required, and affection is key. If you're dealing with Leo ice kings or queens, help them go from polar to solar by melting through a few of those self-protective layers.

HOW TO END IT FAST

Date outside of your royalty level, like Leos Jennifer Lopez and ex-husband/backup dancer Cris Judd. Sorry, guys—King of the Sandbox and Queen of the Universe may both be royal titles, but the rank is not compatible. Pride and arrogance will also shred this relationship faster than a wildebeast caught in a lion's powerful jaws. If you turn off the lights and ice each other out with ego games, it will be sunset on your relationship. A little drama will keep the show running for seasons, but generate too much—as did Leos Madonna and ex-husband Sean Penn—and you'll only get a curtain call.

LEO
(July 23–August 22)

+

VIRGO
(August 23–September 22)

STAR COMBO: singer/actress Madonna (Leo) and director Guy Ritchie (Virgo), married

THE BREAKDOWN

This is the relationship of the Leo star and the Virgo director. If their egos don't clash, they may produce a hit—or a box-office bomb (*Swept Away*, anyone?). Virgo likes to serve. Leo loves to serve *and* be served. These two control freaks will have to stay off each other's turf and give each other the space to do things their own way.

COMMON GROUND

In spite of Virgo's reputation as vanilla-ice-cream plain, this sign is secretly capable of great theatrics and spitfire. Leo is a traveling Broadway show that comes in one hundred different flavors of drama. Both signs can be haughty and snobbish, even self-righteous. They like to pamper their friends, and may be self-sacrificing as a way of getting attention and praise. Integrity is important to both of them, and neither one takes kindly to being told how to live their lives. Perfectionism and attempts to do everything themselves can lead them both to burnout.

VIVE LA DIFFÉRENCE

It's a matter of temperature—fire-sign Leo is warm and open, while earth-sign Virgo can be cool and composed. Virgo is the sign of service, and tends to be selfless. Leo rules the ego, and is often self-centered. Even Leo's "insecure" rants are designed to get reassurance and praise, two things that embarrass Virgo, who never wants to appear needy. Virgo likes simplicity and neutral colors, where Leo likes glamour, excess, and a rainbow of royal colors.

HOW TO MAKE IT LAST

Service-oriented Virgos should treat Leos like rising stars in need of guidance. Help them practice their lines, land the leading role, *and* stay on top once they get there. Micromanager Leos should stop trying to do everything themselves, and give Virgos a chance to prove how well they can come through in a crunch. Virgo can organize Leo's life and help the sun god/goddess prevent burnout. Leos can warm up introverted Virgos, and teach them to worry a little bit less. Virgo needs plenty of quiet time, and Leo needs lots of talk and attention. Compromise will be required in this area. When you're both at your best, Leo is a great talker, and analytical Virgo is a great listener. Just don't burn each other out with your demand for perfection.

HOW TO END IT FAST

In insecure moments, a desperate Leo will ask things such as "Was I good enough?" or "Do you think I'm attractive?" This is not the time for Virgo to offer criticism, even if those eagle eyes have seen just the flaw to fix. Unless Virgo wants a roaring lion to rip his head off, the answer is always "Yes! Of course! You're amazing!" On the flip side, Virgos deal with insecurity by quietly retreating into their thoughts. Silence is their sanctuary, and Leos had better not invade it. This is not the time for Leos to make it all about themselves: "Did I do something wrong?" or "Don't you love me?" If Leos can't get over themselves long enough to give Virgos some time alone, Virgos may pack their things and move the hell out of the jungle.

LEO
(July 23–August 22)

+

LIBRA
(September 23–October 22)

STAR COMBO: Halle Berry (Leo) and Eric Benet (Libra), married

THE BREAKDOWN

It's love, elegance, and beauty without a limit when sun-ruled Leo shines where Venus-ruled Libra glows. Both signs love attention and nights on the town, and they bring beauty to everything they touch. At times, Libra may be a bit "cool" for fiery Leo, and Leo's aggressive style could throw Libra a little off kilter. In general, they'll want similar things from life, and the combo is quite harmonious.

COMMON GROUND

Love is the ultimate happiness for both signs, who live to spoil and be spoiled. Both are highly sensitive to color and love to surround themselves with luxury and beauty. Sentimental by nature, they both have a soft spot for friends and family, and enjoy giving lavish gifts. They both like to be king or queen of their castle, and can be a bit snobbish in their tastes. Vanity is a weakness for both, who spend their fair share of time gazing in the mirror and fussing over their appearance. Both can be perfectionists with an eternally nagging feeling that they're never quite satisfied. Libra is always looking for the perfect balance, and Leo is always privately struggling to stay at the top of the game. Life can feel like an endless search to both signs.

VIVE LA DIFFÉRENCE

Leo is passionate and aggressive and quick to act, where Libra is gentle and slow to decide. Leo can make anything seem more dramatic than it is, which can be both captivating and exhausting. Fair-minded Libras don't like to exaggerate, and will be a bit less dramatic in their expression—though they will ponder a subject for hours, which can bore hyperactive Leos.

HOW TO MAKE IT LAST

Don't battle for leadership; share the throne. Respect each other's need to feel like royalty, and make it a twenty-four-karat romance. Libras' gentleness will have to be tempered with a bit of strength—Leos respect action and need to see that their partner has a spine. Leo, take it easy and don't push your agenda too hard. Libra's scales will be thrown off balance by too much aggression. Also, tame down some of that wild Leo energy—Libra needs to see class and refinement first.

HOW TO END IT FAST

Chill on the overindulgence and snobbery, at least long enough to make sure your bills get paid. If you start acting like "beautiful people," you could get too caught up in image and forget to add enough substance—as did Leo Ben Affleck and his Libra ex Gwyneth Paltrow. Leo pushiness could spark Libra's rebellious side. If Libras are pushed too hard in one direction, they'll balance things out by doing the opposite. Libras, don't take forever to commit or warm up. Passion and devotion are a must for Leos, and they need to see some flagrant expressions of it.

LEO
(July 23–August 22)

+

SCORPIO
(October 23–November 21)

STAR COMBO: actors John Stamos (Leo) and Rebecca Romijn-Stamos (Scorpio), married

THE BREAKDOWN

Which will reign supreme—Leo's royal breeding or Scorpio's magical powers? They'll need to balance the glamorous life with a good amount of nurturing and attention. Both signs love status and are secretly insecure about their own hold on the number one spot. As a result, neither one realizes how strong he comes on sometimes. They'll either threaten each other or be turned on by the power surge of their blended energies.

COMMON GROUND

Both signs have magnetic personalities, and simmer with a quiet power that is often interpreted as arrogant. Control freaks by nature, they can be image-obsessed and ruthless when pursuing their ambitions. Both need high doses of attention and loyalty and have the stamina to return the same to their mates. They may be attracted to partners who can somehow help them get ahead—and they'll likely sense this opportunity in each other.

VIVE LA DIFFÉRENCE

Showy Leo puts it all on the table, while Scorpio hides behind a mask. Like their ruling planet Pluto, Scorpios simmer with an enigmatic power. Sun-ruled Leos can blind you—and even burn you—when they shine. Scorpios may prefer to control things from behind the scenes, while Leo steps directly into the spotlight to command attention. Although both are possessive, Scorpio jealousy and suspicion is unrivaled here. In the face of hurt feelings, Leo roars and pouts, while Scorpio quietly delivers a deadly sting.

HOW TO MAKE IT LAST

Scorpio, you'll have to lengthen that short leash you put your partner on—Leo rules the jungle and must be free to roam. Remember, Leo prizes loyalty as much as you do. Like cats, they'll always come back to a comfortable home, no matter how far they wander. Leo, remember that privacy is a virtue to Scorpio. Keep your paws to yourself in public and show some restraint. Scorpios admire control, and they'll chase what doesn't come easy. Scorpios also like mystery, so Leos may want to modify their open-book style, and release only an enticing preview.

HOW TO END IT FAST

Refuse to take orders or direction from each other. Focus all your energy on your ambitions and neglect each other's needs. Compete for stardom instead of collaborating. Do something to tarnish the other's public image or security. (The star-studded relationship between Leo Jennifer Lopez and Scorpio P. Diddy went downhill after he was tried on gun charges.) Orchestrate a manipulative drama to get revenge or attention. Bulldoze each other to get your way.

LEO
(July 23–August 22)
+
SAGITTARIUS
(November 22–December 21)

STAR COMBO: actors Christine Taylor (Leo) and Ben Stiller (Sagittarius), married

THE BREAKDOWN

These friendly fire signs pump up each other's confidence level, and inspire each other to make bold moves. There won't be a whole lot of rest between activities. An energy-conservation program will be needed to keep them from burning out. Leo's demands for attention may drain Sag at times, and Sag may frustrate Leo by wandering too far from the royal kingdom. Still, when these playful, dynamic souls connect, the chemistry can be off the map.

COMMON GROUND

Both signs like to please people and usually have a large circle of friends. Their thirst for adventure is insatiable, and they seek the joy in life—they love to laugh and celebrate. With their supersize goals and need for constant action, they may take on more projects than they can handle, then burn out temporarily. In general, they are fun-loving, passionate, and wise—but can also be intensely serious or silly.

VIVE LA DIFFÉRENCE

Sun-ruled Leos want to be the center of the universe; Jupiter-ruled Sags are caught up in their own world, and don't like to be disturbed when they're immersed in a project. When Leos commit to a project or relationship, they see it through to the end. They'll burn out their own solar-power reserves to keep their word. Impatient Sag has more trouble working within a structure, and drops things before they're fully bloomed. Why waste time if something better has come along? Sags are gamblers, and no risk is too big for them, at least until they crash and burn. Leo, on the other hand, pretends to be timid, but likely has the greater courage in the end.

HOW TO MAKE IT LAST

Sags, focus! A little attention goes a long way with Leos. Pay it now to avoid additional taxations in the future. Support Leos in their commitments, and don't ask them to be as impulsive as you (unless you're shopping). Sit still and give them some affection. Leos, stop bugging Sags for attention and reassurance—and don't smother the independent archers. Respect Sags' need to do things their way, and don't try to win them through bulldozing, pouting, and manipulation.

HOW TO END IT FAST

Gamble away everything on luxury and wild times. Spend more time on your hobbies than with each other. Royal-lion Leo will lose the throne by trying to order free-spirited Sag around. Sags smell a manipulative tactic a mile away, and they'll call Leos on it outright, paying no attention to the lions' pride. This disrespect to Leos' dignity will send them roaring, or they'll simply ice Sags out. If Sag fails to give Leo enough romance or attention, Leo will smother Sag until the archer can only break down, or break for the border. Watch those tempers!

LEO
(July 23–August 22)

+

CAPRICORN
(December 22–January 19)

STAR COMBO: model Iman (Leo) and singer David Bowie (Capricorn), married

THE BREAKDOWN

This first-class couple loves to see and be seen, and may be attracted simply on the basis of how good they look together. If they don't get too caught up in playing Ken and Barbie, they'll accessorize their strong chemical attraction with an enduring bond. With their matching abilities to be self-centered, they may develop a bit of a love-hate thing. In spite of their many differences, they may be continuously drawn to each other for reasons they can't quite explain.

COMMON GROUND

Both signs are ambitious and are quick to defend their honor. Integrity and admiration are important to them, and they like to be seen as people of strong character. Image-conscious types with first-class tastes, Leos and Capricorns both want to look good in public. They love to have the best of everything and can both play a little rough at times. Selfish tendencies can flare, especially when pursuing a goal.

VIVE LA DIFFÉRENCE

Leo is the sign of play, while Capricorn is the sign of work. Dramatic Leos are famous for gushing out their emotions, while poker-faced Capricorns would rather grunt or go silent. Fiery Leos like action and quick results, while earth-sign Capricorns move slowly and steadily, and may take years to reach their destinations. While both signs like the finer things in life, Capricorn makes solid, well-thought-out investments. Leo goes ultra-cheap, then breaks into random bursts of impulsive self-indulgence.

HOW TO MAKE IT LAST

Dress up in your finest and head to the hottest spot in town. Make sure you do it VIP style with eye-catching outfits and a luxe set of wheels. Leo, bring out your traditional side—show that your good taste also makes good sense. (A Leo like Martha Stewart would do well with a Capricorn.) Capricorn, get in touch with your animal instincts—put down the work and play a little more. Team up on common goals; Leo can be the star, and Capricorn can be the executive producer. Creating a platinum hit together can provoke passion in this materialistic matchup.

HOW TO END IT FAST

Work-first-play-later Cap could leave Leo feeling attention-starved and neglected. Their refusal to worship each other won't go over too well, either, especially since they both expect to be revered. If earthy Capricorn doesn't dig below the surface, Leo's passion could lie buried and untapped—and there's no life for Leo without passion. Capricorn pessimism will be a downer to Leo's sunny optimism. Leo's natural confidence can seem naïve to Cap, who believes that everything must be earned the hard way. As a result, Capricorns could see Leos as a shaky investment, and may place their bets elsewhere.

LEO
(July 23–August 22)

+

AQUARIUS
(January 20–February 18)

STAR COMBO: singers Whitney Houston (Leo) and Bobby Brown (Aquarius), married

THE BREAKDOWN

These opposite signs both have a way of snapping up the spotlight just by standing in it. As a result, they can either be costars or competitors, especially if their powerful egos get in the way. Busy Aquarius may not have time to catch every act of Leo's drama. Lovey-dovey Leo may not be able to fully express her passion with cool-and-collected Aquarius. With well-defined roles, they make great costars, as is the case with Aquarius Jennifer Aniston and Leo Lisa Kudrow, or 'N Sync band mates Justin Timberlake (Aquarius) and JC Chasez (Leo). Shared levels of success are the key to balance. As rivals, they'll bring out each other's worst qualities.

COMMON GROUND

Leo and Aquarius are both fixed signs, meaning they like to declare goals, then steadily reach them. Both signs take disappointment hard, and may demand perfection of themselves and/or others, then explode from the pressure. It's hard to tell if they're naughty or nice—they can flip between the roles of teacher's pet and rebellious show-off. They make powerful managers, team leaders, and creative coordinators. Both signs can be forceful and manipulative when they want to get their way.

VIVE LA DIFFÉRENCE

Leos are clingy and praise-hungry; detached Aquarians freestyle to their own beat. Aquarius doesn't like to get too heavy too soon, while Leo wants commitment *yesterday*. Leos love kids, family, and affection; wandering spirit Aquarians may be indifferent to family matters, and can only take so much of the "mushy" stuff that Leo loves. While Leo is often an open book, Aquarius is casual and private about his feelings.

HOW TO MAKE IT LAST

Leo is the sign of love and the self, while Aquarius is the sign of friendship and groups. As a result, this is a match between a solo act (Leo) and a team player (Aquarius). Leo, don't dim your lights so Aquarius can shine. Aquarius, don't try to crowd Leo out of the spotlight; follow your individuality and stage your own unique production. Focus on your differences instead of your similarities so that everyone feels like a star.

HOW TO END IT FAST

Competition is the road to ruin. A cool Aquarian response to Leo's dramatic displays of affection will cause temperatures to drop dangerously low. Leo drama could also bust up Aquarius's chill vibe. Aquarius will lose by refusing to praise Leo, or by tearing down Leo's ego to pump up her own. Affection-hungry Leo will have to recognize that Aquarius shows love through friendship, not worship—so lower those demanding expectations. The lion's temper tantrums and pouting will not be played here. If Leo tries to make Aquarius into a backup singer, Aquarius will back on up—and out—of this match.

LEO
(July 23–August 22)

✛

PISCES
(February 19–March 20)

STAR COMBO: actors Tom Green (Leo) and Drew Barrymore (Pisces), divorced

THE BREAKDOWN

There's plenty of romance and chemistry here, but these signs may throw each other a bit off balance. There could be too much reality for escape-artist Pisces, and not enough stability for Leo. Pisces could feel especially vulnerable and moody next to sunny, confident Leo, and they'll have lots of control issues to work through. The bond will be intense and mysterious, and they may feel like strangers to each other at times.

COMMON GROUND

Both signs are creative, dramatic, and romantic. Their vivid imaginations conjure up some interesting fantasies and artistic creations. They're both self-sacrificing as a means of getting people to do what they want, and have sent their friends on fantastic guilt trips. Insecurity lies beneath the lion's arrogant roar and the fish's toughest scales. Throughout life, they're both haunted by the question "Am I good enough?" They're both a bit narcissistic and paranoid—Leos need to hear constant applause, and Pisces have such active imaginations, they think everyone's judging them.

VIVE LA DIFFÉRENCE

Leo is an aggressive, dynamic fire sign who loves tradition; Pisces is a moody, reflective water sign who fears commitment and hates other people's rules. Where arrogant Leos may have an inflated idea of their abilities, insecure Pisces are always doubting their own talent. Leos rule the ego, and don't apologize for putting themselves first. By contrast, Pisces are the sign of self-sacrifice, and they feel a guilty embarrassment if they don't put themselves last in line. As the last sign of the zodiac, Pisces is said to carry the karmic memories of all twelve signs. As a result, the boundaries between themselves and others are blurred. Thus, where Leo has a strong sense of self, Pisces has a hazy one at best.

HOW TO MAKE IT LAST

Pisces lack confidence, and Leos have too much of it—spread it around, and it all evens out. Leo wants to see action, and Pisces' active imagination won't do the trick after a while. Pisces will have to show Leos that they have commitment, drive, and goals to turn all their creative ideas into reality. (Pisces' least favorite word is *reality,* so that won't be easy.) Leo will have to go easy, and recognize that the fish needs time to dream and reflect. Although Leo is usually the needier party in relationships, in this case, Pisces will probably be the clinger. Pisces will have to be loyal and supportive, instead of pouty and brooding. Let the lion roam the jungle and the fish swim the sea—only a generous amount of freedom will inspire you both to come back to each other.

HOW TO END IT FAST

Avoid dealing with reality, or play passive-aggressive games. Refuse to take responsibility for your own moods and happiness. Too much Piscean insecurity could kill off Leos' passion, since it will require the lions to give more attention than they receive. Pisces' gloom can bring Leo's hopeful spirits down, and if Leo demands that Pisces paint on a happy face the fish will only resist. Leo's royal routine may cause authority-hating Pisces to rebel. Pisces' slippery-fish act may frustrate Leos, driving them into a sad state of neglect.

VIRGO IN LOVE

VIRGO: (August 23–September 22)

★ What They Need in a Mate

✳ To be needed

✳ A chance to "fix" your flaws and fuss over you

✳ Patience and honorable intentions—to feel safe before opening up

✳ Cleanliness—keep it pure for the "virgins" of the zodiac

✳ Intelligence and common sense

✳ A perfect match—fit their checklist, or don't bother

☆ What They Offer a Mate

✳ Responsibility—they'll always take care of you

✳ A sweet, helpful desire to please you

✳ Sharp opinions that can seem preachy or critical at times

✳ A great eye for detail and a patient ear for listening

✳ A willingness to work hard—this is the sign of the perfectionist

Virgo-Aries: *See Aries-Virgo.*

Virgo-Taurus: *See Taurus-Virgo.*

Virgo-Gemini: *See Gemini-Virgo.*

Virgo-Cancer: *See Cancer-Virgo.*

Virgo-Leo: *See Leo-Virgo.*

VIRGO
(August 23–September 22)

VIRGO
(August 23–September 22)

STAR COMBO: model Claudia Schiffer (Virgo) and magician David Copperfield (Virgo), exes

THE BREAKDOWN

There's always a touch of practical magic when two no-nonsense Virgos join forces. With their constant analyzing and their ability to find any fact or fault, this relationship could become a game of Trivial Pursuit. They'll be fine as long as it doesn't get *too* trivial—Virgos have a tendency to get stuck in the details. Since Virgos represent service to others, they could be bound by a strong sense of duty and may enjoy sharing easy times and outdoor activities.

COMMON GROUND

Virgos like privacy and time alone, and love to analyze everything. At best, they're sweet, devoted, and helpful. On bad days, they can be judgmental and preachy—as Virgo rapper-turned-minister Mase has been. Don't let the innocent facade make you think they're no fun. Many Virgos have a dash of spice in them—as do Pink, Adam Sandler, and Beyoncé Knowles. Ruled by Mercury, their active minds can be quite mischievous, and they'll smugly deliver lip service with a smile.

VIVE LA DIFFÉRENCE

Some Virgos are data wizards who prefer the company of books or machinery to that of human beings. Others apply a more personal touch, and use their analytical skills to help friends solve problems. Theirs is often the shoulder that everyone cries on—as a result, they have all the latest gossip. Many Virgos are drawn to the healing arts and can create a soothing atmosphere where everyone feels well fed and rested. The Virgos who get *too* caught up in the details can become high-maintenance, and may resort to catty criticism and complaining.

HOW TO MAKE IT LAST

Keep it innocent, but not naïve. Strong opinions are welcome, as long as you don't push them on each other. Bring a touch of freshness to everything, and try to curb the pickiness and perfectionism—let yourselves be human. Use plenty of soap and water (Virgos like cleanliness), and respect each other's privacy. Since Virgos need to be needed, create opportunities to serve and help each other. Be a sensible soul mate the other Virgo can feel safe around. Enjoy long conversations, simple pleasures, and plenty of fresh air.

HOW TO END IT FAST

If you criticize each other or set the standards too high, Virgo could say, "Analyze *this*" . . . while the door slams behind him. Reject Virgo's help or refuse to open up, and your mate will find a new soul to save. Make impractical decisions, or spend all your time indoors—active Virgo will grow restless. Show weak opinions and a lack of judgment, and Virgo will lose respect. At the same time, if your judgment abilities become too snobbish or gossipy, Virgo will look for someone a little more down to earth.

VIRGO
(August 23–September 22)

+

LIBRA
(September 23–October 22)

STAR COMBO: No Doubt band mates Tony Kanal (Virgo) and Gwen Stefani (Libra), exes

THE BREAKDOWN

Down-to-earth Virgo is focused on the daily grind, while up-in-the-clouds Libra is always daydreaming. Still, they may be able to teach each other a thing or two. Libras can lighten up Virgos and help their critical eyes see a little more beauty. Virgos can offer wishy-washy Libras stability and help them make more sensible, thorough decisions. This will only work if they *want* to try each other's foreign approach to life—it could take hard work to balance Libra's extravagance with Virgo's practical nature.

COMMON GROUND

Few signs spend as much time evaluating everything as these two. Virgo is ruled by analytical Mercury, and Libra is represented by the scales of judgment. Both signs can get "analysis paralysis" when it's time to make a move. With their baby faces, they have a similar freshness to their flirting. Both signs like to take care of people, and have critical eyes—Virgos see every flaw, and Libras are sensitive to color, style, and order. When these signs feel down on themselves (which happens often), they may share a scathing sense of humor and a weakness for gossip. Meow!

VIVE LA DIFFÉRENCE

Libra's practicality has its limits, while Virgo's has few. While Virgos pinch pennies, Libras drop ducats—Virgos' favorite shopping words may be *dollar store*, while Libras' are *designer outlet*. Ruled by beauty planet Venus, Libra loves rich colors; earthy Virgo is happiest when everything is khaki, white, or navy. Virgo can be a bit of a wet blanket when Libra gets playful, and may react awkwardly to Libra's open gestures of affection. Libras like to meet new people; Virgos can be a bit introverted, and tend to stick with a trusted few.

HOW TO MAKE IT LAST

Libras can help Virgos see life's beauty, and bring out their sensual sides. Virgos can be a grounding force for Libras, teaching them the power of simplicity and self-sacrifice. This kind of discipline may be uncomfortable for Libras, who like to indulge. Fortunately, Virgos are always happy to serve, so Libras probably won't go without nurturing, as long as they request it in a noncritical way. Since you both like to help people, join forces to make someone happy—visit an older relative or volunteer with kids. Libra can provide the charming talk, and Virgo can be the attentive listener.

HOW TO END IT FAST

Both signs can be quick to judge and slow to forgive. Too much Virgo "sensibility" could be a downer for Libras, bringing their scales crashing back to reality. Serious-minded Virgo may think Libra is impulsive and childish; Libra may think Virgo is uptight and parental. Virgo's tendency to give their best away to others could clash with Libra's habit of saving the best for themselves (even if they share it). Different philosophies about life and happiness will have to be balanced.

VIRGO
(August 23–September 22)

+

SCORPIO
(October 23–November 21)

STAR COMBO: singer Shania Twain (Virgo) and record producer Mutt Lange (Scorpio), husband-wife team

THE BREAKDOWN

There's a lot going on below the surface for these kindred spirits, who usually want similar things from life. With Virgo's analytical skills and Scorpio's research abilities, they can build quite a mystery together. If they scatter a few clues, the other is sure to follow the trail, and will likely stick around once the case is opened.

COMMON GROUND

Both signs take life—and themselves—pretty seriously. They're fascinated with details and internal wiring and want to know how everything works. Micromanagers by nature, they can analyze for hours, and few flaws escape their critical eyes. They share a tendency to be tight with cash and to dress in low-key colors or conservative cuts. Both like to hang at home and are slow to share their secrets. However, they want to hear everything about *you,* and are great at getting people to pour out their own confessions. Both signs have been known to use this information as a weapon later, should you cross or betray them.

VIVE LA DIFFÉRENCE

Earth-sign Virgo appears calm next to Scorpio, who burns with a quiet intensity. Virgo energy feels like soothing background music, while Scorpio's is like an agitated, enchanting beat you can't ignore. Virgos like a bit more variety and room to change their minds. Scorpios prefer to put down roots and establish a solid foundation for their empires. When done wrong, Scorpio can obsess over an enemy for years, and may unleash a few poisonous strikes. Virgo will just deliver a self-righteous parting shot and cut off foes when things get messy.

HOW TO MAKE IT LAST

Communication and friendship are key, and will be easy to come by in this relationship. Without these essentials, Scorpio jealousy could flare and Virgo could lose interest. Scorpios should make sure to channel their energy into lots of hobbies, since even Virgos may not be able to give them the intense attention level that they need. Virgos' helpfulness will be appreciated, and they can teach Scorpios a little anger management.

HOW TO END IT FAST

Broken trust, revenge, and hurt will follow if Virgos turn their critical eye and harsh judgment on Scorpios. An icy rebellion will also follow should Scorpio try to micromanage Virgo, or cling when Virgo needs time alone. Scorpio loyalty tests and head games will not be welcomed—Virgo likes things clean and consistent. If Virgo is too "pure" or basic, bad-boy/bad-girl Scorpio will swiftly solve the mystery and move on to a more intriguing case. These signs' shared tendency toward perfectionism, and their hesitance to forgive, could also burn them both out.

VIRGO
(August 23–September 22)

✛

SAGITTARIUS
(November 22–December 21)

STAR COMBO: singer Beyoncé Knowles (Virgo) and rapper Jay-Z (Sagittarius), exes

THE BREAKDOWN

Anything can happen when a Virgo teacher's pet meets a Sagittarian class clown. They may not understand or approve of each other's way of doing things, but they'll certainly learn through their differences. Sag could feel surprisingly vulnerable with Virgo, and may wish Virgo would open up more. Virgo will be frustrated and awed by Sag's risk-taking and refusal to play by the rules. Over time, Sag may end up on the honor roll and Virgo could wind up in detention for a day. It will be a refreshing role reversal for both, even if it doesn't last forever.

COMMON GROUND

These are both mutable signs, meaning they can adapt to their surroundings and like to communicate. As a result, they can probably adjust to their differences. Both signs are people pleasers—Virgo likes to help and serve; Sag wants everyone to have a good time. Both signs love to learn, and probably have plenty of books on their shelves. When challenged, they can be preachy know-it-alls. Virgo likes to analyze and Sag likes to philosophize, so conversation will never be boring. Both signs are active, curious types who love to spend time outdoors.

VIVE LA DIFFÉRENCE

Earth-sign Virgo is more of an introvert, while fire-sign Sag is more of an extrovert. Although both appreciate sarcasm, Virgo speaks seriously and properly, while Sag uses playful, colorful language and is quick to talk smack. In life, Virgos pursue simplicity, and are happiest serving people or working in a structured environment. Impatient Sags hate routines and rely on their natural luck (a gift from their ruler Jupiter) to complement the hard work. Virgos' analytical minds help them see what *is*; Sags' philosophical minds conjure up a glimpse of what *could be*. As a result, Virgo finds the present interesting enough to stay grounded in it, while Sag is always on to the next project, even before a current one is finished.

HOW TO MAKE IT LAST

Take long walks, and keep a healthy balance between private time and hanging out. Virgos can ground Sags by helping them think before they act. Those great Virgo listening skills will be handy when Sags start bubbling over with talk about their latest idea. Try not to offer a critique unless Sag asks for your feedback, and keep it extremely constructive. Sags, cheer Virgos up when they get down on themselves, and keep them hopeful. Virgos can get stuck on details, and Sags have the power to inspire them to see beyond that—just don't push Virgos to jump into a high-risk scheme without thinking it through.

HOW TO END IT FAST

If Virgo nags or judges Sag, or if Sag mocks or judges Virgo, it will be a verbal showdown at the theater of pain. Virgo hates to be rushed, and Sag hates to wait—unless they compromise on a speed, this could be a blood-boiling traffic jam. Sag's high-intensity pace and big-baller dreams could exhaust methodical Virgo. Virgo's fault-finding and love of trivia could annoy Sag, and the party could end early if Virgo acts stuffy when Sag wants to get wild.

VIRGO
(August 23–September 22)

CAPRICORN
(December 22–January 19)

STAR COMBO: actress Rose McGowan (Virgo) and singer Marilyn Manson (Capricorn), exes

THE BREAKDOWN

These two highly compatible earth signs have their feet so firmly on the ground that they may have to push hard to get their heads lost in the clouds. Neither sign wants to invest in anything that isn't practical or built to last. Together, they can retire from their solo careers and team up for a solid payoff, set on a strong foundation.

COMMON GROUND

As earth signs, they need a certain amount of structure, and prefer to stay grounded in reality. They're hardworking and loyal, the kind of friends who come through in a crunch. These family-oriented signs can be dutiful sons and daughters, and are often patient with kids. A bit on the picky side, they each may have a long list of "rules" or expectations for a partner, which could lead to lengthy breaks between long-term relationships. Both have a bit of the loner in them—they don't mind spending time on their own, and would rather hang solo than waste energy on fools.

VIVE LA DIFFÉRENCE

Who wants to be a millionaire? Thrifty Virgos are happy wearing natural fibers, shopping at the discount store, and driving a secondhand Toyota. Classic Capricorns dream of diamonds, leather, and luxury cars—if they can't have the best now, they're saving up for it. Ultra-ambitious Capricorns can be selfish at times, especially when pursuing their own agendas. Dutiful Virgos put other people's needs above their own, and will delay a goal to help everyone else.

HOW TO MAKE IT LAST

Build something concrete together, and try to avoid getting stuck in routine. Prioritize your time together to keep the relationship on track—Capricorn will have to put the work aside, and Virgo will have to say no to a few needy friends. Capricorn, don't be so goal-focused or set in your ways—Virgo likes to talk, contribute, and analyze. Both signs' version of reality can look a little too much like pessimism at times, so use those organizing talents to arrange some *fun*. Virgo, indulge in the luxury that high-rolling Capricorn loves. You don't have to suffer to build character, so let Capricorn treat you like the lady or gentleman that you are.

HOW TO END IT FAST

Virgo fault-finding and Capricorn pessimism can make this too much of a reality check, with not enough fantasy. All work and no play could lead them straight to dullsville. Capricorns play a little too rough sometimes, and their repression-fueled freakiness may shock innocent Virgos beyond their tolerance. Virgo's "helpful" criticism may seem unsupportive to Capricorns, who need to be admired and encouraged. If Virgo pinches pennies or dresses in rags when Capricorn wants to feel like a class act, the embarrassment may cause Cap to find a new executive partner.

VIRGO
(August 23–September 22)

✛

AQUARIUS
(January 20–February 18)

STAR COMBO: actors Charlie Sheen (Virgo) and Denise Richards (Aquarius), married

THE BREAKDOWN

This match can seem almost bizarre, like Virgo Michael Jackson's short-lived marriage to Aquarius Lisa Marie Presley. The attraction will likely occur through conversation, since both signs have quick minds and are curious about almost any topic. As friends, your bond can be deep, and you may share secrets that you're not likely to reveal to many others. Despite the strong mental connection, though, your emotional needs may be too mysterious for the other to figure out.

COMMON GROUND

Both signs are intellectual and like to have meaningful conversations that cover unusual subjects. When you make up your minds, nobody can change them. You're concerned about helping the world, and you're loyal friends to anyone in need. You shine as a second-in-command to a team captain or class president, since you're both responsible, thorough, and devoted to any job. Because of your strong compassion for others' suffering, you could both have a long list of needy friends who call you in every crisis. It also helps you both avoid dealing with your own emotional issues.

VIVE LA DIFFÉRENCE

Virgo is methodical, practical, and down to earth. Aquarius is impulsive, imaginative, and eccentric. Aquarius likes groups and friends, and is always meeting new people. Virgo can be shy at times, and sticks to a safe, close-knit crew. Air-sign Aquarians are big on change and action—you never know who they'll be on any given day. Earth-sign Virgos are more creatures of habit, with simple tastes and consistent personalities.

HOW TO MAKE IT LAST

These signs get along best when they have some responsibility to bind them together. Collaborate on a money-making venture, like Destiny's Child duo Aquarius Kelly Rowland and Virgo Beyoncé Knowles. Step out of character—Aquarians will have to learn to love routine, and Virgos will have to let their wild side out. Talk about ideas, share books, confide in each other, and give advice. Because of your different natures, you can offer each other valuable perspective. You're both independent in your own way, so give each other the space and freedom you both need.

HOW TO END IT FAST

Virgo pettiness and gossip will annoy Aquarius, who can't stand to hear people being talked about unfairly. Aquarian impulsiveness or lack of discipline could bring out Virgo's critical side, which will lead Aquarius to accuse Virgo of uptightness. Some of Aquarius's radical or experimental ideas could shock the more traditional Virgo, sending him searching for a "saner" partner.

VIRGO
(August 23–September 22)

✚

PISCES
(February 19–March 20)

STAR COMBO: Luke Wilson (Virgo) and Drew Barrymore (Pisces), exes

THE BREAKDOWN

Virgo is the service sign, and Pisces rules self-sacrifice. As a result, this attraction often starts with one of them being needy or weak, and the other rushing in for the save. They'll have to work to balance their own needs with their desire to be needed by others. Both signs like to help people, and they can create a healing sanctuary together. At times, it's a battle between Virgo's desire for reality and Pisces' attempt to escape it.

COMMON GROUND

Virgo is the "health" sign of the zodiac, and Pisces rules hospitals and illness. Many of them are drawn to nursing, psychology, nonprofit work, and the healing arts. At the very least, they'll both have a lot of compassion for people's suffering. At times, both will suppress their own needs, then resent the world instead of speaking up for what they want. Both have been known to deliver high doses of nagging, blame, guilt trips, and criticism—as well as amazing TLC. Solo time and freedom are important to both of them. They need long hours to chill at home and get lost in their thoughts.

VIVE LA DIFFÉRENCE

Although they both are drawn to healing, water-sign Pisces is far more needy and emotionally vulnerable than earth-sign Virgo. When it comes to their goals, Pisces are slow-moving and dreamy, while practical Virgo quickly puts plans into action. Virgo likes things clean and simple; Pisces tends to prefer life cloudy and complicated.

HOW TO MAKE IT LAST

Build a healing sanctuary together. Let yourselves help *and* be helped—open up, already. Team up to heal the world, instead of always trying to fix each other. Virgo, dig down and bring up some "impractical" passion—Pisces love romance and need a break from reality. Pisces, keep your Virgo sane by handling your basic responsibilities. Be sure to ask for plenty of Virgo's help along the way. Virgo, ask for a massage in return.

HOW TO END IT FAST

Between Pisces' secretive tendencies and Virgo's reluctance to open up, they may never build the kind of intimacy needed to sustain a relationship. Besides, Virgo can sense a secret agenda a mile away, and won't be happy about it. Some Pisces are drawn to self-destructive habits. If Virgos have to rush in for too many saves, they may burn out and walk away. Virgo criticism could wound the insecure, self-conscious Pisces—the fish could strike back by trying to make Virgo jealous or guilty. Unless these two step up and communicate openly, they could be torn apart by manipulation and unexpressed resentment.

LIBRA IN LOVE

LIBRA: (September 23–October 22)

★ What They Need in a Mate

✳ Love, love, and more love—a chance to give and receive it

✳ Balance, order, and attention to detail

✳ Fair-mindedness—extreme types will throw them off balance

✳ Peace, love, and harmony—this is the sign of beauty and equality

✳ To be spoiled and feel like the top dog—they want the best of everything

✳ An active social life with plenty of room to mingle and meet new people

✳ A committed but nonpossessive partner

✳ Beauty, grace, and good manners

✳ Pressure-free time to make up their minds—don't rush them!

☆ What They Offer a Mate

✳ Charm, romance, and beauty—you'll always go first-class

✳ Gentleness and love—even the stern Libras are soft inside

✳ Clever conversation, especially if it's a debate

✳ Calm without boredom

✳ Fairness and equality

✳ A lesson about stopping to smell the roses—impatient types should look elsewhere

✳ Sugar *and* spice

Libra-Aries: *See Aries-Libra.*

Libra-Taurus: *See Taurus-Libra.*

Libra-Gemini: *See Gemini-Libra.*

Libra-Cancer: *See Cancer-Libra.*

Libra-Leo: *See Leo-Libra.*

Libra-Virgo: *See Virgo-Libra.*

LIBRA
(September 23–October 22)

LIBRA
(September 23–October 22)

STAR COMBO: actors Catherine Zeta-Jones (Libra) and Michael Douglas (Libra), married

THE BREAKDOWN

This romantic duet can make beautiful music together, as long as they can commit fast enough to record a demo. Balance will be a major theme. They can help each other achieve it, or send each other's scales swinging. Libra is also the sign of fairness, and will fight for equality. They'll have plenty of debates to negotiate their roles.

COMMON GROUND

With the double shot of Venus energy, this could be one of the most loving relationships around. Both Libras are in love with love—they can build a dreamscape filled with romance and beauty. These two gentle souls love to spoil and be spoiled, and they'll spread the love to friends as well. On a good day, Libras are all Prince Charmings and Princess Brides. Give them a pair of one-way tickets to La-La Land and they'll live there happily ever after.

VIVE LA DIFFÉRENCE

Some Libras are very expressive of their loving natures. Others are too sensitive to show how delicate they really are, and may hide behind a controlled or defensive front. Again, it's all about balance. The steady Libras shower their people with sentimental gifts, wear beautiful clothes, and fill photo albums with well-composed shots of their friends. The imbalanced Libras can be tortured souls who brood for hours or rage against the machine as they struggle for equilibrium.

HOW TO MAKE IT LAST

Remember that Libra is the sign of partnership and "other people." No matter how much they love to be spoiled, Libras need to give *and* receive love to stay happy. Surround yourselves with mutual friends who need you, as well as those who feed you. Be true friends to each other, and stay socially active—you were born to be in the mix. Treat this relationship like an equal partnership, and your scales will stay balanced.

HOW TO END IT FAST

Act like two spoiled brats, pouting and whining, "That's not *fair!*" In your fight for so-called equality, forget to consider the other Libra's point of view and make it all about you. Pull the prince/princess routine and demand that things be done your way. Criticize each other's ideas of what's beautiful, and laugh at the other's most sensitive dreams. Refuse to compliment your Libra, or to accept their compliments. Stop nourishing your beautiful mate with love, and the garden will never grow.

LIBRA
(September 23–October 22)

+

SCORPIO
(October 23–November 21)

STAR COMBO: No Doubt vocalist Gwen Stefani (Libra) and Bush front man Gavin Rossdale (Scorpio), married

THE BREAKDOWN

Libra and Scorpio are two very different signs, who may be attracted to each other simply because one has so much of what the other doesn't. The tension and mystery can crank up the heat, and their good times will rock the charts. Unless they respect their vastly different agendas, however, peace may fall apart as quickly as it does in the Middle East.

COMMON GROUND

Both signs like to dialogue, and they'll probably be drawn together through conversation. Libras love long, rambling talks in a one-on-one situation, and they'll debate any topic. Scorpios will hang until the wee hours, and have a sharp insight on any subject Libras throw on the table. Libras will enjoy the challenge of Scorpios' detailed ideas; Scorpios will mellow in the glow of Libras' soothing vibe. Physical attraction will be supercharged.

VIVE LA DIFFÉRENCE

Libra is the astrological flower child, spreading good vibes to everyone like a clown tossing candy to kids at a parade. Unfortunately, this can make possessive Scorpio feel like he got the candy with the razor blade in it, and he'll start throwing even sharper knives back. Scorpio gets jealous at the slightest hint that Libra loves somebody else as much as she loves Scorpio. It doesn't matter if it's Libra's own family and friends—Scorpio must be Numero Uno. Unless they both compromise, Scorpio will get manic and Libra will get claustro.

HOW TO MAKE IT LAST

Libra must give Scorpio truckloads of reassurance. Scorpio must give Libra a warehouse of credit. In social situations, Libra should regularly break from mingling and check in with Scorpio—giving Scorpio focused, one-on-one attention. In exchange, Scorpio can chill with the jealousy and give Libra breathing room. Libra is the sign of relationships—this sign needs other people to stay balanced. Scorpios should stay confident, keep plenty of hobbies, and remember that Libras will always come home to them in the end.

HOW TO END IT FAST

Libras can neglect Scorpios, ignoring their indirect pleas for attention when they feel hurt. Stand back and watch Scorpios strike where it counts. Scorpios can try to limit Libras' love only to them, and attack at the slightest sign that Libras are paying attention to somebody else. Libras will bounce faster than a canceled check. Scorpios can refuse to forgive Libras, bringing up a past offense over and over again until Libras' delicate nerves are fried. Libras can give in to their selfish side and forget to treat Scorpios with the same detailed attention that Scorpios always give them.

LIBRA
(September 23–October 22)

+

SAGITTARIUS
(November 22–December 21)

STAR COMBO: manager Sharon Osbourne (Libra) and rocker Ozzy Osbourne (Sagittarius), married

THE BREAKDOWN

These natural-born friends move at different speeds and will have to set their odometers to a happy middle pace if they want to travel together for the long haul. Although their passion tanks may run out of gas now and then, Libra and Sag have a natural understanding for each other, and they'll stay friends forever.

COMMON GROUND

These two could fall in love as coauthors of a cynical advice column, or performing stand-up comedy in the school talent show. They both appreciate sarcastic jokes and could get kicked out of class for talking too much smack. Both signs get lost in their heads and tend to sweat the small stuff. They're great at giving everyone else perspective, though, and can pull each other out of some rough moods. When insecurity strikes, they may cover it up with cutting or judgmental humor.

VIVE LA DIFFÉRENCE

Moodiness and even depressed spells can hit both signs, but Libras' downswings can last a lot longer. Sags are ruled by Jupiter, the planet of optimism and good luck. Like symbolic archers, they pick up their arrows and shoot for the target again. During bluer times, Libras tend to isolate themselves or brood solo. Sags recover their sunshine more quickly after they talk it out. If their bad moods hit at the same time, Libra may be MIA when Sag sends an SOS. Likewise, Sag may try to cheer Libra up with easy-breezy advice, or push Libra to "get over it," and Libra hates to be rushed.

HOW TO MAKE IT LAST

Stop looking for constant fireworks, and savor the beauty of friendship. This may not be a passionate emotional roller coaster, but the two of you are a walking amusement park, and that's worth the ride. Buy a scrapbook and fill it with all your memories—the funny notes Sag passed in class, the long letters and artistic photos that Libra composed. Refer to this treasure whenever you start to wonder, "Is he the One?"

HOW TO END IT FAST

Turn the sarcasm and judgment on each other—there will be no survivors when your verbal brutality meets in the ring. Refuse to communicate about your "commitment issues" when they come up (and they will, since you both cherish your independence). Sag can give in to reckless impulses and shatter Libra's delicate sense of balance. Libra can tarnish the innocence of Sag's hope by refusing to commit full-on, or by moping when Sag wants to play. Libra longs for true romance, and Sag may be too buddylicious to bring on the hearts and flowers. Impulsive Sag loves action, and Libra's constant, cautious weighing of every option may send Sag bungee-jumping into somebody else's arms.

LIBRA

(September 23–October 22)

CAPRICORN

(December 22–January 19)

STAR COMBO: musician Sting (Libra) and actress Trudie Styler (Capricorn), married

THE BREAKDOWN

It's good to be king—but can these two signs share the throne? It could be a throw-down for the crown. In times of peace, Capricorn provides the solid weight that balances flighty Libra. But if the weight is too heavy, Libra will fly off the scales and into the great beyond. When earthbound Caps get stuck in a rut, airy Libras can lift them to higher ground. But if the winds of change are too strong, Libra's effect will be more like a tornado than a breath of fresh air.

COMMON GROUND

Nobody likes to rush in this combo. Libra weighs each decision; Capricorn takes everything slowly and steadily. They'll understand each other's need to move at a gentle pace toward commitment. Traditional romance is cool with both of them—there will be plenty of long-stemmed roses, chocolates, and Hallmark moments exchanged. In the limelight, they'll fly first-class, since both signs like to look good in public and rock top-of-the-line gear.

VIVE LA DIFFÉRENCE

Ambitious Caps put their goals above everything else, including relationships. "No romance without finance" is their motto. Libras put relationships above everything else, including some of their goals. Ideally, Libras want finance *and* romance, but they'd toss a few coins away in the name of love. Socially, these signs mix it up a little differently. Libras love to meet and mingle—to them, life is all about other people. Capricorns are fine on the solo circuit, content to hang with family and a couple of lifelong pals. They'll step out only to further their own agendas, which could leave Libras frustrated at times.

HOW TO MAKE IT LAST

Instead of making this a royal rumble, form a tag team that lets you enjoy your common ground without stepping on each other's turf. Start an enterprise together. Libra can charm the investors and work the parties; Cap can write a solid business plan and manage the operation. Use your social time to enhance your public profile: Spend time at concerts, award shows, and restaurants where the paparazzi linger. Busy Caps can remind Libras that love is still in the picture, sending flowers, and cards and making other sentimental gestures to make up for lost face-time. Libras can understand that gruff Caps may not be mushy on the outside, but they're definitely soft on the inside. Give Cap a little of that "time to think it over" that you're always asking for yourself.

HOW TO END IT FAST

Capricorn will lose by being selfish and withholding. Libra will lose by being selfish and demanding. Libras need to feel adored, and Capricorns can lose if Libras have to wait in line for a few crumbs of affection. Unfortunately, Caps' families have lockdown on the number one spot. Integrity and achievement are important to Capricorns. If Libras push too hard for attention before Caps' work is done, or question Caps' loyalty in any way, the goats will go earn their MVP trophy from another team.

LIBRA
(September 23–October 22)

✛

AQUARIUS
(January 20–February 18)

STAR COMBO: actors Neve Campbell (Libra) and Matthew Lillard (Aquarius), *Scream* costars and exes

THE BREAKDOWN

This is a heavenly combo of two compatible air signs who may get lost in the clouds at times. Aquarians can inspire indecisive Libras to take action and imagine an exciting future far and away from what they know. Libras can bring out the friendly Aquarians' more passionate side, and will cheer from the sidelines as Aquarians let their creativity flow. They'll float away *somewhere* together. Where they'll end up is anyone's guess.

COMMON GROUND

Because Libra and Aquarius are both air signs, they approach the world through their thoughts first. Conversation will never be dull. Both signs are concerned with justice and human rights. They could meet at a rally or volunteering at an after-school literacy program or simply at a party where they find themselves deep in a lovely debate. Together, they'll rage against the machine, creating peace, love, and harmony everywhere they go.

VIVE LA DIFFÉRENCE

Aquarius can be eccentric and unpredictable, while Libra is a creature of habit. Cautious Libra's balance may be thrown off by sudden bolts of Aquarius "inspiration"—like going to the drive-in on a February night or organizing an after-school search team to discover the lost city of Atlantis. Libra is romantic at heart, while Aquarius is most comfortable with a casual, friendly vibe. Libra kisses could meet Aquarius disses if Libra tries to get too mushy in public. Also, Libra is more talk while Aquarius is more action. Once they get past discovering their similar ideals, they'll either part ways or combine forces.

HOW TO MAKE IT LAST

Talk about ideas and dreams. Get involved in a cause you're both passionate about—keep your eye on something bigger than just the two of you. Travel together, stopping in both quirky and romantic destinations.

Aquarians, remember that even the most punk-rock Libras are traditional about romance. Give them candy and flowers, instead of the hot-pink baseball glove and bubble-blowing squirt gun you were eyeing at the novelty shop. Libras, remember that even the most conservative-looking Aquarians have a deep appreciation for weirdness and originality. Buy them trapeze lessons and a rubber monster mask instead of the generic chocolate-and-Hallmark number.

HOW TO END IT FAST

Say unfair and unkind things to each other. Criticize each other's dreams and ideas. Libras can be more emotional than logical, causing cool-as-a-fan Aquarians to lose their composure. Aquarius can use too much logic and not enough emotion, which will leave love-hungry Libra starved for affection.

LIBRA
(September 23–October 22)

✦

PISCES
(February 19–March 20)

STAR COMBO: singers Usher (Libra) and TLC's Chilli (Pisces), flames

THE BREAKDOWN

These two artsy, romantic signs approach life differently, but often have enough common traits to adapt. Once they bond, they can build a fantasyland together. Air-sign Libra has a breezier, more outgoing approach than emotional Pisces, who needs periods of privacy and deep reflection. Because Libra is the sign of "other people," and Pisces absorbs feelings like a sponge, they'll have to be careful not to get lost in each other's moods.

COMMON GROUND

Romance and fantasy are big with these two, who want love to look a little bit like a Hallmark card or a classic novel. Both can be tortured souls in their own ways, and may need to channel their agony into a creative outlet. (Think of Libra Avril Lavigne or Pisces Kurt Cobain.) Without this, they can become depressed and self-destructive. Many Libras and Pisces are drawn to photography, writing, and other arts. They have refined tastes and a knack for spotting beauty.

VIVE LA DIFFÉRENCE

Libras find comfort by talking with other people, and Pisces heal through alone time. Pisces is the last sign of the zodiac and is said to carry the karma of all the other signs. Venus-ruled Libras can be spoiled and demanding at times—this sign won't compromise on having their favorite creature comforts. Pisces is the sign of self-sacrifice, and feels guilty asking for anything directly. Although both are sensitive, Libra is most comfortable in the world of ideas, and Pisces in the land of emotions. Libra will deal with worries by thinking, and Pisces by feeling—a subtle but important difference.

HOW TO MAKE IT LAST

Become an artistic tag team. Talk about ideas and dreams. Grab your cameras and go on an all-day photo excursion. Chatterbox Libras will have to respect Pisces' need for silence; moody Pisces will have to let Libra burn out their cell phones talking to friends. Listen to lots of music together, then analyze the lyrics—few signs are as specific in their musical tastes as these two. Make a digital movie together, with Libra recording and Pisces directing.

HOW TO END IT FAST

Tears will never dry if Libras try to limit Pisces' alone time, or suggest that Pisces take a "logical" approach to their feelings. Libras love to debate, and Pisces hate conflict. A strong dose of Libran skepticism will kill the dreamy Pisces vibe, and send the fish swimming away. Pisces have been known to send their friends around the world on a guilt trip. Libras' balance could be thrown if Pisces dumps too much negativity on them. Pisces can accuse Libras of being selfish or spoiled. Libras are turned off at the first sign of cheapness or unfairness. If Pisces tries to bring the world's suffering into their happy space, Libra will run for comfort somewhere else.

SCORPIO IN LOVE

SCORPIO: October 23–November 21

★ What They Need in a Mate

* Undying loyalty
* Ambition and goals—free birds can fly somewhere else
* Emotional security and tons of reassurance
* To feel in control and invincible—don't challenge them!
* Mystery and seduction—anything too easy to figure out is a bore
* Respect for their privacy and property—don't meddle without their permission
* Strength, as long as it doesn't challenge theirs

☆ What They Offer a Mate

* Amazing intuition and insight
* A touch of risk and danger
* An unsolved mystery—you'll never be bored trying to put together this puzzle
* A taste of power, straight from their own generators
* Passion and intensity like you've never known
* Transformation—you'll never be the same again

Scorpio-Aries: *See Aries-Scorpio.*
Scorpio-Taurus: *See Taurus-Scorpio.*
Scorpio-Gemini: *See Gemini-Scorpio.*
Scorpio-Cancer: *See Cancer-Scorpio.*

Scorpio-Leo: *See Leo-Scorpio.*

Scorpio-Virgo: *See Virgo-Scorpio.*

Scorpio-Libra: *See Libra-Scorpio.*

SCORPIO
(October 23–November 21)

✛

SCORPIO
(October 23–November 21)

STAR COMBO: actor Julia Roberts (Scorpio) and musician Lyle Lovett (Scorpio), divorced

THE BREAKDOWN

This same-sign match usually works well in love—since they're both so intense, they bond faster than Krazy Glue. At best, two Scorpios neutralize each other a bit, since they finally find a base of security in each other. As a team, they're more tuned in to each other than a pair of synchronized remote controls. But if they try to turn those "controls" on each other, the reception will create an unfortunate amount of static.

COMMON GROUND

With their ability to pick up on signals and "vibes," these magnetic personalities share a scary level of intuition. Both like security and loyalty and are devoted to their friends and families. They take injuries hard, and will strike back at suspicious behavior. Scorpio rules other people's property and large chunks of cash—hence, the sign has produced mega-moguls such as P. Diddy and Microsoft don Bill Gates. Most Scorpios like to hang on to what they've got, and are great at putting other people to work to build a tight base of operations.

VIVE LA DIFFÉRENCE

Some Scorpios are reckless party animals, who can be destructive to both themselves and others. Others channel their control and concentration into a hobby or passion. Legend has it that Scorpios are either scorpions or eagles. The less-evolved scorpions are easily threatened creatures who deliver deadly stings from the ground. The eagles are noble and sharp creatures who rise powerfully above the drama, and use their amazing vision to swoop down on their targets.

HOW TO MAKE IT LAST

Make it intense, passionate, and loyal. Share some things, but also have your own dominions to rule—disperse your focus into separate interests. Keep the mystery alive, since Scorpios love all things enigmatic. Since you both can get stuck in the details, bring in other people to help you see the big picture.

HOW TO END IT FAST

Power trips and revenge plays will be nothing but destructive. If you hold on to hurt and refuse to forgive each other, the war will go on forever. Secrets and lies will get you nowhere. Don't bother trying to hide from each other, since the other Scorpio is equally intuitive, and will always know when something's up. If you try to control each other, or become too homebodyish, you could stunt each other's growth. Skip the head games, too—trying to make each other jealous will bring out the worst in you both.

SCORPIO
(October 23–November 21)

+

SAGITTARIUS
(November 22–December 21)

STAR COMBO: Rappers Pepa of Salt 'n Pepa (Scorpio) and Naughty by Nature's Treach (Sagittarius), divorced

THE BREAKDOWN

These two signs are intense, but in different ways. Scorpio is focused on power and security, while Sag seeks thrills and freedom. Hunter Sag bores easily without a challenge, and Scorpio will keep the archer's head twisted, giving a more interesting chase than *Grand Theft Auto*. Scorpios will have to do some chasing of their own, since active Sags are hard to pin down. They may both drop from exhaustion, but it won't be boring.

COMMON GROUND

Both signs are a blend of crazy-sexy-cool (though in different proportions), and operate at an intense pace. Secretly, they both want to be admired, and strive to achieve on a large scale. Though their communication can be a little tactless, they're also supersensitive. Both signs love a challenge, and will provide plenty of that for each other. They can also be judgmental and will often befriend each other on the basis of a common enemy. Both have been known to lose their minds when angry—beware to those who push either sign's buttons.

VIVE LA DIFFÉRENCE

Secretive Scorpios shroud themselves in mystery while tactless Sags let it all hang out and blow their own cover—a trait that frightens Scorpios no end. World-traveler Sags like to gamble and take risks; homebody Scorpios like to accumulate piles of money and keep it tightly in their grasp. Scorpios are a mysterious force whose power can be felt without words. Sags are more comedy than mystery, and their power is often underestimated *until* they speak.

HOW TO MAKE IT LAST

Team up to balance each other's strengths. Scorpio can handle the money and details, while optimistic Sag helps Scorpio see the big picture. Comical Sags should diffuse Scorpios' anger by making them laugh. Scorpios can flex their intense listening skills when Sags lose perspective. Sags should respect Scorpios' need for security, and curb the wandering eye. Scorpios should tame their jealous flame to avoid provoking Sagittarian anger and claustrophobia.

HOW TO END IT FAST

Scorpio can act controlling, which freedom-loving Sag will not tolerate. Sag can act out of control, which will threaten Scorpio's security. Tactless Sag comments can sound like attacks, and Scorpios will strike back with vengeful stings. If Sag gambles with Scorpio's property, Scorpio's trust will be replaced with outrage. Sag's efforts to pry information out of secretive Scorpio won't extract much at first, and the impatient archer may get restless. Scorpio's own questions may elicit *too much* information. The archer's wild tales could scare Scorpio away before Sag gets a fair chance to be faithful.

SCORPIO
(October 23–November 21)

+

CAPRICORN
(December 22–January 19)

STAR COMBO: actors Anne Heche (Scorpio) and Ellen DeGeneres (Capricorn), exes

THE BREAKDOWN

This is a meeting of two goal-focused superachievers, both looking for a permanent spot in the executive suite. Once they arrive, though, Capricorn eases into a robe and slippers, while Scorpio treats the victory as the mere beginning of her reign. Working together can help them clock a few more hours. If steady Cap can be the muscle and intense Scorpio can be the hustle, they can make quite a team.

COMMON GROUND

Besides being work-obsessed and traditional, these signs also like status symbols—leather, diamonds, luxury cars. They'll work hard to make sure they have simply the best. Both signs have been accused of coming off as cold and dismissive, and may have stepped on a few toes in their quest to lock down security. They're both calculating, and may prefer to figure things out in their heads—it's easy for them to get lost in their thoughts. Among those thoughts are some freaky fantasies. Don't ask unless you're sure you want to know.

VIVE LA DIFFÉRENCE

Scorpio is secretive, manipulative, and highly intense. Low-key Capricorn is pretty straightforward and doesn't enjoy toying with people's emotions beyond a certain point. As a water sign, Scorpio has powerful intuition, and picks up on people's vibes in a near-psychic way. Earth-sign Capricorn may not dig below the surface so much, and remains levelheaded in situations that upset Scorpio's balance. Both signs like security, though Scorpio's main drive is for emotional security, while Cap's is for material comfort.

HOW TO MAKE IT LAST

Put down the work and spend some time together, already. Capricorn will have to pay close attention to Scorpio, who needs to be the object of intense focus. Scorpio, go easy on the accusations—Capricorns need to be appreciated for their efforts in making you happy and don't like to have their integrity questioned. Speaking of integrity, both of you can be drawn to shady affairs on the side. Don't start creeping around on each other—Scorpio will find out, and Capricorn will be haunted forever by the moral slipup. Without honor and security, this relationship feels like a sham. Save the spicy stuff for each other.

HOW TO END IT FAST

Capricorn gloom and Scorpio doom can sink this battleship, unless some outside force comes along to let the sunshine in. Self-absorbed Caps may forget to give Scorpios the attention they crave, or could fail to be passionate enough when Scorpios turn up the heat. Scorpios may misinterpret Caps' mellowness for lack of interest or caring, and might start playing head games to test their devotion. Scorpio intensity could scare Capricorns, especially when the goats want to be left alone to chill. Competition could get ugly between these two if they forget to help each other rise to the top.

SCORPIO
(October 23–November 21)

✛

AQUARIUS
(January 20–February 18)

STAR COMBO: actors Brittany Murphy (Scorpio) and Ashton Kutcher (Aquarius), flames

THE BREAKDOWN

Although these signs may have many conflicting approaches, they allow each other to see vulnerabilities that they don't often show. Both are control freaks in their own way. Scorpio may feel extra-needy with independent Aquarius, which makes this control-loving sign uncomfortable. Aquarians feel understood at their core, and may feel that Scorpios can help them reach their goals. With a willingness to work hard and handle each other with care, this relationship can teach them how to toughen up their "weak spots" and soften their stubbornness.

COMMON GROUND

These are both fixed signs who like to mark their territory and build a solid foundation right there. Ambitious by nature, neither one is easily stopped by obstacles that would frighten other signs away. Both are intrigued by mystery and the unexplained, and love to dig at any information that piques their curiosity. They're competitive perfectionists who can be very hard on themselves, and expect nothing short of top billing as their ultimate goal. Although they're both loyal to trusted friends, they can give off a cool facade—Aquarian detachment and Scorpio ice can be intimidating to encounter.

VIVE LA DIFFÉRENCE

Independent Aquarius likes things cool and casual, while passionate Scorpio can never get too close or intense. Ruled by Uranus, the planet of sudden change, Aquarius is happiest when life is a little unpredictable. Scorpio hates abrupt change, because it makes him feel out of control—a big no-no. Aquarius is also the sign of groups and friends, and loves to be surrounded by buddies. Scorpio prefers focused, one-on-one conversations.

HOW TO MAKE IT LAST

Home-loving Scorpio can set up a solid base where wandering Aquarius can rest between adventures. Scorpios should make Aquarians a "pet project," and welcome them into the inner circle with open, nurturing arms. Aquarians, tone down the surprises and play up your ability to be loyal, consistent friends—the only kind that Scorpios trust. Scorpios, contain your possessiveness and jealousy—accept that Aquarians may give their attention to a wide circle of friends. Balance your private time with a few solid hours of hanging out in public.

HOW TO END IT FAST

Scorpio control issues could suffocate freewheeling Aquarians with their jealous accusations. Aquarians can't stand unfairness, and won't tolerate having their good intentions second-guessed. Because of these two signs' relationship to each other. Scorpios may feel neglected and extra-needy, no matter how much love Aquarians shower them with at times. Aquarians' lack of consistent attention, or their slowness to commit, could drive Scorpios mad—first with desire, then with rage. Too much switching between hot and cold will give you both a fever . . . and it might be for another flavor than this.

SCORPIO
(October 23–November 21)

✛

PISCES
(February 19–March 20)

STAR COMBO: actors Demi Moore (Scorpio) and Bruce Willis (Pisces), divorced

THE BREAKDOWN

Finally—two equally intense and passionate souls connect. Scorpio is happy to control the agenda, and free-floating Pisces can stand for a little direction. With Scorpio providing stability and focus, and Pisces introducing creativity into their romance, they can build a fantasyland while still remaining safely grounded in reality.

COMMON GROUND

Neither sign will open up or trust unless they feel a deep level of emotional security and connection. Nor will they commit to anything unless it's supercharged with passion. Both signs are naturally suspicious and critical, and may hide their insecurity beneath protective layers. Their ability to tune in to people and keep secrets is unparalleled. Both must manage a tendency to fall into self-destructive habits.

VIVE LA DIFFÉRENCE

Pisces can be dreamy and unfocused about their goals, while Scorpios have a laser-beam focus on their targets. Creative Pisces are at their best in a loose environment where they can let their imaginations roam. Scorpio energy needs to be channeled and focused, or its intensity can be destructive. Scorpios are also a tad possessive, and need a solid commitment to feel secure. Pisces hate feeling trapped; like slippery fish, they're ready to swim away if they see a dangerous hook coming to catch them.

HOW TO MAKE IT LAST

Create a safe haven together, then dive into the depths. Play up fantasy, romance, and passion—the best manifestations of your powers. Give gifts that build each other's sense of security, and give them as often as possible. Vulnerable Pisceans will have to toughen up their scales if they don't want to become fish food—Scorpios eat the weak for breakfast. Scorpios need direct attention, so escape-artist Pisces will have to snap out of dreamland. Since Pisces resist being "hooked," Scorpios are best off keeping a mysterious air and letting the intrigued fish swim up to them.

HOW TO END IT FAST

Pisces' tendency to be too self-sacrificing could cause them to periodically resent Scorpios for controlling the relationship. Instead of brooding silently, Pisces will have to speak up and take charge of a few situations. Too many secrets could tear at your trust—open up, already. You'll also lose by withholding affection instead of dealing directly with anger. Both of your abilities to be punishing (Scorpio, directly; Pisces, passive-aggressively) can cause great destruction. Keep the jealous rages and hurtful accusations in check.

SAGITTARIUS IN LOVE

SAGITTARIUS: November 22–December 21

★ What They Need in a Mate

* Freedom and adventure—they must feel like the world is their playground
* Endless and fascinating conversation
* An equally curious partner who likes to travel, learn, and try new things

* Patience and forgiveness when they put their foot in their mouth
* A great sense of humor—somebody to laugh at their jokes
* Open-mindedness and a big appetite for life

☆ What They Offer a Mate

* Expansion—of your mind, your views, and your life
* Las Vegas in your own backyard—it's always a crazy carnival
* Perspective and optimism—they can see the big picture, and your future looks bright
* Fun and learning mixed together
* Honesty, even if it's brutal at times
* Strong, no-b.s. opinions, which can seem judgmental at times, and totally on point in other instances

Sagittarius-Aries: *See Aries-Sagittarius.*
Sagittarius-Taurus: *See Taurus-Sagittarius.*
Sagittarius-Gemini: *See Gemini-Sagittarius.*
Sagittarius-Cancer: *See Cancer-Sagittarius.*
Sagittarius-Leo: *See Leo-Sagittarius.*
Sagittarius-Virgo: *See Virgo-Sagittarius.*
Sagittarius-Libra: *See Libra-Sagittarius.*
Sagittarius-Scorpio: *See Scorpio-Sagittarius.*

SAGITTARIUS
(November 22–December 21)

SAGITTARIUS
(November 22–December 21)

STAR COMBO: magazine publisher John F. Kennedy Jr. (Sagittarius) and actress Daryl Hannah (Sagittarius), exes

THE BREAKDOWN

While they may end up on a friends-only basis, the funnies won't stop once these two clowns get on a roll. When the face paint comes off, the clowns may cry just as hard as they laughed, since Sag moods usually arrive full-blast. With their carnival spirits, they'll always be looking for the next circus to join. Whether their relationship will last once the show is over is anyone's guess.

COMMON GROUND

Both are entrepreneurial risk-takers who inspire friends to see the world through the biggest possible lens. Like Sagittarians Steven Spielberg and Walt Disney, they think large-scale. Most Sags strive to enjoy life and will work obsessively at their goals, as long as the goal is fun for them. They can both be know-it-alls and are extremely stubborn about doing things their own way. Knowledge-seeking Sag is represented by the centaur, a half-human/half-horse archer who shoots arrows tirelessly until reaching an ultimate target. Because of this split personality, many Sags are a curious mix of self-consciousness and total shamelessness. Variety and stimulation are important in their relationships, since Sag passions tend to cool once their arrows hit the bull's-eye. As eternal wanderers, they're full of burning questions and restless energy, and need a partner who can handle their independence.

VIVE LA DIFFÉRENCE

Which half of the centaur are they—horse or human? Some Sags take after the animal half, and can be wild and reckless, as Christina Aguilera, Ozzy Osbourne, and Anna Nicole Smith have been. Others are more the down-to-earth, human types such as Brad Pitt or Tyra Banks. The grounded Sag can be bookish and introverted (since Sag rules the higher mind), always ready to travel the globe in pursuit of knowledge. The wild ones gamble everything and rely on their Jupiter-fueled luck to save them when they crash.

HOW TO MAKE IT LAST

Schedule megadoses of fun, adventure, and variety, but put your paychecks in a vault to prevent yourself from impulse-shopping all your cash away. Travel together and expand your minds—cheer each other up and offer wisdom when one gets stuck. Avoid lecturing each other or spouting your know-it-all opinions as though they were absolute fact. Remember you can lead a horse—or centaur—to water, but you can't make him drink.

HOW TO END IT FAST

Your impulsiveness and hot tempers could burn this relationship out fast. Learn how to compromise, instead of insisting that your way is the right way. True, Sag Frank Sinatra self-assuredly sang "I did it my way," but this attitude will have you passing like two ships in the night. Shoot each other with too many arrows of truth, and the wounds may not heal. As the zodiac's travelers, you may never be in the same place long enough to solidify a bond. Flirtatious Sags should heed this traveler's advisory: A wandering mind is cool; a wandering eye isn't. Head to Sizzler if you want to sample a buffet.

SAGITTARIUS
(November 22–December 21)

CAPRICORN
(December 22–January 19)

STAR COMBO: model/actress Tyra Banks (Sagittarius) and film director John Singleton (Capricorn), exes

THE BREAKDOWN

Sag and Cap can amuse and frustrate each other in equal doses. Impulsive, adventurous Sags may feel as though they're dating a grandparent when they tangle with a cautious, rule-abiding Capricorn. The goats can feel as though they're baby-sitting a hyperactive "problem child" with an unruly Sag's endless demands on their energy supply. If the two strike a balance, Capricorns can build a solid platform for Sags to launch their big ideas, and Sagittarians' fire can save Caps from getting stuck in an earthy rut.

COMMON GROUND

Both signs are driven and can be quite hard on themselves, at times becoming self-absorbed. When things don't work out as they envisioned, both can fall into depressed spells. Fortunately, they're both survivors, and they'll emerge ready to step up to the plate again. They have wacky senses of humor, and appreciate the amusing side of life. Capricorn is a realist, and Sag likes to keep it real. Nobody will be offended by blunt jokes, as long as they shed light on the truth.

VIVE LA DIFFÉRENCE

Sag is ruled by Jupiter, the planet of expansion and optimism. Cap is ruled by Saturn, planet of restriction and pessimism. Capricorns like to follow a solid life plan, with goals and milestones along the way. The only thing Sags really enjoy planning is a vacation. Even then, they'd prefer that somebody else handle the details and let them simply show up. In life, impulsive Sags rely on luck and inventiveness—they crave a certain degree of risk. Methodical Capricorns prefer to play it safe, trusting only in hard work and time-tested strategies.

HOW TO MAKE IT LAST

Team up on ventures and adventures, with Capricorn supplying the basic ingredients, and Sag adding the spice. Impulsive Sag had better exercise some serious patience and prepare to wait in line behind Capricorn's goals, job, family, and possessive childhood friends. Hey, Sag, remember all those hobbies you used to have? Get back into them, because you're gonna need to entertain yourself. Capricorn, catch up on your sleep while you can, if you hope to hang with Sag's wild style, long conversations, and around-the-clock schedule.

HOW TO END IT FAST

Sag's lack of interest in family and tradition could be a turnoff to loyal Cap, who cherishes people from the days of old. Even if Sags aren't overly attached to their *own* family, they'd better learn to love Capricorn's. And Caps had better prepare to welcome some spontaneity into their tightly scheduled lives. If Sag demands for fun aren't met by work-first Capricorn, the archer will go crazy from neglect. Mountain-goat Capricorns are used to a rocky climb, but they won't tolerate Sags trying to mess up their footing with distractions like, oh, fun. If Sag's impulsiveness threatens to gamble away Capricorn's hard-earned security, the goat will find a new mountain to climb.

SAGITTARIUS
(November 22–December 21)

AQUARIUS
(January 20–February 18)

STAR COMBO: singers Britney Spears (Sagittarius) and Justin Timberlake (Aquarius), exes

THE BREAKDOWN

As with many couples two signs apart, this pairing often grows out of long-term friendship (Britney and Justin were fellow Mouseketeers long before their love spawned). These kindred spirits usually have a mind-soul-*then*-body connection, which arises once they discover that they share a similar level of energy and independence.

COMMON GROUND

These free spirits prize their individuality more than life itself. Born to be megastars, they can sell you anything, and will keep things moving at an active pace. Although they're generally cheerful and joke around, their tempers are fearsome—both signs are known to have sudden mood swings. This is because they often repress their needs—Sag, in an overextended effort to please people; Aquarius, for the "good of the group." Both signs may have a collection of eccentric friends, who depend on them for wise advice and comic relief.

VIVE LA DIFFÉRENCE

Aquarius is a rational air sign, and detaches from feelings more easily than fiery Sag can, who goes down in self-created flames when emotions get heated. Although both signs are goal-oriented, Sags may multitask their way all over the map, while Aquarians have an easier time sticking to one subject. Their intensity levels can be different, too. As a half-human/half-horse centaur, Sag's animal instincts may be a little more primal than Aquarius's casual, down-to-earth vibe.

HOW TO MAKE IT LAST

Sagittarius Brad Pitt and Aquarius Jennifer Aniston refer to their marriage as "the adventure," and this pretty much sums up the best approach for these two freedom-loving signs. They should label their love with any word besides *relationship* or *commitment*—something to distract them from the idea that they've sacrificed their individuality by teaming up. Their colorful collection of friends keeps the good times rolling, but this crew can cut into their precious one-on-one time. They should remember to send their pals home and leave the party early here and there, or the romantic connection could weaken.

HOW TO END IT FAST

Too much individuality can keep them from bonding, and their ambitious schedules can scatter them in different places. They may forget that a healthy relationship does call for *some* dependency, as long as it's a reasonable amount. Because they're both star material, they may become competitors, and resentment could rip them apart. Aquarius's unpredictable temper outbursts can hurt sensitive Sag's feelings. Sag's rude or judgmental comments could anger fair-minded Aquarius, who always sticks up for the little guy. Sag can be insecure in love, and may foolishly test cool Aquarius's passion by flirting or playing games. Rebellious Aquarians can provoke a fiery rage from Sag by getting a little too "friendly" with an adoring fan.

SAGITTARIUS
(November 22–December 21)

PISCES
(February 19–March 20)

STAR COMBO: actors Katie Holmes (Sagittarius) and Chris Klein (Pisces), flames

THE BREAKDOWN

Both signs like change and adventure, but they may have trouble translating their intense romantic chemistry into the structure of a "real" relationship. As two of the zodiac's biggest reality avoiders, they prefer to keep an element of fantasy about their bond, even if they've been together for years. Midnight bike rides, costume parties, a round of Truth or Dare—both signs will be in at a moment's notice. Yet, when it comes to something as "normal" as a commitment, they both get weirded out. At least they'll understand each other.

COMMON GROUND

Both signs want to live life in the land of make-believe. Sag rules travel and the higher mind, and Pisces rules the imagination—so they're always packed for some kind of head trip. They're both constantly searching for new dimensions of reality, and sometimes lose their own perspective in the quest. Moody spells always seem to follow, since both are particularly hard on themselves as well. As mutable signs, they love change and adventure—a certain amount of freedom is key.

VIVE LA DIFFÉRENCE

Pisces is a calm water sign, while Sag is an action-packed fire sign. Their paces can be very different. As the zodiac's truth seeker, Sag is ultimately on a quest for reality, while Pisces is on a mission to escape it. Sagittarius values the truth above all else. On Pisces' ruling planet Neptune, everything appears as an illusion—what does it matter to them whether something is true or not? Sag strives to be upbeat and can be a tad insensitive. Pisces is easily depressed and can be a tad *over*sensitive. The fish may suffocate from Sag's shallowness, or the archer could drown in Pisces' murky depths.

HOW TO MAKE IT LAST

Balance security and freedom. If you won't say, "I do," at least agree to be exclusive, then call it anything you want—just make sure the terms are clear. Cheery Sag can lighten up the Pisces gloom, and Pisces can dream up secret escapades that entice Sag's love of adventure. Sag should relax and take in some low-key evenings at home. Pisces, try not to be overly passive and wishy-washy—Sag needs to see some action.

HOW TO END IT FAST

Sag can live by a soundtrack of cheesy pop music, while Pisces spins one of angst-filled grunge. (Think Sag Britney Spears versus Pisces Kurt Cobain to get the idea.) During insecure spells, they can kill the party atmosphere by introducing too much reality—by asking, for example, "Do you think we could consider ourselves a couple?" Overindulged hedonism could leave them feeling like the morning after a Halloween candy binge. Pisces guilt trips and gloom will make claustro Sag want to break free. Sag bluntness can wound sensitive Pisces' feelings, and the archer's impulsiveness can leave Pisces feeling insecure and drained.

CAPRICORN IN LOVE

CAPRICORN: December 22–January 19

 What They Need in a Mate

* Integrity—say what you mean, and mean what you say
* Ambition and a solid work ethic

* Strong character and admirable values
* Respect for family, and any other traditions they cherish
* Consistency and patience—work comes first, so don't be too needy

☆ What They Offer a Mate

* Mentoring and discipline—Capricorn is the "father" of the zodiac
* A lesson on hard work and self-discipline
* Endurance—they'll be there when everyone else is gone
* A touch of class or luxury—Capricorns like to spoil you
* A secret freaky streak they'll reveal with time
* Rock-solid loyalty—once they truly commit, they're in 110 percent

Capricorn-Aries: *See Aries-Capricorn.*
Capricorn-Taurus: *See Taurus-Capricorn.*
Capricorn-Gemini: *See Gemini-Capricorn.*
Capricorn-Cancer: *See Cancer-Capricorn.*
Capricorn-Leo: *See Leo-Capricorn.*
Capricorn-Virgo: *See Virgo-Capricorn.*
Capricorn-Libra: *See Libra-Capricorn.*
Capricorn-Scorpio: *See Scorpio-Capricorn.*
Capricorn-Sagittarius: *See Sagittarius-Capricorn.*

CAPRICORN
(December 22–January 19)

CAPRICORN
(December 22–January 19)

STAR COMBO: singers R. Kelly (Capricorn) and Aaliyah (Capricorn), divorced

THE BREAKDOWN

Will these high achievers score a goal, or will they be too focused on their own ambitions? Since they're both workaholics and slow-moving earth signs, they may have to pencil each other a little higher on the priority list to get this one off the ground. With a common agenda, they'll be inducted into the millionaire's club together.

COMMON GROUND

Both Caps are ambitious, practical, and work hard at their goals. They're loyal to family and friends, and appreciate the simple humor of life. They also value tradition and anything that has the enduring quality to last through the generations. Both may have a freaky side lurking below the composed surface. Since they rule the teeth, jaw, and bone structure, they may have "classic" faces as well—think of Caps Christy Turlington and Elvis Presley. Even the wilder Capricorns have an acute sense of the past—Cap Marilyn Manson, for example, named himself after historical figures Marilyn Monroe and Charles Manson.

VIVE LA DIFFÉRENCE

Some Caps are "old souls" with heavy spirits and somber faces—as are Kid Rock, R.E.M.'s Michael Stipe, and model Kate Moss. Then there are the ageless Capricorns who endure the shifting trends, such as Rod Stewart (famous for his hit song "Forever Young"), Nicolas Cage, and David Bowie. Ruled by Saturn, planet of restriction, Caps are known for holding back or even repressing themselves, which can cause the quirkier parts of their personalities to come out in shocking ways—as with Jim Carrey, Dolly Parton, and Marilyn Manson.

HOW TO MAKE IT LAST

Loosen up the work-first-play-later policy, even if it seems sensible to both of you. Treat each other to some luxurious (but practical) gifts, since Capricorns swoon at a material expression of love. If your goals keep you apart, send flowers, cards, jewelry, or spicy emails—anything substantial to keep you connected. Find a way to work together—long hours on the job can be spiced up with some interesting breaks.

HOW TO END IT FAST

Treat each other like a chore and stay together out of duty instead of passion. Or, be overly status-oriented, and use each other to get ahead in your goals. Forget to dig below the surface to find out what lies beneath—Cap wants to be admired and known. Be cheap and overly practical—if you forget that your mate also has a naughty inner child underneath the J. Crew button-down, he'll search for fantasy elsewhere. Be rude to each other's family and oldest friends, and you'll find yourself moved to the bottom of each other's to-do list. Throw away anything a Cap saves—if it's still around, it has meaning to her.

CAPRICORN
(December 22–January 19)

✛

AQUARIUS
(January 20–February 18)

STAR COMBO: Nicolas Cage (Capricorn) and Lisa Marie Presley (Aquarius), divorced after three months of marriage

THE BREAKDOWN

These ambitious souls are both reaching for the number one spot. Once they get there, Capricorn wants to stay forever, while Aquarius is already off on the next vision quest. Their karmic bond will be tight, and Aquarius will have a natural sympathy for Capricorn's paint-by-numbers approach to life, even if it seems overly simple to them. Capricorns will sense that Aquarians can teach them how to think outside the box, even if the rebellious approach makes Caps a tad uncomfortable.

COMMON GROUND

Both signs are a surprising mix of mainstream and eccentric, though Capricorn's weirdness is a result of repression, while Aquarius's just comes naturally. Traditional Caps prefer to tone down their eccentricity, while Aquarians wear theirs proudly. Neither one is overly touchy-feely in the public eye; they both like to keep it cool and composed to guard their reputations. Speaking of which, fame has a special appeal to their tastebuds. Both signs are goal- and fame-driven, with strong workaholic tendencies.

VIVE LA DIFFÉRENCE

Capricorns are symbolized by the mountain goat, who reaches its goal by persisting through a slow and rocky climb. Aquarians are the mad scientists of the zodiac, so they're more likely to scale a mountain by flying up there in a purple polka-dot helicopter. As a result, these signs usually have different agendas for success. Capricorn's three favorite letters are *CEO*, preferably of an established major corporation that's lasted for generations. Aquarians feel trapped at the top unless it's an institution they invent themselves. Although both value long-term relationships, most Aquarians marry more than once, and often on a whim (four-times-married Christy Brinkley wed her third husband on a ski lift). Caps take their time and look for a lifelong investment.

HOW TO MAKE IT LAST

Check your agendas. If Aquarius wants a light adventure and Capricorn wants to settle down, find out fast. Team up on common goals that boost your status. Aquarians will have to follow a few more traditions than usual—they should prepare to buy Caps diamond solitaires instead of mood rings, or a top-quality leather jacket instead of vinyl hot pants. Caps will have to question the rules more than they're used to, and prepare to open your arms to Aquarius's eclectic collection of friends.

HOW TO END IT FAST

Capricorns' snobbish tastes and heavy spirits can be a turnoff to Aquarians, who befriend every character they stumble over in a dark alley. Capricorn could go ballistic when Aquarius asks too many questions, or refuses to just accept things as they are. Aquarius lives in the future, and Capricorn cherishes the past. If they don't meet somewhere in the present, Caps could still be spinning the classics while Aquarians are off inventing the remix with a brand-new DJ.

CAPRICORN
(December 22–January 19)

+

PISCES
(February 19–March 20)

STAR COMBO: Foo Fighters vocalist Dave Grohl (Capricorn) and Smashing Pumpkins bassist Melissa Auf der Maur (Pisces), flames

THE BREAKDOWN

Rule-maker Capricorn and rule-breaker Pisces can balance each other out. Both like a certain amount of tradition and security—at least in relationships. If Capricorn is established enough to give Pisces the freedom to daydream, Cap will gladly handle the daily chores, and Pisces will spice up the evening's plans. Romance has its best chances if they build a solid friendship first.

COMMON GROUND

Both signs can be depressive, and need a certain amount of alone time to process their feelings. They like traditional romance and courtship, especially when combined with tasteful gifts. Luxury and quality take top billing, as neither of these label hounds likes cheap stuff, and can be a bit snobbish.

VIVE LA DIFFÉRENCE

Capricorn works hard, and Pisces hardly works—at least, when it comes to making a major move. It's not that Pisces are lazy; they'd just rather be at a movie or a poetry reading than sweating the class-president position or MVP title on their sports team. Pisces hates "the man" and Capricorn wants to *be* the man. Uh-oh. Cap's conventional tastes could seem cheesy to ultrasensitive Pisces, whose tastes are a tad more artsy. Pisces can seem overly emotional to Cap, especially when the fish takes offense to Cap's good-natured teasing.

HOW TO MAKE IT LAST

Balance hardworking Capricorn's realism with escape-artist Pisces' thirst for fantasy. Capricorn can be the business manager, and Pisces can be the event planner. Caps will always be excited to come home to the latest adventure Pisces dream up. Capricorns may not enjoy the more "alternative" side of Pisces' artistic tastes, so find a happy medium between mainstream and underground before you reserve concert tickets. Romantic Pisces can melt down Cap's tough facade—as long as the fish shows his practical side, too. Divide roles and responsibilities so that Capricorn feels assured that important matters are covered, and Pisces has enough free time to dream.

HOW TO END IT FAST

If Cap makes it all about the benjamins and fails to have compassion for the underdog, charitable Pisces will be out of there faster than you can say "Scrooge." Pisces needs passion and emotional security, and Cap has a hard time letting it all hang out. If Capricorn laughs at Pisces' sensitive dreams, the fish will toughen her scales and ice Cap out. If Pisces acts like a directionless flake and never sets any goals, Capricorn may search for a more reliable partner in crime.

AQUARIUS IN LOVE

AQUARIUS: January 20–February 18

★ What They Need in a Mate

✳ Friendship and a "team" vibe

✳ Respect for their individuality and goals

✳ Love of their eccentricity—and plenty of your own quirks, too

✳ Fairness and equality—never falsely accuse them

✳ Plenty of personal space—don't push them to show affection, even if they seem cold

✳ One trait that they absolutely adore—they'll forgive all your other flaws

☆ What They Offer a Mate

✳ True friendship

✳ A life of adventure and unpredictable changes

✳ Freedom to be yourself—they'll cherish your uniqueness

✳ Inspiration, particularly creative

✳ A radical view of the world that may just blow your mind

Aquarius-Aries: *See Aries-Aquarius.*

Aquarius-Taurus: *See Taurus-Aquarius.*

Aquarius-Gemini: *See Gemini-Aquarius.*

Aquarius-Cancer: *See Cancer-Aquarius.*

Aquarius-Leo: *See Leo-Aquarius.*

Aquarius-Virgo: *See Virgo-Aquarius.*

Aquarius-Libra: *See Libra-Aquarius.*

Aquarius-Scorpio: *See Scorpio-Aquarius.*

Aquarius-Sagittarius: *See Sagittarius-Aquarius.*

Aquarius-Capricorn: *See Capricorn-Aquarius.*

AQUARIUS
(January 20–February 18)

+

AQUARIUS
(January 20–February 18)

STAR COMBO: actors Diane Lane (Aquarius) and Josh Brolin (Aquarius), flames

THE BREAKDOWN

If these two gypsy souls manage to bond romantically before floating away, they'll make a dynamic duo. Aquarius is the sign of groups, friendships, and humanity, and they'll probably need a common cause or crew to glue them together. Since Aquarians are drawn to the unusual, they may not be stimulated enough by dating somebody just like them. If they are, it will be a fast-talking freak show full of surprises and adventure.

COMMON GROUND

Most Aquarians are so charming, they can sell you your own clothes—right out of your closet. They work hard and stay true to the game when they've committed to a cause. They value friends and feel comfortable hanging in group situations. Ruled by Uranus, planet of sudden events, they'll be unusual and fascinating, and could also have unpredictable temper flare-ups. When their buttons are pushed or they can't take the pressure, the peaceful Aquarius pals disappear, and it's enter the dragons. Beware!

VIVE LA DIFFÉRENCE

Even as team players, Aquarians prize their individuality and will always stand out—think of Aquarius boy-band front men Nick Carter and Justin Timberlake. The immature Aquarians will insist on being an individual at the expense of the group, and could display rash, anger-driven behavior that they later regret. The focused Aquarians, such as Oprah Winfrey, are so great at bringing groups together, they literally have the power to revolutionize the world.

HOW TO MAKE IT LAST

Collaborate. Balance your individuality with your team status, and make sure both of you have a rewarding role that makes you feel like a star. Keep it fair and make it an eccentric adventure—surprise tickets to the circus, a sci-fi novel, and bizarro gag gifts will always go far. Also remember to make it an anger-management tour, or things could get ugly when tempers blaze up. Find a way to ground yourselves—team up on a solid venture or project—or this could never materialize past the talking stages.

HOW TO END IT FAST

Stick to your "friends-only" comfort zone, and you'll never make it into the next dimension. Blow up at each other out of nowhere. Try to run your slick games on each other, or compete for lead-singer status. Spend all your time listening to your nutty friends' head trips or gazing into space through your homemade telescopes, and forget to pencil in romantic evenings for the two of you.

AQUARIUS
(January 20–February 18)

✚

PISCES
(February 19–March 20)

STAR COMBO: talk-show host Oprah Winfrey (Aquarius) and CEO Stedman Graham (Pisces), flames

THE BREAKDOWN

This hazy relationship can be a chamber of secrets as powerful as a sorcerer's stone. Wanderer Aquarius feels a strange pull to settle down with Pisces, who may be a slippery fish to grab. Pisces' selflessness and gentle spirit will touch Aquarius deeply; Aquarian toughness will make Pisces feel safe. Secretive Pisces may be even more hush-hush than usual, which could drive Aquarius mad with curiosity. A spiritual connection or common cause can secure the bond.

COMMON GROUND

Aquarius's and Pisces' respective ruling planets, Uranus and Neptune, are neighbors who often move through the zodiac together. Both signs are drawn to healing and have love for the underdog. They can be self-sacrificing, even self-destructive, if their powerful imaginations run too wild. They both often give their best energies to their friends-in-need, and forget to save some mojo for themselves. Both signs like their freedom, and need their own space in relationships.

VIVE LA DIFFÉRENCE

Slow-moving Pisces need private time to reflect and change their minds, while group- and goal-oriented Aquarians are driven to follow a single mission. Aquarius is a tough comedian who delivers opinions directly; Pisces can be a sensitive brooder who would rather drop hints and keep you guessing. Aquarius feels uncomfortable with open displays of affection and prefers to keep everyone a casual friend; Pisces is a classic romantic who needs to swim into the depths of a loved one's soul.

HOW TO MAKE IT LAST

A common cause will keep this relationship locked in its full upright position. With your shared healing powers, you can sew yourselves matching superhero costumes and go save the world. At the same time, neither sign likes to be forced into anything, so give each other the space to fly some solo missions. Aquarians should take care of the everyday details, and give Pisces time to swim the seas of their imaginations. Pisces, be sure to let Aquarius into your secret world, or you can cause even this independent sign to get lonely.

HOW TO END IT FAST

Pisces pouting and guilt trips will anger Aquarians, who will see this behavior as petty and unfair—not to mention a threat to their freedom. In an effort to guard their individuality, Aquarians may neglect to develop the bond, preventing Pisces' trust from fully forming. Changeable Pisces is represented by two fish swimming in separate directions, and goal-focused Aquarians can drive Pisces into depression by pushing them to swim faster or along a single path. Even a wizard won't be able to bring back the magic if they don't respect each other's need to do things their own way, in their own time.

PISCES IN LOVE

PISCES: February 19–March 20

★ What They Need in a Mate

✳ Fantasy and romance—Pisces rule the imagination and may avoid reality
✳ Consistent stability that they can't give themselves
✳ Respect for their secrets and solitude
✳ A healing touch—and a desire to be healed by them
✳ Steady nurturing for their fragile, poetic souls
✳ A partner who helps them learn to love and stand up for themselves

☆ What They Offer a Mate

✳ A passionate escape from reality
✳ Worship—they'll romanticize you
✳ A storybook romance (warning: may last only as long as a paperback novel)
✳ Sacrifice and devotion—they'll serve you selflessly
✳ Lots of drama, passion, and glamour

* A gentle artistic soul—sometimes tortured
* An occasional guilt trip, since they feel uncomfortable asking for what they want

Pisces-Aries: *See Aries-Pisces.*
Pisces-Taurus: *See Taurus-Pisces.*
Pisces-Gemini: *See Gemini-Pisces.*
Pisces-Cancer: *See Cancer-Pisces.*
Pisces-Leo: *See Leo-Pisces.*
Pisces-Virgo: *See Virgo-Pisces.*
Pisces-Libra: *See Libra-Pisces.*
Pisces-Scorpio: *See Scorpio-Pisces.*
Pisces-Sagittarius: *See Sagittarius-Pisces.*
Pisces-Capricorn: *See Capricorn-Pisces.*
Pisces-Aquarius: *See Aquarius-Pisces.*

PISCES
(February 19–March 20)

+

PISCES
(February 19–March 20)

STAR COMBO: actors James van der Beek (Pisces) and Heather McComb (Pisces), engaged

THE BREAKDOWN

These soul mates can form a deep, healing bond and may intuitively understand each other without even speaking. As fellow fish, swimming in the same school can make the journey less lonely. But do they have enough direction? They may need an outside force to put some motion in their ocean, and keep the waters from getting stagnant.

COMMON GROUND

They'll both be reflective and self-sacrificing and will always want to heal each other in some way. Commitment could be slippery, since fish don't like to be caught. As emotional water signs, they'll appreciate art, music, and film, and could have many artistic talents of their own. Both will need solitude to dream and use their Neptune-powered imaginations. Most Pisceans undervalue their worth in some way—they'll both have to guard against spells of pessimism and depression.

VIVE LA DIFFÉRENCE

Pisces is represented by two fish swimming in opposite directions. Some Pisces swim down to the murky underworld, where they can get caught up in depression and self-destructive habits, as did Kurt Cobain. Other Pisces are like fish who've narrowly escaped getting hooked, and may develop tougher scales—or even become sharks. (Think of no-nonsense Pisces such as Queen Latifah, Thora Birch, and Cindy Crawford.) The Pisces that swim in the clearest waters are creative, calm, and sensitive—as are Pisces Billy Crystal and Chris Klein—and their effect can be soothing to all.

HOW TO MAKE IT LAST

Bring in a no-bull third party to snap you out of fantasyland if your day-dreaming starts to affect you in a negative way. Push yourselves to communicate openly—check that tendency to be passive and secretive. Take control and swim—don't let the currents sweep you along, or you could end up pulled away from each other, and lost at sea. Play up your shared love of romance and creativity—surround yourselves with film, music, and art. Roses and poems will go over fine, too.

HOW TO END IT FAST

Drag each other down with depression, self-doubt, and destructive habits. Build private worlds and shut each other out of them. Project your low self-esteem onto each other and withdraw support when the other is hurting. Get stuck in a bully-victim cycle—if one Pisces is a shark and the other is a goldfish, the weaker partner could end up as fish food.

section 4
YOUR ASTROSTYLE

THE BEST LOOKS FOR EVERY SIGN

Can the stars determine your style? After all, Capricorns Tiger Woods and Marilyn Manson are about as different as they come. The answer is simple: Some like to keep things under control, and others like to let it all hang out. When it comes to style, each sign of the zodiac has a radio-friendly mix as well as an uncut version of the same track. In this chapter, we'll show you both sides of the coin. Let the stars guide you to a new look or send you scurrying away from a fashion emergency. The choice is yours.

ARIES STYLE
(March 21–April 19)

COLOR: Red

FABRIC: Cotton

FOCUS AREA: The head, face, and hair

STYLE EQUIPMENT: Clippers, makeup, earrings, hats, hair ornaments, button-down shirts

ROCK IT OUT: Layered basics with a pinch of glam

PUT IT BACK ON THE RACK: Dull colors, untrendy classics

ARIES GIRL

 ## Under Control: The Fresh-Faced Firecracker

WHO'S GOT THE LOOK: Sarah Jessica Parker, Reese Witherspoon, Mandy Moore, Kate Hudson, Sarah Michelle Gellar, Amanda Bynes

HOW TO PULL IT OFF: Your face has a rosy glow, but there's a fire burning behind those eyes. Smile, and wear something daring à la Sarah Jessica Parker who still managed to look adorable—and electric—wearing a tutu at age thirty-five. Show the world that simple doesn't have to mean boring. Pile basics together to create a complex masterpiece, and add a splash of red. Aries rules the head, so let your hair be your crowning glory. Sweep yours into a classic updo, or add accessories and earrings to draw attention to your face

 ## Out of Control: Viva la Diva

WHO'S GOT THE LOOK: Jill Scott, Diana Ross, Mariah Carey, Chaka Khan, Celine Dion, Aretha Franklin

HOW TO PULL IT OFF: You're the reason VH1 dreamed up *Divas Live*. Dress like you know it. Prove to the world that glitter, sequins, and gold lamé do have a purpose. Use your hair to add volume to your performance—the bigger, the better! Dye it red, or sport a colorful head wrap. Leave something to the imagination, no matter how tempted you may be to show off your hot body. Anything too revealing will cost you points in the class department.

ARIES GUY

 ## Under Control: Masculinity Unleashed

WHO'S GOT THE LOOK: Jackie Chan, Russell Crowe, Colin Farrell, Steven Seagal, Method Man, Heath Ledger

HOW TO PULL IT OFF: You've got a raw, masculine quality about yourself, and you dress to show it. You're a restless, impulsive Aries, and you need clothes that move the way you do. Stick to the basics—shirts that come in three-packs, baggy jeans, sneakers, baseball caps, a shaved head. Follow an open-shirt policy, or just don't wear one at all. On those rare occasions that you do get decked out, stick to suits in navy or tan.

Resist the urge to wear black, as it can make you fade into the background—you were born to lead! Thumbs-up to pinstripes, which add a surge of electricity to your already charged-up looks.

Out of Control: Costume Party

WHO'S GOT THE LOOK: Steven Tyler, Eddie Murphy, Martin Lawrence, Hugh Hefner, Q-Tip, Martin Short

HOW TO PULL IT OFF: Forget about beating the other guys at the same old game—invent a whole new competition. Create a signature style, as *Playboy* icon Hugh Hefner did with his red smoking jacket, or Steven Tyler with his tight jeans, bare chest, and pouting lips. The goal is to be unmistakable. Bonus if your fans can spot you from a mile away. If you want to take it all the way, make every day Halloween. Choose an alter ego or two, and lead a double life through them—as Aries Eddie Murphy did in *The Nutty Professor,* or Martin Lawrence in *Big Momma's House.*

TAURUS STYLE
(April 20–May 20)

COLOR: Green

FABRIC: Wool

FOCUS AREA: The neck and throat

STYLE EQUIPMENT: Choker, chain, perfumes, cologne, body lotion, hair gel

ROCK IT OUT: Classic, well-made clothes amplified by tiny details

PUT IT BACK ON THE RACK: Bright colors, big patterns

TAURUS GIRL

Under Control: Grace under Fire

WHO'S GOT THE LOOK: Uma Thurman, Penelope Cruz, Kirsten Dunst, Kelly Clarkson, Jessica Alba

HOW TO PULL IT OFF: Picture yourself as a classic movie star, like Taurus Audrey Hepburn. She looked great in black and white, and you do, too.

Keep it elegant and simple. Choose solid colors amplified by tiny details such as beads and embroidery. Black velvet and a strand of pearls were practically made for you. Your sign rules the throat area, so play yours up with colorful chokers and scarves. You're a thrifty girl, but stay out of that ten-dollar store! Your sign needs quality and a little luxury, too. If you want to save money, hit an outlet mall or designer warehouse sale.

Out of Control: Bullfight

WHO'S GOT THE LOOK: Janet Jackson, T-Boz, Donatella Versace, Jamie Lynn Siegler, Jordana Brewster, Cher

HOW TO PULL IT OFF: Like the bull that represents your sign, your look is sweet *and* fierce. You'll wear outfits that require a stylist—or a really good friend—to help you get in and out of them. So shred your clothes as though you've just been in a bullfight. Now add the details—buckles and buttons and belts. Lace-up boots and corsets. Leather pants and bone chokers. All the small things add texture and create contrast against your skin (think Janet Jackson). Brown, black, and ivory make you radiate like the natural woman you are.

TAURUS GUY

Under Control: Men in Black

WHO'S GOT THE LOOK: George Clooney, Trent Reznor, Tim McGraw, Bono, David Boreanaz, Al Pacino, Cedric the Entertainer

HOW TO PULL IT OFF: No songs about rainbows here—you're all about the black, from your shoes to your jeans to your leather jacket to your hat. You're living proof that Tauruses are stubborn. Use black to announce yourself with authority and even stir up a little mystery and fear. Don a tailored black suit like the one Al Pacino wore in *The Godfather*. Rage poetically in black molded rubber as tormented Taurus Trent Reznor has. A little color will go a long way, so push yourself to add a splash here and there. Otherwise, you run the risk of looking like a vampire.

Out of Control: Material Boy

WHO'S GOT THE LOOK: David Beckham, Dennis Rodman, Enrique Iglesias, Busta Rhymes, Lance Bass

HOW TO PULL IT OFF: Your sign is ruled by beautifying Venus, so pay attention to your five senses. You've gotta look good, smell good, and taste good. Make friends with the "freshmaker." Don't leave the house without a hit of cologne. Pick your brands carefully and splurge on well-made basics. Don't be afraid to play around with products, either. Dye your hair blond as soccer star David Beckham did, or gel your locks into spiky, manmade bull's horns. Warning: Unless you want the pretty-boy label, throw in a masculine touch, like a sloppy ski cap. After all, does the world *really* need to know how much you love to stare in the mirror?

GEMINI STYLE
(May 21–June 20)

COLORS: Orange, yellow, magenta

FABRIC: Corduroy

FOCUS AREA: Arms, hands

STYLE EQUIPMENT: Bracelets, cufflinks, large watch, rings, costume jewelry

ROCK IT OUT: An eclectic mix of basics and ethnic-inspired pieces

PUT IT BACK ON THE RACK: Anything too dull or untrendy

GEMINI GIRL

 ## Under Control: Always on Time

WHO'S GOT THE LOOK: Courtney Cox, Kylie Minogue, Nicole Kidman, Lauryn Hill, Natalie Portman

HOW TO PULL IT OFF: As a Gemini, you're all about staying on top of the trends, and you use the Gemini double standard to your advantage. Like trendsetter Kylie Minogue, you can create a style that's both easy and difficult to copy. Contrast is key, so mix and match. Combine basic pieces with one-of-a-kind items. Pair ethnic-inspired tops with all-American Levis, as Lauryn Hill does. Keep it casual and comfortable, with an original splash. Don't spend a fortune on clothes, since your sign bores easily.

Out of Control: All over the Map

WHO'S GOT THE LOOK: Helena Bonham Carter, Jewel, Alanis Morrisette, Cyndi Lauper, Venus Williams

HOW TO PULL IT OFF: Give new meaning to the word *eclectic* by piling on a bizarre mix of layers. Done tastefully, you can bring together the best of many worlds. Push it too far, and you might be mistaken for a bag lady. Your sign rules the hands and arms, so pile on the rings and bracelets. You'll sparkle in costume jewelry like a funky fortune-teller. Borrow from different sources, then add your own signature touch. The late Lisa Lopes accented her left eye with a patch, football grease, even a condom! Your ability to push the envelope may bring stares, but it will also inspire the rest of the world to express their daring sides.

GEMINI GUY

 Under Control: Well-Groomed Bad Boy

WHO'S GOT THE LOOK: Mark Wahlberg, Maxwell, Ice Cube, Joshua Jackson, Shane West, Johnny Depp

HOW TO PULL IT OFF: From far away you may look like an ordinary guy, but up close is another story. That twinkle of mischief in your eyes will let the world know not to underestimate you. Shave your head to military regulations. Trim your goatee to a pencil-thin line. Then jump onto your motorcycle and gun the engine. Throw on some "old man clothes" and make them look young again, sort of like a golfer gone wild. Polo shirts, windbreakers, and tweed caps aren't headed for the retirement home when you wear them. Borrow from the past, and add some funky touches to your look, like a retro suit jacket or vintage watch.

 Out of Control: Crossing That Line

WHO'S GOT THE LOOK: Prince, Dave Navarro, Lenny Kravitz, Mike Myers, Andre 3000, Boy George

HOW TO PULL IT OFF: It's a girl! It's a boy! No, it's just Gemini, proving that there are two sides to his personality. Why choose when you can be both? Strange things happened when Prince put on a skintight bodysuit and high heels. Dabble with feminine touches as Dave Navarro or Outkast's Andre 3000 has. Wear something that causes people to question you—and themselves. You love this. When the media circus begins, no one makes a better ringmaster. Warning: Your outfits can feel like disguises after a while. Take off the costume and just be nakedly human sometimes. You'll get both sides of the story that way, which is just how your sign likes it.

CANCER STYLE
(June 21–July 22)

COLOR: Silver, pearl white

FABRIC: Silk

FOCUS AREA: Chest, stomach

STYLE EQUIPMENT: Necklace, belt, belly chain, short jacket, oxford shirt, silver jewelry, pearls, lace

ROCK IT OUT: Fitted styles that are both sporty and romantic

PUT IT BACK ON THE RACK: Vamped-out styles, anything too baggy

CANCER GIRL

 Under Control: Runway Casual

WHO'S GOT THE LOOK: Liv Tyler, Selma Blair, Michelle Branch, Michelle Rodriguez, Missy Elliott

HOW TO PULL IT OFF: As a mood-swinging Cancer, getting dressed for the day can be a difficult task. By noon you may hate what you put on in the morning! You need versatile clothes that are both sporty and romantic at once. With a little layering, you can pull together outfits that are stylish enough to be found on the runway and casual enough to be worn to wherever the day takes you. You like comfort, but steer clear of the tomboy look. Cancer Missy Elliott spent the early days of her career drowning in baggy clothes, but now she looks just as powerful in curve-hugging styles. It's all about being comfortable in your own skin, so don't use your clothes to form a protective shell.

✳ Out of Control: Naughty Baby Doll

WHO'S GOT THE LOOK: Pamela Anderson, Lil' Kim, Juliette Lewis, Courtney Love, Deborah Harry

HOW TO PULL IT OFF: Remember that dolly you used to play with as a little girl? The one in the lacy dress with the huge, blinking eyes and the bright Cupid's-bow lips? You're kinda like her, all grown up. That doesn't mean you'll blink and say "mama" though. You're sugar *and* spice—and like Cancer girls Lil' Kim and Pamela Anderson, you've got the low-cut minidress to prove it. You've got a weakness for makeup. Glossy lipstick, powdery blush, creamy eyeshadow—these are your poisons. Be prepared to deal with stares—this isn't always easy, since deep down, you're actually shy. Of course, if you didn't want them to look, why would you make it so damn hard for them to turn away?

CANCER GUY

⬟ Under Control: The Sensitive Jock

WHO'S GOT THE LOOK: Vin Diesel, Tom Cruise, Carson Daly, Josh Hartnett, Prince William, Derek Jeter

HOW TO PULL IT OFF: Like Cancer Tom Cruise, you're the kind of guy who likes to do his own stunts. To keep your competitive edge, choose clothes that are active rather than restrictive. You do best in stylin' guy classics like button-down shirts and designer denim—even if the shirt is half hanging out of your jeans. When it's time to clean up, just surrender and take it all the way. Holding on to your inner jockboy can create unfortunate results. Case in point is Carson Daly, who's been known to pair sneakers with a tux. Talk about a state of confusion! Choose a theme and stick with it. At the end of the day, people will appreciate you for your consistency above all else.

✳ Out of Control: Boy in the Band

WHO'S GOT THE LOOK: Beck, Tobey Maguire, David Spade, Jason Schwartzman, Billy Crudup

HOW TO PULL IT OFF: Start with the accessories: scissors, paper, gluestick and a Kinko's copy card. You've got flyers to make for that show your band is playing next week. Next, add mussed hair a la Beck and a wrinkled "Bob's Bowling Alley" T-shirt that you got for five cents at a yard sale. Voila! One man's junk is another man's treasure. Your sign loves history and you prefer relics from the past to the spankin' new. Shop around for that rare find and wear it with pride. Just make sure you wash it first. If you get too carried away with the dirty boy look, people might be afraid to come close. A little laundry detergent will help you stay in the running and take it to the finish line.

LEO STYLE
(July 23–August 22)

COLOR: Gold

FABRIC: Fur

FOCUS AREA: Heart, upper back

STYLE EQUIPMENT: Scarf, trench coat, shawl, gold jewelry, hat, sunglasses, fur coat, cape

ROCK IT OUT: Wild patterns, bright colors, dramatic accessories

PUT IT BACK ON THE RACK: Clothes that make you fade into the background

LEO GIRL

 ## Under Control: Society Lady

WHO'S GOT THE LOOK: Monica Lewinsky, Martha Stewart, Angie Harmon, Charlize Theron, Geri Haliwell, Hillary Swank

HOW TO PULL IT OFF: Imagine yourself as a lioness on the hunt to bring food back to her young. Camouflage yourself and deceive your prey. Opt for clothes that are plainer or sweeter than your fierce and ambitious nature. Society-approved suits, white button-down shirts, berets, and anything that resembles a uniform will appeal to you. They may think you're playing by the rules, but in the end you'll be making them. Add a dash of color—you're a fire sign, and you need a little heat. A streak of crimson lipstick can make you glow like a burning ember.

Out of Control: Spotlight Queen

WHO'S GOT THE LOOK: Madonna, Iman, Whitney Houston, Jennifer Lopez, Kelis, Halle Berry

HOW TO PULL IT OFF: As the queen of the jungle, you understand the power of raw energy and primal passion. Skip the neutral solids, and step into bold colors and wild patterns. Shiny, sparkly, glittery things give you red-carpet radiance. Choose styles that accentuate your womanly curves. Leo Jennifer Lopez taught the world the beauty of the big ol' booty. Ain't no shame in your game—but that doesn't mean you should forget that you are royalty. Hold yourself in a regal pose, and never let them see you sweat. Like Madonna, you could wind up leading a revolution for women's empowerment while wearing lingerie.

LEO GUY

 Under Control: Who's That Guy?

WHO'S GOT THE LOOK: Ben Affleck, Daniel Radcliffe, Ed Norton, Matthew Perry, Matt LeBlanc, Tom Green, Bill Clinton

HOW TO PULL IT OFF: As a fiery Leo, you're alive and full of energy. You're a modest king, though, and you'd rather not hit people over the head with the fact that you are royalty. Dress down and blast 'em with a surprise attack. The contrast between your plain clothes and your daring moves will create a dramatic effect. Looking like a regular ol' guy helped Leo Tom Green pull some outrageous stunts—and get away with them. Suit jackets and oxford shirts look great on you, and you could wind up spending a fortune on them, as Leo Ben Affleck has. If you're feeling extra daring, wear a pink shirt or one made from shiny fabric.

 Out of Control: Lead-Singer Appeal

WHO'S GOT THE LOOK: JC Chasez, Billy Bob Thornton, Scott Stapp, Fred Durst, Mick Jagger, Hulk Hogan

HOW TO PULL IT OFF: As the zodiac's star, you were born to take center stage. All eyes will be on you whether you like it or not. Have some fun while you're at it. You're a lion king, so pay attention to your mane. Grow your hair long like Creed lead Scott Stapp has, or don't leave home without a trademark red baseball cap like Fred Durst's. Take that passionate part of yourself—the one that's hurt and angry—and wear it on the sleeve of your leather jacket. Break the rules of fashion and invent your own. So what if no one else wears leather pants to graduation? You'll stand out in the crowd, which is your reason for living anyway.

VIRGO STYLE
(August 23–September 22)

COLOR: Brown, cream

FABRIC: Wool

FOCUS AREA: Abs, hands

STYLE EQUIPMENT: Belts, navel piercing, nail polish, blazer, delicate rings, thin earrings, glasses

ROCK IT OUT: Low-rise jeans, vintage suits

PUT IT BACK ON THE RACK: Complicated clothes, anything too revealing

VIRGO GIRL

 Under Control: Glamour Girl

WHO'S GOT THE LOOK: Faith Hill, Shania Twain, Claudia Schiffer, Salma Hayek, Sophia Lauren, Raquel Welch

HOW TO PULL IT OFF: As a Virgo, you like everything simple and pure. Undyed wool sweaters come to life when you pull them on. So do simple gowns. With your earthy glamour, you can make even the most basic piece look stunning. Like Virgo singer Faith Hill, your wholesome beauty helps you cross over into the mainstream. If you aren't careful, however, you also run the risk of fading into the background or looking a little too untouchable. Make sure to add a few original details here and there to avoid the disappearing act.

Out of Control: I'm Not That Innocent

WHO'S GOT THE LOOK: Beyoncé Knowles, Pink, Macy Gray, Cameron Diaz, Fiona Apple, LeAnn Rimes

HOW TO PULL IT OFF: Like blushing Virgo Pink, you've got a baby face. But being treated like a six-year-old ain't your thing. What's a girl to do? Shop like it's your first trip to the mall without parental guidance. Load up on the half tops like midriff-baring Beyoncé Knowles. Defy the neutral Virgo color palette and rock some jewel tones, even black. Dust your angelic eyes with smoky shadow. You may be sweet, but you're not *that* innocent. They key is finding the balance between sugar and spice—the quantities you use can be a recipe for either success or disaster.

VIRGO GUY

Under Control: Sports Center

WHO'S GOT THE LOOK: Kobe Bryant, Marc Anthony, Adam Sandler, Nas, Prince Harry, Paul Walker, Mario, Hugh Grant

HOW TO PULL IT OFF: Your sign likes things to be in perfect order, and that includes your clothes. You're Mr. Clean-Cut, from your perfectly trimmed hair to your crisp white socks. (Virgo Michael Jackson actually started a trend with his white socks.) Life is a spectator sport for analytical Virgos, and your idea of a good time is lounging in athletic gear watching TV, particularly ESPN. Granted, you've probably ironed your team jersey. Anal, perhaps, but you'd prefer to err on the side of being too neat rather than too messy. A thin, guy-approved earring is often as daring as you'll get.

Out of Control: I Just Rolled Out of Bed

WHO'S GOT THE LOOK: Macaulay Culkin, Luke Wilson, Jimmy Fallon, Liam Gallagher, Ryan Phillipe, Julian Casablancas

HOW TO PULL IT OFF: Your style inspiration comes from a time before you cared about style. (Isn't it ironic?) Like back in the day, when you rolled out of bed with your hair sticking up straight and wore the same, slightly tight Metallica T-shirt four days in a row. In fact, many of your clothes are one size too small, as if you outgrew them but didn't have the heart to give them away. For the most part, your boyish charm is irresistible. Just make sure you wake up on the right side of the bed, or your youthful appeal can turn you into a spoiled brat like Virgo badass Liam Gallagher.

LIBRA STYLE
(September 23–October 22)

COLORS: Blue, pink

FABRIC: Satin

FOCUS AREA: Lower back

STYLE EQUIPMENT: Button-down shirts, expensive jewelry, tuxedo or ball gown, lingerie or silk boxers, cologne and perfume

ROCK IT OUT: A harmonious (and expensive) mix of casual and elegant styles

PUT IT BACK ON THE RACK: Wash-and-wear fabrics

LIBRA GIRL

Under Control: Material Girl

WHO'S GOT THE LOOK: Toni Braxton, Ashanti, Sharon Osbourne, Gwyneth Paltrow, Mya, Donna Karan

HOW TO PULL IT OFF: Ruled by beauty-loving Venus, you've turned shopping into an art form. To you, the best of both worlds means looking both elegant and sparkly at once. Whether diamonds, clothes, or beauty products are your best friends, your appetite for luxury can border on insatiable. Lucky Libra Gwyneth Paltrow managed to make friends with designer Valentino. You'd be wise to make some connections of your own in the fashion industry, or just get a job! Learning to balance bargain finds with expensive classics can save you from breaking the bank.

Out of Control: Punk-Rock Girl

WHO'S GOT THE LOOK: Gwen Stefani, Avril Lavigne, Rachel Leigh Cook, Janeane Garofalo, Betsey Johnson, Shannyn Sossamon

HOW TO PULL IT OFF: Libra is the sign of justice, and you hate when anything is unfair. That includes the dress code. Like designer Betsey Johnson, you prefer to make your own rules. Spiky or studded details are the perfect replacements for the gems your more materialistic Libra sisters crave. You're the original punk-rock girl and like Libras Avril Lavigne and Shannyn Sossamon, no one wears black eyeliner quite like you. Balance is the key to success here. Avoid going head to toe in one color or going overboard with the mismatching, or your outfit could wind up looking like a costume.

LIBRA GUY

 ## Under Control: Boy-Next-Door

WHO'S GOT THE LOOK: Matt Damon, John Mayer, Will Smith, Seann William Scott, Usher, Eminem

HOW TO PULL IT OFF: Ruled by harmonious Venus, you're the well-groomed boy-next-door. Like Libra Matt Damon, you've got the dimples, the charming smile, the nice manners. You're not afraid to spend money on a quality item as Libra Usher does, who has a collection of ice-encrusted *U* necklaces. Some may even accuse you of being pretty. If you want to avoid this, go easy on the feminine touches such as longer hair and earrings. You look best in a mixture of basic and elegant pieces. Adding masculine touches such as a tie, jacket, or big ol' pair of Timberlands can help bring the look into balance.

 ## Out of Control: Pimped Out

WHO'S GOT THE LOOK: Snoop Dogg, Tommy Lee, Flea, Ginuwine, Shaggy, Weird Al Yankovic

HOW TO PULL IT OFF: Life is a balancing act for most Libras, and from the looks of you, you're determined to push things as far as they can possibly go. Zoot suits will never die in your world, and like Libra Snoop Dogg, you'll take yours with a matching feathered pimp hat. Decoration is not something you fear—the more bling-bling the better. You may cover yourself in tattoos and piercings as does Tommy Lee or Flea of the Red Hot Chili Peppers. As the tickets from the fashion police pile up, you'll only laugh. Your sign loves to rebel, and these are simply markers of success.

SCORPIO STYLE
(October 23–November 21)

COLOR: Black

FABRIC: Leather

FOCUS AREA: Crotch

STYLE EQUIPMENT: Leather jacket, black T-shirt, push-up bra, fishnet stockings, hair dye, tattoos, piercings (hidden and revealed), silk boxers

ROCK IT OUT: Tight clothes, leather

PUT IT BACK ON THE RACK: Loose and baggy clothes, unsexy cuts

SCORPIO GIRL

 ### Under Control: Simply Sexy

WHO'S GOT THE LOOK: Julia Roberts, Thandie Newton, Calista Flockhart, Demi Moore, Monica

HOW TO PULL IT OFF: They say the eyes are the windows of the soul. As a secretive Scorpio, you're not exactly offering a box-office view into yours. Shield yourself with a pair of glasses. It will only make things more dramatic when you finally take them off. When it comes to your clothes, you're all about the details. Like Scorpio Julia Roberts, you like simple clothes with sexy little touches. A white oxford shirt with the top buttons half undone, a tank top with delicate lace trim—these details may be small, but they're enough to drop a hint. Interested parties are sure to get a clue quickly.

 ### Out of Control: Vamp Around the Edges

WHO'S GOT THE LOOK: Winona Ryder, Eve, Björk, Brittany Murphy, Kelly Osbourne, Chloe Sevigny

HOW TO PULL IT OFF: Are you a good girl or a bad girl? It's kinda hard to tell. Like Scorpios Eve and Brittany Murphy, your face may be sweet, but your eyes tell another story. *Look, but don't touch* is the message you often wind up sending out. You're a trendsetter. Like Kelly Osbourne, you constantly reinvent your look, taking fashion dares few would dream of.

Vampy styles turn you on, especially if they're made of black leather. This should be used sparingly, or you may wind up looking like a runaway cast member from *Buffy*.

SCORPIO GUY

 ## Under Control: International Man of Mystery

WHO'S GOT THE LOOK: Sean "P. Diddy" Combs, Leonardo DiCaprio, David Schwimmer, Matthew McConaughey, Bill Gates

HOW TO PULL IT OFF: You're a power dresser, and you do it in a formal and understated way. Like Scorpio mogul P. Diddy, you like people to see how important you are. You look great in a suit and tie, especially in Scorpio black. You could almost blend into the background, if only you weren't wearing Versace sunglasses at 10 P.M. While mysteriously alluring, you can also be frustratingly hard to read. Every now and then, it wouldn't hurt to show people a little bit of your dirty laundry. Scorpio Matthew McConaughey has been busted playing the drums naked at home, and this didn't hurt his ratings one bit.

 ## Out of Control: Dark Angel

WHO'S GOT THE LOOK: Anthony Kiedis, Jack Osbourne, Joaquin Phoenix, Gavin Rossdale, Scott Weiland

HOW TO PULL IT OFF: You may have a baby face, but there's something smoldering below the surface. It's pure Scorpio energy, and it may even intimidate people. Not that you mind. You're a Scorpio, and you don't do anything unplanned. You like to dress in black from head to toe and you'll throw in a couple of Dungeons & Dragons–inspired tattoos for good measure. Being "different" from the crowd is important to you. Like Scorpio Jack Osbourne, you may rely on an ever-changing haircut to stay one step ahead of the game.

SAGITTARIUS STYLE
(November 22–December 21)

COLORS: Purple, royal blue

FABRIC: Lycra

FOCUS AREA: Hips and thighs

STYLE EQUIPMENT: Well-cut jeans, funky accessories, miniskirts, knee-high boots, backpack, sneakers

ROCK IT OUT: On-the-go styles with an individual twist

PUT IT BACK ON THE RACK: Anything labeled "dry clean only"

SAGITTARIUS GIRL

Under Control: Sporty Spice

WHO'S GOT THE LOOK: Nelly Furtado, Katie Holmes, Tyra Banks, Kim Basinger, Anna Faris

HOW TO PULL IT OFF: Adventurous Sagittarians are the travelers of the zodiac. Since you never know where a day will take you, you're at your best choosing versatile clothes that let you move around. Jeans, baby tees, and flip-flops are a few of your favorite things. Like Sag girl Nelly Furtado, you look great in funky colors and know how to make sporty gear look sexy. Just try not to get *so* comfortable that your sweatpants become a second skin. Taking little fashion dares gives you a charge. If you're going to wear tube socks, cut off the toes and pull them on as arm warmers. Think outside the box, and you won't go wrong.

Out of Control: Tease

WHO'S GOT THE LOOK: Britney Spears, Christina Aguilera, Alyssa Milano, Christina Applegate, Anna Nicole Smith, Trina, Lucy Liu

HOW TO PULL IT OFF: Meow! Who let the kittens out? Your style is an unpredictable combination of elements, kind of like you raided a locker room and a lingerie shop and put it all together. The result is a mixed message . . . and a serious tease. Like Sagittarius Britney Spears, you're both girl and woman at once. At times, you've been known to take it too far and wind up looking a little . . . ahem . . . trashy, like Anna Nicole

Smith, who appears to apply her makeup with a trowel. Knowing when to say "enough" is the key—although this can be a challenge, since your sign craves more, more, more!

SAGITTARIUS GUY

 ## Under Control: Big Man on Campus

WHO'S GOT THE LOOK: Jay-Z, Ben Stiller, Mekhi Phifer, Benjamin Bratt, Frankie Muniz, DMX, Tom DeLonge

HOW TO PULL IT OFF: Sagittarius is the sign of higher learning, so take your inspiration straight outta the dorms. T-shirts, jeans, and sneakers are a few of your favorite things. Athletic gear makes a good uniform for you, too. Show some school spirit with a team jersey as Sagittarius Jay-Z does. Make sure to study your reflection before you go racing out the door, since getting too sloppy can cost you points. A strong canvas backpack is a must for throwing in your books and equipment. Pack for the day, since you'll usually be gone 'til sunrise.

Out of Control: My Way or the Highway

WHO'S GOT THE LOOK: Ozzy Osbourne, Brad Pitt, Mos Def, Samuel L. Jackson, Johnny Rzeznik, Chris Robinson

HOW TO PULL IT OFF: The seventies have come and gone, but you will remain an eternal hippie. Like Sag rocker Ozzy Osbourne, you've got the long hair to prove it. Flowy beatnik tops with strange prints add cool points to your rep—not that you care. "Live and let live" could be your motto. You're not interested in following or leading; you just wanna be free to do your thing. Your devil-may-care style gives the fashion industry a big "talk to the hand," and yet they can't help but trail your every move. Just picture Sagittarius Brad Pitt on one of his shaving strikes if you still don't understand.

CAPRICORN STYLE
(December 22–January 19)

COLORS: Black, forest green

FABRIC: Flannel

FOCUS AREA: Knees, skin, teeth

STYLE EQUIPMENT: Hiking boots, lip balm or lipstick, cashmere sweater, leather gloves, antique jewelry, button-down shirts, watch

ROCK IT OUT: Expensive fabrics in muted colors, athletic gear

PUT IT BACK ON THE RACK: Loud colors, trendy clothes

CAPRICORN GIRL

Under Control: Simply Stunning

WHO'S GOT THE LOOK: Kate Moss, Sade, Estella Warren, Kristin Kreuk, Amanda Peete, Kate Bosworth

HOW TO PULL IT OFF: Being a practical Capricorn, you prefer low-maintenance styles. Fortunately, you've got classic good looks that don't require much work to keep up. Like model Kate Moss and soulful singer Sade, you look simply stunning with your hair pulled back into a tight bun. Capricorns rule the bones, and your facial structure is quite interesting on its own. A single coat of matte lipstick is often more than enough to give you a little extra light. When it comes to your clothes, you stay true to your earth-sign ways. Thick turtleneck sweaters in undyed wool bring you the fresh, clean, and cozy feel you crave.

Out of Control: Steel Magnolia

WHO'S GOT THE LOOK: Mary J. Blige, Dolly Parton, Joey Lauren Adams, Annie Lennox, Dido, Eartha Kitt, Donna Summer

HOW TO PULL IT OFF: Capricorn is the sign of ambition, and even if you take the road less traveled, you'll still find a way to make it to the top. Your path? To become an icon of female strength. Like Mary J. Blige, you reach into the depths of your soul and share your pain so that others won't feel alone. Your sign is known for persistence, and you are famous for establishing a style and sticking with it through the decades. Like

Dolly Parton and her wigs or Annie Lennox and her cropped orange hair, your look can easily become a timeless classic.

CAPRICORN GUY

Under Control: Clean-Cut

WHO'S GOT THE LOOK: Taye Diggs, Jude Law, L.L. Cool J, Ricky Martin, Tiger Woods, Morris Chestnut

HOW TO PULL IT OFF: With your clean-cut good looks, you fit right into society's picture of a handsome fella. Hello, confidence! Your sign rules public image, so you like to appear as though you've got it all together. "Never let them see you sweat" could be your motto. Like Capricorn Tiger Woods, you remain cool under pressure. Should your preppy shirts become dampened by perspiration, you'll whisk them off to the dry cleaners—even the washable ones, since you like things that last. Your sign rules the jaw and teeth and, like those of Jude Law and Morris Chestnut, yours may be strong and picture perfect.

Out of Control: Freaky Rock Star

WHO'S GOT THE LOOK: Kid Rock, Marilyn Manson, Dave Grohl, A. J. McLean, Jonathan Davis, Zack de la Rocha

HOW TO PULL IT OFF: They say Capricorns are uptight, play-by-the-rules kind of guys. Well, all that repression has to find balance some-where. When you let loose, your look can get a little freaky—sort of like the love child of a rock star and a zombie. Women's clothes hold a strange and special appeal, and you might dabble with black nail polish and eyeliner as Backstreet Boy AJ McLean has done. You're all about creating a mixed message, as you dress in medieval torture devices and pontificate about politics and religion as Marilyn Manson does. You're not afraid of traditions such as marriage. Like Capricorn Kid Rock, you may tie the knot, but you won't be bound to anyone's rules but your own.

AQUARIUS STYLE
(January 20–February 18)

COLOR: Violet

FABRIC: Denim

FOCUS AREA: Calves, ankles

STYLE EQUIPMENT: Tube socks, leg warmers, friendship rings, unusual jewelry, lace-up boots, ankle bracelets, baseball caps, beads

ROCK IT OUT: Quirky pieces with a futuristic bent

PUT IT BACK ON THE RACK: Dull colors, cookie-cutter clothes

AQUARIUS GIRL

Under Control: Girl-Next-Door

WHO'S GOT THE LOOK: Brandy, Jennifer Aniston, Mena Suvari, Kelly Rowland, Oprah Winfrey, Natalie Imbruglia.

HOW TO PULL IT OFF: Aquarius is the sign of friendship, and you've got the girl-next-door look to prove it. Like Aquarians Oprah Winfrey and Jennifer Aniston, you're popular with the masses. There's something about you that people can relate to. Jeans paired with high-heeled boots, hair pulled into a ponytail—boring on other people, but not on you. Staying in the game is important for you, but so is inventing your own. Even if you're dressed in the basics, don't hold back from adding a bizarre little twist that marks you as an individual.

Out of Control: Gypsy Girl

WHO'S GOT THE LOOK: Shakira, Alicia Keys, Christina Ricci, Heather Graham, Sheryl Crow, Minnie Driver

HOW TO PULL IT OFF: Like a gypsy on an interplanetary shopping spree, pull your inspiration from as many sources as you wanna. You're an Aquarius, and originality is your specialty. Transform a football jersey into a puffy-sleeved girly masterpiece as did Aquarius Alicia Keys. You were born to wander so let your style show it. A little rock-and-roll goes a long way with you, and so does a little bit of country. Pair a cowboy hat with leather pants, and get your a$$ on the tour bus. Like Aquarius

Sheryl Crow, you're the kind of girl who plays her own instruments—
even if you're just shaking a tambourine.

AQUARIUS GUY

 ## Under Control: Pop and Jock

WHO'S GOT THE LOOK: Justin Timberlake, Michael Jordan, Dr. Dre,
Chris Rock, Nick Carter

HOW TO PULL IT OFF: Like Michael Jordan, you're one of the original
team players. Fitting in is not a problem for you—and neither is standing out. If you're not dressed in basic jock clothes, you may take a cue
from Aquarius Justin Timberlake and tread onto pop-star territory,
adding an unthreatening piercing or trendy jacket to your preppy look.
You prefer to stand out just enough to be recognizable but not so much
that you risk being labeled a misfit. Your boyish charm and adorable
smile win you fans and score you points time and again.

 ## Out of Control: Rebel Without a Cause

WHO'S GOT THE LOOK: Ashton Kutcher, Billie Joe Armstrong, Wes Borland, Axl Rose, John Travolta

HOW TO PULL IT OFF: Aquarius is the sign that rules unpredictable
change. Work that to your advantage, and hit 'em up with a style that
only a mind like yours could dream up. Cover your entire pupil with a
black contact like Wes Borland. Why? Who cares why? There doesn't always have to be a reason. It's all about the surprise attack with you. Your
sign also rules electricity, so any high-voltage accent will charge up your
appearance. The current you send out could actually shock people, as
was the case with the comebacks of both John Travolta and Guns n'
Roses front man Axl Rose. When you enter a room, the world will sit up
and take notice.

PISCES STYLE
(February 19–March 20)

COLORS: Sea green, violet

FABRIC: Rubber

FOCUS AREA: Feet

STYLE EQUIPMENT: Shoes made for walking/dancing/jumping around on stage, tattoos, nail polish, piercings, leather pants, lace

ROCK IT OUT: Fashion-forward clothes with a theatrical flair

PUT IT BACK ON THE RACK: Anything lacking rock-star appeal

PISCES GIRL

Under Control: The Lovely Nurse

WHO'S GOT THE LOOK: Cindy Crawford, Queen Latifah, Chelsea Clinton, Jessica Biel, Kristin Davis, Elizabeth Taylor

HOW TO PULL IT OFF: Pisces are the helpers/healers of the zodiac, and you prefer to dress like someone who can be counted on, as hip-hop matriarch Queen Latifah does. The prescription is this: Be polished and theatrical all at once. Your hair and nails? Done. To avoid looking like an actual nurse, balance strong, structured pieces such as jackets and preppy sweaters with frilly and funky accents such as lacy or striped shirts in unusual colors. Be warned: Your shoulder will be cried on, so don't go overboard with the dry-clean-only pieces. Like the little mermaid, you're tough enough to survive on dry land, but you also understand the enchanted mysteries under the sea.

Out of Control: Flower Girl

WHO'S GOT THE LOOK: Drew Barrymore, Thora Birch, Jennifer Love Hewitt, Chilli, Kate Dillon, Lauren Ambrose

HOW TO PULL IT OFF: You've got the face of an angel, so why not create a halo? Adorn your flowing hair with tiny jewels and floral accents as has Pisces Drew Barrymore, who even named her production company Flower Films. Like Thora Birch, you are known to have large and dreamy eyes. Dust on glowing makeup that makes you glisten and gleam. You like clothes that are both edgy and ethereal at once—sparkly, glittery fabrics and winged sleeves help you build your stairway to heaven.

PISCES GUY

 ## Under Control: Prince Charming

WHO'S GOT THE LOOK: Freddie Prinze Jr., Chris Klein, Shaquille O'Neal, Bow Wow, Mark McGrath, Benicio del Toro

HOW TO PULL IT OFF: Ruled by dreamy Neptune, you're the zodiac's answer to a romantic fantasy boy. Charming and sweet, you disarm the opposition with your smile. Your look is friendly and unthreatening—preppy sweaters and khaki pants are your style staples. Like Freddie Prinze Jr., you may like to add the dapper touch of wire-rimmed glasses. Pisces are known for their sensitivity, and even if you're a notorious bachelor like fellow fish Mark McGrath, you can't help but look like "take home to mama" material.

 ## Out of Control: Tortured Artist

WHO'S GOT THE LOOK: Kurt Cobain, Johnny Knoxville, Jon Bon Jovi, Chris Martin, Seal, Billy Corgan

HOW TO PULL IT OFF: Pisces have a special relationship with pain—it's what fuels you and shapes your identity. Your ability to tap into these twisted emotions makes you the perfect poster boy for tortured artists. And, like *Jackass* star Johnny Knoxville, you may actually be willing to torture yourself for your art! No piercing needle has the power to scare you away. Your pain? You'll wear that on your sleeve in the form of tattoos. Like singer Seal, you may even make a fashion statement out of your scars. Even your clothes look like they've been through the wringer—but the story behind them is what keeps people captivated.

section 5
MAKE THE STARS WORK FOR YOU!

PLAN IT BY THE PLANETS: YOUR ASTROLOGICAL EVENT GUIDE

Wouldn't it be nice to know when to try out for a starring role, and when to just stay in bed? Certain cosmic events stir up energies that you can use to promote your best interests. The exact dates change every year, so consult an annual astrological guide to plan. Here are a few events that exert influences you can work to your advantage.

NEW MOONS AND FULL MOONS

Schedule: once a month

Following moon cycles can be a fun way to set goals and reap their benefits. Astrologers believe that our energy begins to build at the new moon, then peaks two weeks later at the full moon. New moons mark beginnings and are the perfect time to kick off any new project or idea. Full moons are times for completions, creative outpourings, and harvesting. They're also your cue to cash in on anything you started at the new moon. After the full moon, wrap up your success as the moon dwindles, then begin the cycle all over again at the new moon two weeks later. In many cultures, farmers have planted by the new moon and harvested by the full moon. Why not get a little lunar boost for your own life?

ECLIPSES

Schedule: two to three times a year

Eclipses can bring sudden changes and turning points to our lives. If you've been sitting on the fence about an issue, the eclipse will knock you off and force you to face the facts. Truths and secrets will rise to the surface. Things that aren't "meant to be" will be taken away faster than Winona Ryder's shopping privileges at Saks Fifth Avenue. Eclipses are like giant industrial vacuum cleaners. They either suck away the messes, or clean up what's gotten dusty and leave it shiny and new. Procrastinate if you must, but it's best to find out when the eclipses are so that you deal with your issues in advance—before an eclipse deals them right back to you.

There are two types of eclipses—solar and lunar. Lunar eclipses happen when the earth passes directly between the sun and moon, cutting off their communication. A solar eclipse takes place when the new moon passes between the sun and the earth, shadowing the sun. The effect is similar to a spiritual power outage—it either makes you feel a little off center, or makes your mind crystal clear. The effects of an eclipse can usually be felt from three to five days before and after it. Expect the unexpected, and wait for the dust to settle before you act on any eclipse-fueled impulses.

RETROGRADES

Schedule: varies by planet

You know those times when everything goes haywire, and you can't figure out why? A planet could be in *retrograde*—meaning that from earth, it appears to be spinning backward. While this is just an illusion, the areas that a retrograde planet rules may become weak or out of whack. Two major retrogrades to watch are Mercury and Venus. Mercury, planet of communication, transportation, and technology, goes retrograde for three weeks about three times a year. Arguments and misunderstandings rage, plans fall apart, cars break down, and computers crash suddenly. Back up your digital files beforehand, postpone any deals, and plan to explain yourself a few extra times. Love-planet Venus goes retrograde about once a year, and causes relationship craziness. Astrologers advise against proposals, weddings, and any major relationship moves during this four-to-six-week period.

So what's good about retrogrades? The prefix re-means "to go back"—and retrogrades are a time to polish up projects already in the works, or to dig up ones you've set aside. Old friends and past issues can resurface, giving you a chance to reconnect or revise. This can be a useful time to resolve any arguments, revisit old ideas, research an idea, or renew a commitment. Tighten up your routine during these periods, and you'll be ready to rock when the retrograde planet returns to direct, or forward, motion.

PERSONAL POWER TIMES—
AND POWER OUTAGES

Your ultimate best astro-moment falls at the time of your birthday. The sun is in your sign, giving you the solar power to shine. It's like a personal new year—and it's the best time to start new plans that truly reflect you. If you want to give yourself a new look, update then. If you've been putting your friends first, it's time to pull back and make it all about you. This is the time of year to ask yourself, "Who am I, and what do I want?" The planets will help you come up with some interesting answers.

Other times of the year are better for chilling. Six months after your birthday, the sun is opposite your sign—a bit of an uncomfortable place. You may feel distanced from its power (and your own). You're literally out of the solar spotlight. That's not necessarily a bad thing, though! Use this time to ask others for support, take a vacation, and go easy on yourself. Good news: Around this time, the full moon will fall in your sign. Remember those goals you set at your last birthday? Your half-birthday is the perfect time to cash in on some of those goods. Plan it right, and it's sort of like taking an all-expense-paid vacation.

The other sleepy time happens the month before your birthday. The weary sun has now traveled the entire zodiac since it was last in your sign—and man, are you tired. It's the end of your astrological year, so catch up on rest, wrap up loose ends, and hold off on the new projects until after your birthday.

OUR FAVORITE ASTRO-RESOURCES

ASTROLOGY BASICS

Astrology for Dummies by Rae Orion (includes tables for finding your
   moon and rising signs)
Planets and Possibilities by Susan Miller

ANNUAL GUIDES (NEW MOONS, FULL MOONS, ETC.) AND EPHEMERIDES

Sydney Omarr's Day-By-Day Astrological Guides by Sydney Omarr
Llewelyn's Astrological Pocket Planner
The Year Ahead by Susan Miller

CREATE YOUR OWN FREE CHART ONLINE

Astrology.com—www.astrology.com
Astrolabe—www.alabe.com

ACKNOWLEDGMENTS

We'd like to thank our family for always encouraging us to follow our destiny, even if it took us into outer space—we love you. Thanks to the cosmic crew at *Teen People,* Simon & Schuster, and Vigliano Associates who helped make this book a reality: Molly Aboud; Elisa Albert; our amazing agent, Donna Bagdasarian; Christina Duffy; Isabel Gonzalez; Noelle Howey; Michael Jennings; Barbara O'Dair; our star-spangled editor, Caroline Sutton; and David Vigliano.

A special thanks to Eitan Zachodin for naming the book and offering nonstop support throughout the writing process, proving that Aries really *do* have patience. Thanks to all our friends for nurturing our astro-obsession by letting us do your charts and map your love interests' horoscopes and for humoring our insatiable need to find out the sign of every pop star, waiter, public figure, and perfect stranger who caught our attention. Special thanks to Ramona Watson and Susan Jane Gilman for giving us our earliest charting tools, which launched our planetary passion.

This book is dedicated to the memory of Lavell Jones, who perfected the art of fun, laughter, and Piscean selflessness.

DISCARD